Kabul Beauty School

**Center Point
Large Print**

**This Large Print Book carries the
Seal of Approval of N.A.V.H.**

Kabul Beauty School
An American Woman Goes Behind the Veil

DEBORAH RODRIGUEZ
with Kristin Ohlson

CENTER POINT PUBLISHING
THORNDIKE, MAINE

The text of this Large Print edition is unabridged.
In other aspects, this book may vary from the original edition.
Printed in the United States of America.
Set in 16-point Times New Roman type.

ISBN-10: 1-60285-009-7
ISBN-13: 978-1-60285-009-5

Library of Congress Cataloging-in-Publication Data

Rodriguez, Deborah.
    Kabul Beauty School: an American woman goes behind the veil / Deborah Rodriguez.--Center
Point large print ed.
        p. cm.
    ISBN-13: 978-1-60285-009-5 (lib. bdg. : alk. paper)
        1. Women--Afghanistan--Kabul--Social life and customs--21st century.
    2. Muslim women--Afghanistan--Kabul--Social conditions--21st century.
    3. Kabul Beauty School. 4. Beauty shops--Social aspects--Afghanistan--Kabul.
    5. Kabul (Afghanistan)--Social life and customs--21st century. 6. Large type books. I. Title.

HQ1735.6.R63 2007b
305.48'69709581090511--dc22

2007006940

This book is dedicated to my father, Junior Turner, who passed away June 5, 2002, while I was on my first trip to Afghanistan. Dad, I never got a chance to tell you about Afghanistan and the school.

You left me too soon. I know you would love Sam, my husband—he is just like you, but Afghan style. I know you would be worried, but also very happy that I am following my dream. I miss you.

Luckily, I am a lady
Mariam of my own epoch

I have conscience,
Intelligence and talent
But am fated to continue
Existence
In captivity behind the
Bars of prison of life
As if I am a jail-bird

I want to declare my feelings
But nobody seems to realize me

I am being asked to stay thoroughly out of sight,
In the darkness
Why?
Because it is easy for them to disgrace me and
    discard me

They have covered me from head to toe
Amputated my legs
Shut my mouth

Oh!
I want to be known
If not as I am a female
But through my knowledge

Let the years go
Let them have my written words

One day they will ask whose
unique words are these

Maybe at that time they will
Know me as
a female who can do something

I am hopeful . . .

Farida Alimi

Chapter 1

The women arrive at the salon just before eight in the morning. If it were any other day, I'd still be in bed, trying to sink into a few more minutes of sleep. I'd probably still be cursing the neighbor's rooster for waking me up again at dawn. I might even still be groaning about the vegetable dealers who come down the street at three in the morning with their noisy, horse-drawn wagons, or the neighborhood mullah, who warbles out his long, mournful call to prayer at four-thirty. But this is the day of Roshanna's engagement party, so I'm dressed and ready for work. I've already had four cigarettes and two cups of instant coffee, which I had to make by myself because the cook has not yet arrived. This is more of a trial than you might think, since I've barely learned how to boil water in Afghanistan. When I have to do it myself, I put a lit wooden match on each of the burners of the cranky old gas stove, turn one of the knobs, and back off to see which of the burners explodes into flame. Then I settle a pot of water there and pray that whatever bacteria are floating in the Kabul water today are killed by the boiling.

The mother-in-law comes into the salon first, and we exchange the traditional Afghan greeting: we clasp hands and kiss each other's cheeks three times. Roshanna is behind her, a tiny, awkward, blue ghost wearing the traditional burqa that covers her, head to toe, with only a small piece of netting for her to see out the front. But the netting has been pulled crooked, across her nose, and she bumps into the doorway. She laughs and flutters her arms inside the billowing fabric, and two of her sisters-in-law help her navigate her way through the door. Once inside, Roshanna snatches the burqa off and drapes it over the top of one of the hair dryers.

"This was like Taliban days again," she cries, because she hasn't worn the burqa since the Taliban were driven out of Kabul in the fall of 2001. Roshanna usually wears clothes that she sews herself—brilliant shalwar kameezes or saris in shades of orchid and peach, lime green and peacock blue. Roshanna usually stands out like a butterfly against the gray dustiness of Kabul and even against the other women on the streets, in their mostly drab, dark clothing. But today she observes the traditional behavior of a bride on the day of her engagement party or wedding. She has left her parents' house under cover of burqa and will emerge six hours later wearing her body weight in eye shadow, false eyelashes the size of sparrows, monumentally big hair, and clothes with more bling than a Ferris wheel. In America, most people would associate this look with drag queens sashaying off to a party with a 1950s prom theme. Here in Afghanistan, for reasons I still don't understand, this look conveys the mystique of the virgin.

The cook arrives just behind the women, whispering that she'll make the tea, and Topekai, Baseera, and

Bahar, the other beauticians, rush into the salon and take off their head scarves. Then we begin the joyful, gossipy, daylong ordeal of transforming twenty-year-old Roshanna into a traditional Afghan bride. Most salons would charge up to $250—about half the annual income for a typical Afghan—for the bride's services alone. But I am not only Roshanna's former teacher but also her best friend, even though I'm more than twenty years older. She is my first and best friend in Afghanistan. I love her dearly, so the salon services are just one of my gifts to her.

We begin with the parts of Roshanna that no one will see tonight except her husband. Traditional Afghans consider body hair to be both ugly and unclean, so she must be stripped of all of it except for the long, silky brown hair on her head and her eyebrows. There can be no hair left on her arms, underarms, face, or privates. Her body must be as soft and hairless as that of a prepubescent girl. We lead Roshanna down the corridor to the waxing room—the only one in Afghanistan, I might add—and she grimaces as she sits down on the bed.

"You could have done it yourself at home," I tease her, and the others laugh. Many brides are either too modest or too fearful to have their pubic hair removed by others in a salon, so they do it at home—they either pull it out by hand or rip it out with chewing gum. Either way, the process is brutally painful. Besides, it's hard to achieve the full Brazilian—every pubic hair plucked, front and back—when you do it on your own, even if you're one of the few women in this country to own a large mirror, as Roshanna does.

"At least you know your husband is somewhere doing this, too," Topekai says with a leer. My girls giggle at this reference to the groom's attention to his own naked body today. He also must remove all of his body hair.

"But he only has to shave it off!" Roshanna wails, then blushes and looks down. I know she doesn't want to appear critical of her new husband, whom she hasn't yet met, in front of her mother-in-law. She doesn't want to give the older woman any reason to find fault with her, and when Roshanna looks back up again, she smiles at me anxiously.

But the mother-in-law seems not to have heard her. She has been whispering outside the door with one of her daughters. When she turns her attention back to the waxing room, she looks at Roshanna with a proud, proprietary air.

The mother-in-law had picked Roshanna out for her son a little more than a year after Roshanna graduated from the first class at the Kabul Beauty School, in the fall of 2003, and opened her own salon. The woman was a distant cousin who came in for a perm. She admired this pretty, plucky, resourceful girl who had been supporting her parents and the rest of her family ever since they fled into Pakistan to escape the Taliban. After she left Roshanna's salon, she started asking around for further details about the girl. She liked what she heard.

Roshanna's father had been a doctor, and the family had led a privileged life until they fled to Pakistan in 1998. There, he was not allowed to practice medicine—a typical refugee story—and had to work as a lowly shoeshine man. By the time they returned to Kabul, he was in such ill health that he couldn't practice medicine. Still, he staunchly carried out his fatherly duties by accompanying Roshanna everywhere to watch over her. The mother-in-law had detected no whiff of scandal about Roshanna, except perhaps her friendship with me. Even that didn't put her off, since foreign women are not held to the same rigorous standards as Afghan women. We are like another gender entirely, able to wander back and forth between the two otherwise separate worlds of men and women; when we do something outrageous, like reach out to shake a man's hand, it's usually a for-givable and expected outrage. The mother-in-law may even have regarded me as an asset, a connection to the wealth and power of America, as nearly all Afghans assume Americans are rich. And we are, all of us, at least in a material sense. Anyway, the mother-in-law was determined to secure Roshanna as the first wife for her elder son, an engineer living in Amsterdam. There was nothing unusual about this. Nearly all first marriages in Afghanistan are arranged, and it usually falls to the man's mother to select the right girl for him. He may take on a second or even third wife later on, but that first virginal lamb is almost as much his mother's as his.

I see that Roshanna is faltering under her mother-in-law's gaze, and I pull all the other women away from the waxing room. "How about highlights today?" I ask the mother-in-law. "My girls do foiling better than anyone between here and New York City."

"Better than in Dubai?" the mother-in-law asks.

"Better than in Dubai," I say. "And a lot cheaper."

Back in the main room of the salon, I make sure the curtains are pulled tight so that no passing male can peek in to see the women bareheaded. That's the kind of thing that could get my salon and the Kabul Beauty School itself closed down. I light candles so that we can turn the overhead lights off. With all the power needed for the machine that melts the wax, the facial lamps, the blow dryers, and the other salon appliances, I don't want to blow a fuse. I put on a CD of Christmas carols. It's the only one I can find, and they won't know the difference anyway. Then I settle the mother-in-law and the members of the bridal party into their respective places, one for a manicure, one for a pedicure, one to get her hair washed. I make sure they all have tea and the latest outdated fashion magazines from the States, then excuse myself with a cigarette. I usually just go ahead and smoke in the salon, but the look on Roshanna's face just before I shut the door to the waxing room has my heart racing. Because she has a terrible secret, and I'm the only one who knows it—for now.

Both engagement parties and weddings are lavish events in Afghanistan. Families save money for years and even take on huge debt to make these events as festive as possible, sparing no expense. After all, this is a country with virtually no public party life. There are no nightclubs, no concerts, only a few restaurants—and the ones that have opened since the Taliban left are frequented mostly by Westerners. There are a few movie theaters, but it's primarily men who go to them. If a woman happens to show up, as I once did when I insisted that a male friend take me, then she becomes the show, with every turban in the room turned her way so that the men can gawk at her. There are just about no venues where Afghan men and women dress up and mingle. They don't exactly mingle at engagement parties and weddings, either. At big gatherings, the hundreds of men and women are segregated on two different floors of the hall with two different bands; at smaller gatherings, they are on one floor but separated by a curtain. In both cases, they dress to the nines. When I first came to Kabul, I was amazed by all the stores that sell wedding gowns. There are probably two on every block. Full-size mannequins are lined up in the windows of these stores, heads tilted at a haughty angle, overlooking the street in their colorful dresses spangled with rhinestones and swathed in tülle. They look like giant Barbie dolls— all very tall and Caucasian-looking —and when I was first here, I memorized the dolls in the windows so I could find my way back to my guesthouse. I pretended that they were guiding me home.

Roshanna's parents shook their heads and declined when the groom's mother first came calling with cakes and imported candies and other gifts to ask for her hand, but they were pleased with the offer. Saying no was only part of the ritual, a way of signaling that their daughter was so precious and beloved that they hated to let her leave the family home. It was also the first step in a bargaining process. For the next few months, the fathers haggled over the size of her cash dowry, over the number of dresses the groom's family would have their tailor make for her and the amount of fabric they'd give her family so they could make their own new clothes, over the value of the gold jewelry the groom's family would give Roshanna. Her father had negotiated all this well. The cash dowry that would be paid to her family was ten thousand dollars, and she would receive five thousand dollars in gold as well as many other accoutrements of an upperclass wedding. Roshanna was not consulted about any of this. As with all first marriages in Afghanistan, it was strictly business, a transaction enacted between fathers. But she was eager to be married. In fact, she's one of the only brides I've ever met in Kabul who actually wanted to get married.

From the moment that I met Roshanna during my first visit to Kabul in the spring of 2002, the first spring after the rout of the Taliban, I puzzled over the sadness in her. Why did I respond so strongly to her sadness when there are millions of sad stories in Kabul? It's a city that's dense with sadness. There are so many people who lost loved ones in the twenty-seven years of war in Afghanistan, who have lost homes and livelihoods, who have lost entire towns and families, who have lost every dream they ever had. And there is still the occasional bombing or surprise mine explosion that rips away the happiness people finally think might be theirs. So why did Roshanna stand out amid all that sadness? I think it was her gaiety, her warmth and exuberance, her colorful clothes and bright smile. She was trying so hard to be happy that it hurt me when her sadness showed.

It had taken a few weeks for her to tell me her story. I had noticed that she seemed to light up when a certain young man came into the building where she was a secretary and I was a volunteer with a nonprofit organization. At first, I thought she might be sad because he wasn't interested in her, but then I thought I saw the same light in his face when he caught sight of her from across the room. I started to tease her about it.

"Got a boyfriend?" I'd whisper, and\she'd blush and turn away.

"We don't marry for love here," she told me after I had teased her a few times. "I have to marry the man my parents pick."

I knew that Roshanna and the boy couldn't admit their feelings or be obvious about them—they couldn't do a damn thing about them, in fact, because there isn't any dating in Kabul. But I thought that maybe his mother could talk to her mother and a match could be made that began with love. My mind started to race ahead with the possibilities. Which I mentioned to her one day, but she pulled me into a dark hallway.

"It can't happen, Debbie," she said, her eyes glistening in the faint light. "I was engaged once to someone else. This boy's parents would never let him marry me."

I slumped against the wall. "Why is it a problem if you were engaged before? Aren't you allowed to change your mind?"

"You don't understand," she insisted. "We signed the *nika-khat* at the engagement party."

This other, almost-marriage had taken place when the Taliban were still in power. Her family was living the miserable life of refugees in a camp just over the border in Pakistan. Roshanna was then sixteen years old and so bright that she'd actually found opportunities to get ahead in the camp. She learned English and some computer skills, and then found a job as a secretary with an international aid agency. She often had to cross back into Afghanistan—accompanied by her father, of course—to do some work for the agency.

That brought her into dangerous proximity to the Taliban, then at the height of their power. They would often snatch up young unmarried girls without warning and force them into marriage with one of their men. During this period of time, many Afghan families didn't let their daughters out of the house for fear that the Taliban might see them. Even with these precautions, the Taliban might hear a neighborhood rumor—or get a tip from someone eager to curry favor with them—about a family with a beautiful daughter. They'd break down the family's door in search of her.

So Roshanna's family had a dilemma. They needed her income but were afraid she'd be stolen away from them and end up leading a life of bondage to a man they hated. And they hated the Taliban. Like many Afghan families, they had greeted the Taliban with cautious optimism when they first rolled into the city in 1996. Before their arrival, Kabul was being blown to bits by the mujahideen factions who had trounced the Russians, then turned on one another in a bloody fury, fighting for control of the country. Even though Roshanna's parents weren't deeply conservative Muslims, they wanted to see their country return to normal, and the Taliban seemed determined to make this happen. But her parents were horrified by the growing savagery that the Taliban used to enforce their kind of order.

To keep Roshanna safe, her parents did what many Afghan families did at this time. They searched frantically for a suitable husband among members of their tribe, hoping to marry her off to a good man before the Taliban found out that she was available. They thought they had succeeded when they heard that there was a single male cousin living in Germany. It was a buyers' market for grooms in those days. The girls' families couldn't afford to dicker over dowries, dresses, and gold rings with the Taliban circling like wolves. So an agreement was quickly reached, with

19

only a very small dowry. Because the families wanted the union to take place as soon as possible, the groom came back to Afghanistan for the engagement party right away. And because the actual wedding would take place in Germany months later, they signed the nika-khat that same night.

The nika-khat is the marriage contract drawn up according to Islamic law. This contract, more than the wedding itself, is what makes a couple legal husband and wife. In ordinary times, the nika-khat is signed well after the engagement party to give the groom's family time to put together their resources for the dowry, the clothes, the wedding, and so on. Roshanna's family took the less ordinary step of allowing her to become this man's legal wife before the wedding by signing the nika-khat at the engagement party. His family had insisted upon it, so that she couldn't change her mind about marrying him after he went back to Germany. And everyone agreed that it would be easier for her to emigrate there if she was already his legal wife. But within days her new husband left—without a word, without reason, and without her. She was crushed and humiliated, but it only got worse. Two weeks later, she was told that the cousin had divorced her when he got back to Germany.

"It is so easy for a man," Roshanna told me. "All he has to do is say 'I divorce you' three times in front of witnesses. We found out later that he already had either a girlfriend or a first wife in Germany. When he

20

went back there, he decided to defy his parents' wishes and be with this other woman."

As Roshanna finished her story, she sobbed, and I held her just as I had once held my children. Even though I hadn't been in Afghanistan long, I knew that things could hardly be worse for a girl. People don't dismiss a divorce with a benign label such as "irreconcilable differences" in Afghanistan. If a man divorces you, other people assume there must be something wrong with you. People will whisper that you are lazy or willful or a bad cook or—worst of all—that you were not a virgin. I love the Afghan people, but their true national sport is gossip. As a hairdresser—someone whose professional motto could be "Do tell!" and who takes great pleasure in the whirl of divulged secrets and suppositions that goes on in every salon—I consider myself an expert on the subject. I wondered if the taint of Roshanna's almost-marriage had made its rounds through the tea shops and neighborhood stores. She confirmed this, telling me that many of the Afghan men she encountered while she worked as a secretary had already made the mental leap from divorcee to whore. They'd take every opportunity to push her into dark corners and grope her in a way that they would never treat "nice" girls. Her father had been imploring her to leave her job because of this; when I mentioned that I might want to come back to Kabul and start a beauty school, she leapt at this opportunity. But on that day back in 2002, my heart sank as I realized that this lovely girl

21

would probably never be chosen as a man's first wife again. She would likely be considered only as a second or third wife for a much older man. She was sure of this, too; that was why she cried every time we spoke of it.

Or at least that was why I thought she was crying.

Then this engineer's mother waltzed into her salon two years later, and Roshanna's fortunes changed dramatically. I was back in America when it happened, but still planning to return to Afghanistan as soon as I could. Roshanna and I had been keeping in touch by e-mail, and all of a sudden, the whole tenor of her messages changed—it was almost as if music played when one of them dropped into my in-box. She had always hoped she'd be able to marry a man from a good family and have children. Now it seemed that she would get this wish. I was happy for her and didn't even want to ask about the problem with her first engagement. It seemed impossible that the engineer's family had not heard about it, especially since they were distantly related. Maybe they ran in vastly different circles. Or maybe they were a progressive family who weren't about to think ill of her because some cad of a cousin had toyed with her briefly, not caring if he ruined her reputation. Maybe they saw past the innuendo to Roshanna herself, as perfect a wife as any man could want. I hoped this was the case.

Before the engagement party, there had been yet another party—a sort of seal-the-deal gala to celebrate

22

the end of the families' negotiations. Roshanna invited me to attend as her honored guest, and I was back in Kabul by that time and eager to share my friend's big day. The party was held in a large house in one of Kabul's old neighborhoods. Men and women from both families filed inside, and then the men stayed downstairs and the women went upstairs and into a room heaped with good things to eat. When the mother-in-law arrived, she gave a basket of imported candies to Roshanna's mother, then kissed Roshanna, her mother, and then me and Roshanna's sisters three times on the cheeks. The groom's sisters and seven of his aunts and girl cousins followed with their kisses. There was so much kissing that my neck started to feel unhinged. Then the mother-in-law hung a gold necklace around Roshanna's neck. It was huge, like something a wrestler would win at a tournament. Each of the groom's sisters and aunts placed a gold ring on one of Roshanna's dainty little fingers, until she had gold all the way up to her fingertips. I could hear laughing from the men's room downstairs and then clapping. I went to the landing and peered down, but one of the groom's sisters pulled me back. "They sign the papers now," she explained. Her father was probably giving Roshanna's father the fat envelope stuffed with her dowry.

Then the groom's female relatives started to clap their hands and sing as one of them pounded a small drum. The mother-in-law and one of the groom's sisters unfolded something that looked like a huge umbrella draped with a soft netting stitched with flowers. They held it high, and the other women from the groom's family danced over to take up the edges of the netting; then they floated it over Roshanna's head and circled her, singing still, dancing, keeping step with the beat of the drum. It was as if Roshanna were at the center of a bright, noisy carousel. She stood still as the room turned around her, touching her hands to her hair nervously, her face pale against the moving backdrop of her in-laws' brightly colored dresses, her lips pinched together. In the back of the room, her mother and sisters held one another. They looked at the dancers sadly.

If I'd known then what I know now, I might not have been alarmed by Roshanna's forlorn appearance during this ceremony. Afghan brides aren't really supposed to look happy at these events. Just as her parents turn down the first offer of marriage to show how precious their daughter is—and continue to look sad at all the wedding events—the daughter isn't supposed to act as if she welcomes the union, either. She's supposed to show that she's sad to leave her parents' home for that of her husband's family. Her sadness is a sign of respect for her parents. But even now that I know this, I don't think all the sadness is feigned. After all, the bride is leaving behind the tight embrace of her own family for one that may bring as much pain as pleasure. A mother-in-law sometimes turns into a tyrant after the wedding is over, expecting that her son's wife will become a sort of unpaid household servant who will sweep the floors, bring in the firewood, and even rub her feet when they ache. Husbands sometimes turn into tyrants, too. Or they turn into distant shadows as they spend all their time working and socializing with other men, returning to the home only for a meal or two. A man's new wife will serve this meal without any expectation that he will talk or even eat with her.

But I didn't know then what I know now, so I joined the forlorn-looking Roshanna after the dancing stopped. I took her hand, protective and suddenly apprehensive about her future since I knew so much about her past. She looked at me with terror and leaned toward me to whisper, while her new in-laws continued to sing and clap. "Oh, my God," she said hoarsely. "This is really happening, isn't it? What am I going to do?"

It was then that I divined her secret. She was not a virgin.

I couldn't sleep that night; I couldn't stop thinking about what she must be going through. The next day she came to the beauty school, and we ran out to a quiet place in back, between the building and the compound wall. She leaned against the wall and wept, tears of kohl streaking her cheeks. "My first husband, the one in Germany—he forced me the day after our engagement party!" She gasped. She had never had the nerve to tell her parents about this. They would have been distraught and outraged if they'd known, since there is always a formal consummation ceremony at the beginning of a marriage in which the couple spend their first night as man and wife and the family wait outside for proof that the girl was a virgin. That's the proper, time-honored way to consummate a marriage, but her cousin had grabbed her for a brutal quickie when he got the chance—and then bolted.

Roshanna had even been too ashamed to tell me until this moment.

And now she was headed toward another marriage with another man who lived abroad. Once again, the groom and a representative from her family would be signing the nika-khat at the engagement party because her husband—whom she still hadn't met— would be going back to Amsterdam a few days after the party. He wasn't planning to return to Afghanistan for the wedding party—odd as it may seem, this happens pretty often—and his family had announced that they wanted to have the consummation ceremony right after the engagement party.

I hadn't forgotten any of this in the few months since the contract-signing party. I suppose, like Roshanna, I put it out of my mind because there was nothing I could do about it. Nothing she could do, either, if she intended to go ahead and marry the engineer from Amsterdam. His family would never accept her as his first wife if they knew she wasn't a virgin. Neither would any other family. So when she visited my salon during those months, we talked only about her dresses for the upcoming engagement party and wedding, her

26

hair, the food that would be served, the guests who would be invited, and so on. We chatted about inconsequential matters. We enjoyed the gossip that followed my customers into the salon and filled it like strong perfume. Even when we were alone, we never talked about what might happen at the consummation ceremony. I didn't even want to think about it. I felt sick every time I tried.

But today is finally the day for the engagement party followed by the consummation. In the main part of the salon, I inspect the foils on Roshanna's mother-in-law and help the sisters-in-law pick out the right shades of nail polish to offset their gowns. Then I head back to the waxing room to see the sheets neatly folded on the foot of the bed. I go to look for Roshanna in the facial room, and she's there under a spotlight and Topekai's penetrating glare. Topekai has already shaped one of Roshanna's eyebrows into a delicate arch and is now inspecting the errant hairs on the other one, which she will remove by threading—an ancient technique Afghan beauticians employ to whisk away hair using a piece of thread that is rolled across the skin and looped around individual follicles. Topekai holds one end of the thread in her mouth and has the rest of it wrapped around her fingers like in a game of cat's cradle. She points at the corner of Roshanna's eye, where a tear has formed, and rolls her eyes. She thinks Roshanna is crying because threading hurts. It certainly can be that painful, but I know better.

When Roshanna finally comes downstairs, the skin

on her face is so clean that it looks naked. She is pale except for the red patches where her hair has been yanked off. All the other women applaud when she comes into the room, glad for her that her first big ordeal of the day is over. She fans her face and smiles. Bahar rushes to get a basin of hot water; then she begins Roshanna's pedicure, moving on to her manicure as I finish the mother-in-law's hair. Finally, I begin to work on Roshanna's hair after Baseera washes and blows it dry. I section off small pieces with a rat-tail comb and pin them back, then sink one hand into a special pot of gel that has gold glitter mixed into it. I begin shaping one of the clumps of hair into a big barrel curl on top of her head using the gold glitter gel. It seems as if everyone in the salon holds her breath, waiting to see if the big curl will collapse, but it stands. Then I shape some of the other clumps into big glitter-crusted curls until there is a mass of them on top of her head, like a pile of gold bangles. Next, I work some of the other strands in and around the big gold curls using red, green, and blue glitter gel. Everyone else leans in with suggestions. How about curls that slink across her cheeks like snakes—held in place with gel, of course? When I point out that I've already used all of Roshanna's hair to make the big curls on top of her head, Baseera kindly offers to cut off a few pieces of her own hair and glue them on the bride's cheeks. Roshanna declines.

Finally, everyone crowds around to watch me work

on Roshanna's makeup. It's customary to coat the bride's face with a heavy white matte base, almost like that of a geisha, but I don't like this look, and it bothers me even more today—I feel as if I'm erasing my friend's face. So I use a light hand, and I can tell by Roshanna's look that she approves. After this base is applied, I put green eye shadow—to match her dress—on her lids, then swoop it out to the sides of her face. I put a layer of glittering peach eye shadow above that, just below her eyebrows, then shape her eyebrows with a black pencil so that they arch and swoop, too.

My hands don't feel steady enough for the next step, so I hand Roshanna's little bottle of kohl powder to Baseera. She tells Roshanna to lick the kohl stick, dip it in the bottle, and blow away the excess powder. Then Baseera inserts the coated stick into the inside corner of Roshanna's eye, tells her to close it, and moves the stick across her eye so that it coats the inner lids, top and bottom, with black kohl. If this is done right, the stick glides across the inner lids, just barely missing the surface of the eye. While Roshanna's eyes are closed, Baseera also attaches a huge pair of false lashes. Roshanna opens her eyes and flaps her lids so vigorously that one of the sisters-in-law laughs. "You make the hair on the floor blow away," she says. Finally, I work on Roshanna's lips, lining them in dark reddish brown and filling them in with a bright candy-apple red. I apply some contouring makeup and some rouge, then step back. The mother-in-law takes

Roshanna's chin and inspects her. She's pleased but wonders about gluing a row of rhinestones just under Roshanna's eyebrows, which she saw on another bride several weeks ago. No, her daughters tell her; this is good, more would be too much. Then I have to rush off to do my own makeup and change clothes.

Soon there are cars honking and men shouting outside, and the compound guard comes to knock on the salon door. All of us walk outside in a cluster around Roshanna, the groom's sisters holding their hands around her crown of curls to keep them from blowing over, the mother-in-law trying to lift the hem of her dress enough that it doesn't drag in the dirt but not enough that her legs show. Outside the wall, the groom's male cousins point to the bridal car proudly. They've spent the day decorating it with fabric and flowers, so that it looks kind of like a huge piece of cake with lots of icing. Roshanna and the groom's female relatives pile inside the car, pulling me in as well.

At the hall, the groom's mother and sisters sweep Roshanna inside right away for pictures. There is a blinding fluorescent light overhead in the photo room, and I can barely even look at her with the light shining off all the glitter and gold and spangles. The photographer makes her turn this way and that—arms this way, head angled that way, mouth just so. He wants poses that make her look innocent yet seductive, kind of like the shots of movie stars from the 1940s—assuming that they were getting photographed while their sweating older sisters were holding a Koran over their heads. Roshanna sees that one of her sisters is standing next to me, and she makes a face at us, then folds her hands together under her chin and puts on a dazed-by-romance smile, looking kind of like the heroines in the Indian Bollywood movies that everyone watches in Afghanistan. "Should I start to sing now?" she jokes, because that's what the Bollywood stars do in the unlikeliest moments. The photographer puts down his equipment and shouts. He wants her to look like the haughty wedding mannequins in the stores.

The photographer finally finishes and starts packing away his things. Roshanna stares at him as if stunned that this diversion is actually over. Her sisters and mother flutter around her, and then one of her sisters opens the door to the party room and the noise of all the guests roars in. Roshanna turns a pale face toward me. "Walk with me," she pleads and holds her hand out, so I come over to her and hold her trembling hand and we move through the door.

The room is so full of glitz that even I am dizzy. Ornate chandeliers drip crystal tears over the heads of hundreds of women who are dressed like all the glamorous mannequins. Velvet, gold brocade, tassels, seed pearls, embroidered silk—and that's just one of the dresses! As we make our way down a long white cloth that leads to an archway twined with roses, I see another side to the women of Kabul, who usually dress as if they're headed to a funeral. Here, they truly

31

strut their stuff, with slit skirts, plunging necklines, and heels so high they could swan-dive from them into a pool. Later, I'm told that this is where many potential mothers-in-law find wives for their sons; today, I'm just dazzled by the sight of them. As are the videographers, who pan the crowd and prompt one table after another to preen and smile. One of them walks backward along the white cloth in front of Roshanna and me with a camera the size of a tree trunk, so I smile as if I'm one of those movie stars who escort Oscar winners across the stage. Roshanna looks down at the white cloth, and her mother and sisters follow us, dropping rose petals in our wake. One of her sisters is still holding the Koran over Roshanna's head, but her arms are drooping dangerously and the Koran nearly flattens Roshanna's barrel curls. Over to the side, a band is playing.

As we clear the archway, I see that the room is divided in two by a huge curtain—all the women are on this side, so I figure that all the men must be on the other. As if to prove this, a man's head pops up through a slit in the curtain and he gapes lecherously at the women, then is pulled back and the curtain drops. I see that we are making our way toward a stage on the women's side of the room, where two golden chairs—like those of a king and queen—are set up. There is a table in front of the chairs with what looks like a treasure chest, and a spotlight shines on the empty chairs. As we get closer to the stage, the curtain rustles, and all of a sudden, a man appears on the stage. I can't see his face well because the lights are so bright. "I think that's the groom," I tell Roshanna, but she won't look up. I want to turn around and ask her mother if that's the groom, but she hasn't seen him, either. Besides, the glare of the spotlights is still making it hard to see anything. We keep walking toward the stage, the noise of the crowd pulsing around us, the music picking up tempo, and Roshanna trembling so much that it's hard to keep a grip on her.

Finally, the man on the stage comes into focus, his face pale and dazed—and suddenly there is the mother-in-law, reaching out to Roshanna. The mother-in-law pulls Roshanna up on the stage and takes the groom's hand and places it on Roshanna's, but Roshanna flinches as if his hand were on fire. Then all the members of the families climb on the stage, and I'm jostled away by a crowd of photographers and videographers. Lights flash, cameras whir and click, and the men wielding them push against one another for the best angle. I stand on my toes to see how Roshanna is holding up, and I resist the urge to yell "Smile," as we do at all such events back home. But she continues to look mournful, as do the members of her family. The groom doesn't look mournful, but he doesn't look happy, either. He looks stunned, as if someone knocked him out a few minutes ago and he just woke up to this assault by the cameramen.

Finally, the mothers lead Roshanna and her husband off the stage and pull them through the crowd toward a door at the far end of the room. Women at the tables near me stand and gesture me to join them, and I finally sit down.

"Where did they go?" I ask one of the women wearing a rhinestone headdress who seems to speak some English.

"They get to know each other now," she replies. "And family members get to meet, too."

"Are they going to come back out here to eat?"

"No, not in front of all these people. This is their first meal together as man and wife."

The band starts up again. Everyone stands to watch as the groom's mother and sisters step onto the dance floor. They move around the floor together in slow, graceful steps, swaying toward one another and then falling away, like the pattern in a kaleidoscope forming and re-forming. Sometimes the mother is at the center, her purple-swathed bulk surprisingly sinuous and light. Sometimes her daughters are at the middle, their arms stretched out to the sides, their hundreds of bangles jingling and glistening in the light, their hips swaying. Roshanna's family sit off to the side, their sad faces a stark contrast to all the gaiety.

Then the music changes and the dancing becomes more suggestive. The groom's sisters pump their hips and draw their hands across their faces as if feigning sexual ecstasy. Even the mother does an exaggerated bump and grind for a second; then she laughs and sinks into a chair someone has pushed toward her. And then all the women join the sisters on the dance floor; I am included—the woman with the rhinestone

headdress and her friends insist. There, I'm surrounded by the kind of dancing I would never have
expected from these women who dart down the city
streets—when they go out at all—draped in dark
colors with their eyes down. This is dirty dancing,
Kabul style: they shimmy, they shake, they arch their
backs and thrust their hips. The ones with long hair
whip it around, drape it over their faces, then lift it to
reveal parted lips and smoldering eyes. They snake
their arms behind their backs, to the sides, over their
heads, and their hands move as if they're stroking
imaginary lovers. They dance together and then break
apart, but when they're together they move their
hands along the sides of one another's bodies, sink to
the floor, and sway back up again, grazing cheeks,
arms, hips. And then I peer into the crowd, startled: I
notice that there are men on the women's side of the
room, holding them around the waist, spinning them,
and pressing their hips against them. I wonder if the
police will storm the room and drag them off for
sexual mingling. But then I realize that they're not
men but women dressed as men, acting as men,
standing in for men.

I back off the dance floor, because this scene is
almost too much to take in when I'm right in the
middle of it; then I notice that another man has stuck
his head through the curtain to watch. Sure enough, a
big hand quickly appears to grasp him by the hair and
pull him back, but this makes me curious. I make my
way over to the split in the curtain and arrange a tiny

peephole so that I can look through. It's almost the same wild scene on the other side, only with a different set of clothes and less glitz and the powerful aroma of male sweat. The men are dancing with one another, snaking their arms, thrusting their hips, holding one another close, shimmying to the ground while running their hands down one another's sides— all of it. I'm stunned, and I let the curtain flap open a little more so that I can watch.

The men are obviously very comfortable touching one another, dancing with one another. They show one another not only affection but also sexual vigor. I wonder what would happen if the two sides of the room ever got together, wonder if any of the men and women ever find a way to sneak off together, and then suddenly I don't have any more time to wonder about it. Some of the men have seen me peering through the curtain, and they pull it open wider. There I am, my face poked into their side of the room, looking very much like a woman with her head in a guillotine. It seems as if all the men in the room turn around to look and shout. Blushing, I pull my head back and move away.

The dancing on the women's side has begun to slow down, because the food is on its way. Each of the red-clothed tables seats around twenty people, but enough food is brought for forty or more. Piles of kebabs on platters, pasta stuffed with leeks and covered with a meat sauce, bowls with every known method of food preparation applied to eggplant, rice with nuts and raisins. The delivery of food goes on for what seems like hours, as the family makes sure no one leaves the feast without having stuffed themselves ten times over. There are no utensils on the tables, and everyone eats with her hands. I admire the way the other women are able to eat without spilling so much as a drop of sauce or a grain of rice. A thread of cabbage coated with yogurt falls in my lap, and I whisk it away quickly, but I soon wind up wearing more of my dinner than I eat. I drop so much that I'm actually still hungry when the servers come back to take away the plates. Once the food is gone, the women around me stand, kiss my cheeks, and begin to leave.

I'm not sure how I'm going to get home, but finally I see one of Roshanna's sisters rushing toward me. She tells me that Roshanna wants me to come to her parents' house with some of the other honored guests and the groom's family. So we go outside, and I squeeze back into the bridal car with a dazed Roshanna and about six other women in tight dresses and high heels. As we start driving, a car behind us honks and pulls up, and a man with a video camera leans out the passenger side window. Then an insane race begins as the driver of the wedding car tries to make it as hard as possible for the video car to keep up with us. We race up and down Kabul's streets, dodging people on foot and on bicycle, screeching around corners. We pass a bus and, incredibly, wind up driving on the other side of the oncoming traffic, almost on the sidewalk. We almost sideswipe a patient, dusty water buffalo that's standing near a group of men having an argument. The driver guffaws that he's lost the videographer and we turn a corner, but there the other man is, facing us. He leans so far out of his window that I'm sure he's going to fall, but he wins the game: he's able to film our driver frantically backing out into traffic again as the women in the back of the car—except Roshanna—scream with laughter. Driving in Kabul is never a walk in the park, let me tell you, but I truly thought we were all going to die on the way to Roshanna's house.

When we arrive, we take off our shoes at the door and go into the living room. Roshanna and her new husband sit on the only chairs in the room, and the rest of us drop onto cushions. I wave and put on my biggest smile for Roshanna, but she doesn't respond. She and her husband sit without touching, without smiling, like bride and groom mannequins propped in the chairs. Roshanna's sister takes my arm and leads me to her, pats the cushion next to her, and I sit near my friend, who only glances at me and then resumes staring into space. For a moment, it's hard to believe that this woman with the dead eyes and rigid body is my Roshanna. But I know that the consummation ceremony is the next event on the marital agenda. I realize she's so stunned with fear that she can't do anything other than stare. I don't even see her breathing.

We are all served tea and sweets. There is much talking among the guests and families. I can't understand them because my Dari—the Persian dialect spoken in Afghanistan—is not so good, and the one person in the room who speaks English well—Roshanna—isn't talking. Then the groom's family and the other guests begin leaving in little groups, and I stand, both relieved to go and guilty about leaving my friend. But again, her sister clamps herself to my arm. She shakes her head while she keeps talking. Her mother comes over, too, and tugs on my arm. I don't know what's going on until Roshanna turns to me. "Please stay," she whispers, and then she lays her own cold fingers on my wrist.

Roshanna's mother turns to the bride and groom. She beckons them and they rise, although Roshanna catches her heel on the cushion and staggers forward. They follow her mother down the hall, Roshanna still a little shaky on her feet. She bumps into the wall, as if she's been drinking, but this has been a strictly traditional Muslim affair with no drinking—as for myself, I'm thinking fondly of the bottle of Johnnie Walker Red in my room at home. I hear a door slam in the back of the house; then I'm led to a guest room with four of the other women. We lie down on the cushions in our party clothes, and one by one, we fall asleep. I'm the last to go. I keep listening for noises from down the hall, but all is quiet and I finally let go of my fear. Or it lets me go. Anyway, I sleep.

And awake to someone shaking me. Roshanna's mother is standing over me, waving a white handkerchief, her long black braid swinging over my head.

She's talking rapidly and clutching the Koran to her chest. Every once in a while, she stops talking and covers the Koran with kisses. I look over at one of Roshanna's sisters, who winces and tries to explain. "No blood," she whispers. I remember that this is supposed to be the proof of Roshanna's virginity: a bloody handkerchief, dropped outside the door of the consummation room.

Roshanna's mother is still talking away, rapid, frantic words that might not make any sense in Dari, either; then she grabs my hand and works the handkerchief into my clenched fist. She and the sister start pulling me down the hall. I protest, but it doesn't do me any good. They open the door to the consummation room, and in the dim light, I see Roshanna crouching on one of the cushions at the side of the room. Her husband is sitting on the bed. He turns his face away from the door, and then Roshanna's mother pulls her from the room and closes the door.

"It is not working," the husband says suddenly. I didn't think he spoke English, but he does, at least a little. "It's not working."

I'm not sure what he means, but he seems troubled, not angry. Is he having a hard time getting an erection? Is she having a hard time with lubrication? Even though he's forty years old, is it possible that he doesn't know what to do in here? That he's been told all his life that sex is so dirty and shameful he's never tried it? I decide these questions are too big for me to tackle, even though many of the Afghans I've met seem to think Americans can figure anything out. I try a different angle.

"Sometimes there is no blood, even if the girl is a virgin," I say. "If she works too hard or even falls down a flight of stairs, there is sometimes no blood."

He nods, his dark eyes on the ground.

"Sometimes, it's hard to have sex if the girl is nervous," I continue. "You have to be gentle. You have to touch her very gently so she can relax."

He doesn't say anything. I don't want to use body language to show him where he should touch her. Instead, I stroke my arm. "Like the way you'd pat a dog if it's scared," I add desperately. It's the only thing I can think of, but he gives me a funny look. Then I remember what an Afghan friend told me the other day, that Muslims don't like dogs because one of them was supposed to have bitten the Prophet.

"I know all these things," he says with sudden agitation. "But it's not working."

Then Roshanna's mother is knocking on the door, and she brings Roshanna back into the room. She smoothes her hair and then smiles at me as if I've made everything right again. "Good-bye, good-bye, good-bye!" the mother says, pulling me out the door. Then one of the sisters leads me back to the guest room while the mother settles herself right outside the door of the consummation room.

The other women are awake and waiting for me in the guest room. I bet they'd kill to have a Dari-English dictionary right now so they could ask me what's

41

going on. I just wave my hand as if the problem down the hall is so minor that it need not concern them, then settle myself on my cushion again. I ignore them until they stop talking and fall asleep, and then, amazingly, I too fall asleep. It's a bad sleep, though: I'm back in the car on the way to the wedding and the driver keeps smashing into other cars and I'm afraid, once again, that we'll all die.

Then someone is shaking me. Roshanna's mother is back, waving the clean white handkerchief, kissing the Koran, then hugging it to her chest, rocking back and forth, wailing and crying, talking rapidly to me and to her daughters, who are again urging me up off my cushion. This time, her mother looks even more terrified than before, if that's possible. I don't know how many trial runs Roshanna will be allowed before the groom decides his family has been cheated, that she is not a virgin, that she is a disgrace and a humiliation to both families. I try to act as if this is no big problem, that the couple just need a little bit more prompting. "Let me talk to Roshanna alone," I say.

The groom leaves the room, and I settle my arms around my shivering friend. "I'm afraid," she whispers. "It hurts so much when he pushes into me that I pull away. I can't help it."

"Try to relax," I tell her. "Breathe slowly. It won't hurt as much if you can relax." Then I give her the advice that so many women who don't really like sex cling to—just lean back, open your legs, and try to think of something else. I tell her that it won't hurt after the first few times, that she might even find it as pleasurable as I do. She looks at me as if I'm trying to convince her that she will enjoy chewing broken glass someday.

"One more thing," I tell her. "If this happens again, tell them that you want to talk to me one more time. But this time, don't let your mother take the handkerchief." Then I kiss her and leave. I check my watch, because I know that after the morning call to prayer the in-laws will be coming back to the house. They'll want to see a bloody handkerchief.

This time, I can't sleep. And sure enough, her mother is back in the room in a half hour or so, weeping, kissing the Koran, imploring me to talk to Roshanna again. I'm ready for her this time, with my purse tucked up inside my dress. Back in the consummation room, I ask Roshanna for the white handkerchief and pull a pair of fingernail clippers out of my purse.

"What are you doing?" she asks.

I grit my teeth and dig the clippers under one of my nails, then cut down to the quick until blood spurts out. I wipe my finger back and forth on the handkerchief, then hand it to her. "Here's your virginity," I tell her. "Hide it under your cushion and then pull it out the next time he enters you. Let your mother come in and find it."

She puts her hands over her face again, and I leave the room.

Back in the guest room, I fall asleep once more and

43

am awakened just as the sky is beginning to lighten. The house is in chaos. I can hear Roshanna's mother wailing and screaming. Doors are slamming, people are crowding the hallway, everyone is talking at once. I stagger up from my cushion, filled with dread that the husband has discovered the bloody handkerchief under their bed or that it somehow doesn't look the way it should.

But when I rush out into the hallway, I see that Roshanna's mother is wailing for joy. "Virgin!" she shouts at me triumphantly, waving the handkerchief stained with my blood. "Virgin!"

Chapter 2

I left for Afghanistan in May 2002, that first spring after the fall of the Taliban. I didn't have any idea that I'd still be here nearly five years later doing spiral perms and introducing the art of pubic waxing. I had taken emergency and disaster relief training two months before 9/11 with a nonprofit organization called the Care for All Foundation (CFAF). Then I talked myself into a place on the first team that the organization sent to Afghanistan. I imagined I would spend the month there bandaging wounds, splinting broken limbs, clambering over the rubble, and helping people who were still hiding from the Taliban climb into daylight. I bought my first-ever pair of rugged boots for that trip at the army surplus store. I figured I'd be staying in a tent the whole time and wouldn't be

44

able to take a shower, so half my suitcase was stuffed with Wet Ones so that I could tidy myself up every day behind a tree.

Very little of that trip met those expectations.

I first met my team members at the airport in Chicago, where we identified one another at the gate by the little red hats we had been instructed to wear. Then we flew to Pakistan, where we boarded a United Nations flight for Kabul. I spent the next few hours sleeping, reading, and looking out the window. Mostly, it was too cloudy to see anything, but there were times when I could see the terrain we were crossing. The mountains jutted upward like pitted brown teeth, and the plane seemed frail against such a harsh landscape. As it finally cleared the mountains and started its descent for Kabul, everyone strained toward the windows to see what was coming. Below us was the vast bowl in the middle of the mountains where the city was located, an immense green plain— seven thousand feet above sea level with large, irregular, brown splotches of habitation. At this height, I couldn't really see the scars of war. I remember puzzling over the shapes below me, though. It was as if Kabul was laid out in boxes, like a crossword puzzle.

When we finally bumped down on the tarmac, that vision of sweeping green vanished. I couldn't even see the mountains anymore because the air was so heavy with dust. Instead, I could see only the devastation surrounding the airport. On both sides of the runway, there were jagged holes in the ground from bombs and land mines. They looked like burst blisters, still raw and painful. Nearby, there was also a huge graveyard of tanks and planes that had been twisted and torn by the fighting. On the façade of the main airport building, what looked like a hand-painted sign said WELCOME TO AFGHANISTAN. The building looked as if it hadn't welcomed visitors for many years, though— there were broken windows, scarred bricks, and piles of rubble heaped outside.

Before we climbed down the stairs from the plane, all the women quickly pulled the scarves we had been told to bring over our heads. On the ground, we passed by dozens of stern-looking men with machine guns. It looked more like we were being captured than like we were being welcomed, but I straightened my spine— aching from two days of travel—and followed the line of volunteers into the building. I wasn't afraid. People still ask me if I was worried about the reception we'd get from the Afghan people. Whether they'd love us because America had driven away the Taliban or hate us because we had bombed the bejesus out of their capital and countryside to do it. Whether they shared the fanaticism that had propelled the 9/11 terrorists to kill three thousand people in New York City or whether they feared it even more than we did. But I didn't think about any of these things. I was just excited to be there, and I was trying to make sure I didn't lose track of our group.

Inside the airport was complete and total chaos.

There was a crowd of people pressing up against a man who was checking passports before we could get through to baggage claim. When we finally squeezed through that bottleneck, we found that our bags and equipment were being tossed into a heap by men wearing long pieces of cloth twisted into ragged, mushroom-shaped turbans. Other men and boys swirled around us asking if we wanted them to help with the luggage, but we had been told beforehand by the group leaders that we should get our own bags— that the locals would charge us too much money. So when three men reached out for my luggage, I shook my head. They backed away, disappointed but respectful. I must say that, in all my time in their country, I've never met a rude Afghan. Even when they're pointing a gun at you, they're polite.

Outside, a van and a driver waited for us. Before we could leave, there was a confusing moment when one of the men carrying a machine gun—and there were plenty of them in front of the airport, too—was talking to the driver and shaking his head. I held my breath, wondering if they wouldn't allow us to go, but finally we started to bump along the street leading away from the airport.

"Why was he shaking his head?" I asked the driver. I had to shake my own head to show him what I meant. "In America, this means no."

He flashed a grin at me. "Here, it means 'Okay—go ahead.'"

My overall impression of Kabul in those first

moments was that it was a city of gray. Everything seemed to be the same color, from the crumbling gray walls of the mud-brick houses to the clothes that people were wearing to the sky filled with dust. The roads themselves were long strips of gray mud, with lots of holes and humps of rock and dirt and only occasional flat spaces. But against that basic palette of gray, I started to notice bright colors here and there. Once we got away from the airport, the street turned commercial. Along both sides and all crowded together, there were shops made from old shipping containers—like the kind I used to see going by on trains back in the States. There were shops made from burned-out trucks, shops made from tarps draped over wood or metal frames. Even the shabbiest of these stores had colorful signs above them, with the stores' names written in elegantly flowing Dari—and here and there, an added sign in English. The first few blocks of stores seemed to be selling basic goods, such as tires and tin pipes and big rolls of cotton bat-ting. Often the roofs were heaped with things like car parts or plastic jugs. Extra inventory, I guess.

Then we turned a corner, and suddenly, all the stores were selling food. Our driver swerved around a cluster of old men who were talking in the middle of the road and passed within inches of a huge dead sheep hanging from the front of a shop, its skin and head lying on the ground. A live sheep was tied up on a rope next to it. As we rolled by, I imagined that the live sheep was hoping that everyone would fill themselves on his dead, dried-up, fly-covered brother. There were brightly painted carts along the street heaped with fruits and vegetables that seemed bigger than any I'd ever seen. Were cauliflowers usually the size of basketballs? Were cantaloupes usually so large that you'd need two hands to carry them? We sped past shops that had big white plastic containers that held conical heaps of spices and nuts—red heaps, gold heaps, brown heaps—and shops with hundreds of things that looked like snowshoes hanging from their roofs. I found out later this was the flatbread that Afghans eat with just about every meal. We sped past shops that sold packaged goods in tins and boxes and bags, each colorful and so artistically displayed that the shops almost looked as if they were piled with beautifully wrapped presents. Even though we certainly weren't here to shop, I wished the driver could pull over for a minute so I could wander around. Then we drove past a man who was shaking something in a big pan over an open fire. The smell of roasted corn floated into the van, and I realized I was famished.

Though the Afghans added lots of color to their environment—the painted signs, the vibrant store displays—they didn't wear much in the way of color themselves. We passed people on foot, on bicycles, crowded into wagons, in cars; there were even a few young men who startled us by cantering on horses between the lines of cars. The clothing was almost always the same, either close to white or close to black. The only clothes that seemed to stand out were the blue burqas covering the women. These were just a whisper of color—soft, fluid ripples that moved through the black and white and gray and tan stream of men, usually with a few children attached to their blue fringes. It took me several minutes to realize that, aside from the few women in burqas, there weren't many women on the streets at all. Even on the very busy blocks, there were hundreds of men walking, pushing wheelbarrows, dickering over prices, balancing long, curled-up rugs on their shoulders, calling out to customers, sniffing at bananas, inspecting pomegranates, nodding their heads in conversation, eating kebabs, and peering at us as we drove by, but aside from the few elusive puffs of blue, no women. It was chilling to see this visual proof of the absence of women from public life.

The driver turned another corner, and we were on a street where half the buildings had been blown apart. Some of them were still being used, at least on the lower level. We passed one building where there was a thriving business in metal pots on the first floor, storage on the second floor, and teetering spires of shattered brick on the third. As we kept going, I saw more and more empty spaces between the buildings. I wondered why there were so many children playing on the sidewalks and streets instead of in the open spaces. Later, I found out that these open spaces hadn't been cleared of mines yet. The terrible inventions of war were still there waiting, buried just a few inches underground.

We kept driving until we left the stores and crowds behind. Now we were clattering along streets that were more like canyons—all the buildings on either side were surrounded by high walls made of either exposed mud bricks or bricks covered with stucco or concrete. I remembered all the little squares I had seen from the air and realized that I had been seeing walled compounds. The compounds looked pretty much the same, one after another, except for their colorful metal gates. It was a little like being in a room where everyone wore a gray suit but was allowed one fancy brooch. Some of the walls were topped with long snarls of barbed wire. Many had clusters of holes in them, as if they had been pecked by big, strong birds. I realized that they must have taken some bullet fire during the fighting. The walls often fluttered with glued-on papers that had pictures of stern-looking, bearded men in blue and black ink. Many of the compounds had little houses—not much bigger than phone booths—outside by the road with machine-gun-toting guards lounging against them. It was hard to see what was going on behind the walls. I could sometimes see roofs, sometimes trees with bits of colorful cloth clinging to them, and once in a while one of the big metal gates would be open and I could see gardens and cars inside. Finally, our driver pulled up to one of these walled compounds, honked the horn, and the gate swung open. Instead of living in a tent, I would be staying in a guesthouse—kind of like a bed-and-breakfast—for the foreign aid staff and volunteers.

"Whites? Darks?" I called out as my teammates rose from one of their endless strategy sessions. "I'm filling a tub with hot water, and I actually have some detergent."

Once we settled into the guesthouse, I finally got to know my six teammates better. They were lovely people, every one of them—and all of them had some sort of medical background. They were doctors, nurses, and dentists, some of whom had already done disaster work. I realized that they were probably wondering why the CFAF had bothered to send along a hairdresser. I started to wonder about this myself. I tried to find ways to be useful over the next few days while all the rest of them discussed the most pressing health care issues in the city and started making plans to open a clinic. At first, the only thing I could find to do was everyone else's laundry. Then, when they started to go out to hold clinics in temporary spots—it would take a long time before they found a house to rent for a permanent clinic—I went along to take people's blood pressure. But really, anyone can do that.

When someone else on the team came to tell me she had a job for me to do, I was momentarily excited. But it turned out she just wanted me to make welcome posters for the new team members who would be arriving soon. I started to feel frustrated and restless, wondering if I'd ever have much of an opportunity to do something meaningful. My consolation in those first few days was that, while everyone else was figuring out how to save lives, I had started to make friends with the Afghans who worked around the compound. The lovely girl who was always so kind about helping me figure out how to get hot water and phone cards to call home was Roshanna. The shy, handsome man who drove the van was Daud.

After a few days, our little group of volunteers went to a meeting of other foreigners who had been living in Kabul for a while—including some who had been there for years. We rode to the meeting site in the van, and when we arrived, our group leaders urged us to get out quickly and duck into the building. No one wanted to attract attention to the fact that a big bunch of foreigners was getting together; it might make us an irresistible target to any Taliban sympathizers who were still in town. Inside, there were about 150 people milling around, eating cookies and introducing themselves, passing out business cards and telling one another about the projects they were involved in. I overheard their conversations and had the sinking feeling that everyone else had been trained in something that met a specific and pressing need here. Since the fall of the Taliban, hundreds of foreigners and dozens of nongovernmental organizations (NGOs)—big ones like the Red Cross as well as smaller ones like CFAF—had been pouring into the country. All around me, I heard people introducing themselves as teachers, engineers, nutritionists, agricultural specialists, and experts of all sorts. Not once did anyone introduce herself as a hairdresser.

Toward the end of the meeting, Allen—our group leader—was asked to introduce the team. He stood in front of the room and explained CFAF's plans to open a health care clinic. That got a round of applause. He also got quite a few cheers when he offered the team's services to the other Westerners in the room as well. Some of these people had been working here for months with cavities that needed filling, mysterious rashes that wouldn't go away, and other ailments that they hadn't been able to do anything about. Then he introduced our team members one by one: doctor, nurse, dentist, doctor, and midwife. Everyone in the room clapped as each team member was introduced. When Allen finally got around to introducing me, he gave me a bright smile, as if to assure me that he wasn't going to leave me out. "Finally, we have Debbie Rodriguez," he said. "She's a hairdresser from Holland, Michigan, who did some training—"

He didn't even get to finish his introduction, because the room broke into the wildest applause of the night. A few of the women were actually jumping up and down. It seemed like half the people in the room were pulling at their hair with relief. Allen hesitated, then finished talking about the clinic. The meeting soon broke up. And suddenly I was mobbed.

"We're so glad you're here!" said the woman who got to my side before any of the others. "There isn't a decent haircut within a day's drive of Kabul."

"We have literally risked our lives for highlights," another said. "Once I drove ten hours over the Khyber Pass to get my hair done in Pakistan. I had some other errands to run there, too, but that was the one thing I really couldn't do here."

"Aren't there any beauty salons in Kabul?" I asked.

"I think there used to be a lot of them, before the Taliban took over," the first woman said. "They pretty much squashed them out of existence. I hear some are resurfacing now, but they're in pretty rough shape."

"My kids and I got some kind of bionic lice at an Afghan salon," her friend added. "When we got back to the States, we had to use an industrial-strength pesticide to get rid of them. It took months!"

People were swarming around me, eager to set up appointments. They wanted to know what I was doing the next day and the day after that. They wanted to know how long I was staying in Kabul. They wanted directions to my guesthouse. I couldn't give directions, since I hadn't a clue which streets we had taken to get to the meeting, but I tried to point them toward the people who could tell them. They didn't even ask me whether I had brought any of the tools of my trade with me, but if they had I could have quickly assured them. I always travel with my scissors, my combs, a salon cape, and some product. It's just part of who I am.

And the next day, people started showing up at the guesthouse. I don't know how they found their way there, but they did. Word seemed to spread throughout

Kabul that there was a Western-style hairdresser in town. Soon, all sorts of people—journalists, diplomats, missionaries, aid workers, you name it—were trying to contact me. They couldn't call for appointments because there wasn't any phone service, but they managed to send word that they were coming. Every time I'd go out with the team to do some work, I'd return to find the door to my room covered with sticky notes from people wanting their hair done.

My team had finally figured out some useful tasks for me, including trauma counseling with Afghan children using puppets. But by the end of that first week, there was almost always a little group of Westerners waiting in the yard of our guesthouse for me. I'd take them up to my room between team assignments and cut their hair. Some people came with their kids, and I'd do the whole family. One German woman who had been living in Afghanistan for seven years even showed up with perm solution stored in a brown bottle so ancient that it looked as if it had been dug out of an archaeological site. She told me the Taliban had raided her house a bunch of times, but they'd never taken that bottle. I apologized and told her that I didn't have perm rods, but then she held up a bag—she had the rods, too. So I set her up out in the garden and gave her a perm. Roshanna and I served her tea and cookies while it set, and then I washed the solution off with a bucket of water.

All this time, I'd been making fast friends with the Afghans. While the other team members were busy doing the medical things that only they could do, I'd be hanging out with Roshanna, Daud the driver, Muqim the cook, and several others. There was a swing set in the garden, and Daud, Muqim, and I would sit there and talk and swing, talk and swing, until soon we'd be pumping ourselves up so high that we could see over the wall. Daud and Muqim would let themselves fly off the swings at the high point, tumble on the grass, and joke about who had gone the farthest. I'd have to laugh, remembering that *these* were those scary Afghan men half the world was afraid of.

One day, after I came back from doing trauma counseling at a school, Daud picked up one of my puppets that had a beard and head scarf and examined it. "Is this Osama bin Laden?" he asked. The puppet did look a little like Osama, but it had been Joseph of Nazareth in a former life. A church group had donated the puppets to our team. Now I was turning Joseph, Mary, and Jesus into ordinary Afghans who were trying to become happy families again in the aftermath of the wars. But Daud and Roshanna preferred the idea that the patriarch puppet was Osama. Roshanna picked up the Mary puppet and announced, "I am Osama's wife. I will help the Americans kill him!" And for the next half hour or so, we played "Search for bin Laden" throughout the downstairs of the house. We did some really bad things to the Osama puppet, but he recovered well enough to be an Afghan dad the next day.

I cut their hair, too. The men had been watching as I

cut some of the Westerners' hair—on nice days, I did it out in the garden—and they were intrigued with the kiwi-scented gel that I used to finish up some of the cuts. So I squirted a little on their hands, and they spread it on their hair. They liked it so much that they didn't want to wash it off. For days they walked around with stiff hair coated with dust. Then I offered to trim Roshanna's hair out in the garden. I took a few inches off the bottom and cut a few short angles around her face so that she could have little tendrils poking out of her head scarf. When I finished, I asked Muqim if he wanted a haircut. After a few minutes of deliberation, he said yes. I knew that Afghan men don't get their hair cut by women—they go to barbers, not beauticians—because there is no touching allowed between unmarried men and women, either professionally or casually. So I was careful to snip his hair gingerly, without a lot of physical contact, because I didn't want him to go home at the end of the day thinking he had sinned. But when I finished, he stared up at me with bleary, besotted eyes.

"I love you," he croaked. "I love you, I love you!"

Then I pointed my scissors at Daud. He had a haircut that was pretty typical of the Afghan men I had seen so far—a sort of pompadour trimmed short in the back with a big wad of hair puffed up on the top. It was like the hairdo Elvis had sported in his most hideous days, when he was wearing those tight leather pants and awful capes made by the Ice Capades people. I hated it. Daud backed away, but Muqim,

Roshanna, and some of the other Afghans hanging around decided to nab him for me. I put my scissors down and joined the chase. All of us raced around the yard trying to grab him, slipping in puddles, tripping over the hedges, laughing, hooting. We were so full of our own high spirits that you'd have thought we were roaring drunk. They finally captured him and dragged him back over to my chair, then tied his feet down and put a gag in his mouth. After all that, I only trimmed his hair a little. But when I was in the middle of doing it, Roshanna came running outside with a video camera and taped me standing over Daud, menacing him with my scissors while he rolled his eyes and tossed his head from side to side.

I still wonder if that videotape will show up on Aljazeera television someday, as evidence that American hairdressers are torturing Afghan men.

As I left my room and clomped downstairs, I nearly mowed down Allen, the head of our group. He regained his footing pretty quickly but stared at me for a few seconds too long. "Is something wrong?" I asked.

He reddened a little and cleared his throat. "Is it really necessary to wear such bright lipstick? And all that eye makeup?"

I planted my feet and stared back. "Have you taken a good look at the Afghan women? They wear a lot more makeup than I do."

"I suppose they do," he conceded, then continued on his way.

It was clear that my behavior was starting to make some of the CFAF people nervous. I adored Allen and I still do, but he had started to think of me as a loose cannon. He's a really brainy guy who spends his time doing good deeds all over the world, and I don't think he had ever spent much time around someone like me. Even my appearance made him nervous. Whereas all the other women in the group had neat, conservative hairstyles, mine was short, unnaturally red, and spiked. While this was the first time he had spoken to me about my makeup, sometimes I could feel him wince at the sight of me. I felt vindicated on the makeup issue when four of CFAF's major funders came to visit us at the guesthouse. These were four Texas ladies—we called them the Texas Dolls—who breezed through the gate with the biggest bouffant hairdos, the most extravagantly applied perfume, and the glossiest nails, as well as faces made up as if they were stars in a daytime soap opera. While they were there, there was some discussion about the emergency kits we were all supposed to carry, with things like maps showing where safe places were, a compass, a whistle, a five-hundred-dollar piece of gold, and such. One of the ladies drawled, "I just have plenty of lipstick in mine," and turned on her battery-operated fan to keep the sweat from ruining her makeup. I told Allen that if our funders could wear lots of makeup, so could I.

Still, our head worried and tried to rein me in periodically. My luck turned when a second group of

CFAF volunteers arrived and our team swelled from seven to fifteen people. The guesthouse was now so crowded that everyone was getting uncomfortable, so Allen asked if a few of us would move over to the Mustafa Hotel for the rest of the month. I don't think he had me in mind, because he thought he needed to keep an eye on me for my own safety. He had already asked one of the other girls if she'd move. She was a sober, responsible midwife, and he trusted her to be safe away from the main group. You'd never imagine that this girl and I would be partners in crime, but we had already gotten to be friends, and I asked her to request me as her roommate. She did, promising Allen that she'd watch out for me. We moved into a room at the hotel, and that was the point at which I was turned loose on Kabul.

That wasn't Allen's plan, of course. There still wasn't a lot for me to do with the team because I just didn't have skills that were very helpful to them. So he and some of the others came up with a new job for me for the rest of the month. Good Christians that they were, they figured that, since I had all this time on my hands, I should sit in my hotel room and pray for the team while they were out in the field. I'm a good Christian, too, but there are some things I'm not so good at. Intercessory prayer is one of them. I tried, though. I'd sit in my hotel room and start to pray for the team, and then I'd hear one of the Afghan vendors going by singing about his turnips or whatever, and I'd just have to go outside to investigate. Then I thought I'd try listening to spiritual music to drown out any alluring street noise. I put on a CD and my headset and tried to sit still but quickly got bored. I just decided that I was a naturally fast prayer. Instead of taking three hours, I'd whip those out prayers in about three minutes. Then, arm in arm with Roshanna, I was out the door.

And where did we go? One block away, to Chicken Street!

Once upon a time, Chicken Street was the place where vendors sold chickens—just as Plumber Street is still the place where they sell kitchen sinks and copper pipes, and Bird Street is the place where they sell canaries and parakeets. Now Chicken Street is lined with stores that sell traditional Afghan goods and handicrafts. Roshanna and I clung to each other so that we wouldn't get lost in the rush of people: boys headed to school, men pushing wagons filled with oranges, burqa ladies who were begging for coins. We were immediately surrounded by little boys who shouted, "Let me be your bodyguard!" When we waved them away, they raced after one of the peace-keeping troops who was eyeing a rug hanging in a shop window that had pictures of machine guns and helicopters instead of the traditional geometric designs. "Let me be your bodyguard!" they shouted at the soldier, and he looked at them with a bemused smile.

We walked along the street and peeked in the shop windows. Gorgeous rugs in a thousand different shades of red, with a few other colors thrown in for contrast. Camel bags and donkey bags, which were so beautiful that I didn't believe they were really used on camels and donkeys until I saw it for myself. Intricately painted furniture from Nuristan, an area in northeastern Afghanistan. Wonderfully embroidered fabrics, from purdah curtains—used to separate the women's part of a house from the public rooms—to tea cozies. Thick knitted woolen gloves, sweaters, and slipper socks. Heavy jewelry made of semiprecious stones from Pakistan and the jingly metal jewelry worn by the Kuchis, Afghanistan's nomads. Hookahs, metal pots, horsewhips, colorful tassels to braid in your hair—Chicken Street is the place to go for all that and more.

I loved Chicken Street, and it wasn't just because of the fabulous things I could buy there. The shopkeepers had clung to their businesses through the war against Russia, the war among the mujahideen, and then the bleak years of the Taliban. Now, they were thrilled to have some foreigners back in the country to exclaim over their goods. I didn't have enough money to buy much, but they didn't seem to mind. As soon as Roshanna and I peeked into their stores, they'd jump up from their lunch spread out on a tablecloth at the back of the store or from their game of backgammon on the counter and beckon us inside with gracious smiles. Usually, we'd wind up sitting there and having tea with them for a while. We'd leave with a gift of apples or sugared almonds or biscuits imported from

Iran; they insisted upon sharing whatever sweets they had. After a little less than a week of this, most of the shopkeepers on Chicken Street knew me by name. "Miss Debbie!" they'd shout as I walked by. "Chai for you now?"

Of course, I wasn't supposed to be doing this, because security had gotten even tighter since we'd arrived. The first Loya Jirga since the fall of the Taliban was getting ready to convene. This was the "grand council" elected from all the Afghan tribes that was going to select the transitional government in June 2002. That was why all the walls in Kabul were covered with pictures of stern, bearded men—they were posters left over from the elections. Because there were still Taliban sympathizers and other people who opposed the Loya Jirga, security was being ratcheted up all over town. It seemed as if every vehicle on the street was a tank belonging to the International Security Assistance Force (ISAF), the peacekeeping troops sanctioned by the United Nations Security Council in December 2001.

We were on an 8:00 P.M. shoot-to-kill curfew, and by 7:30, people were really scrambling to get off the streets and back to their quarters. The tension was also high because there was yet another crisis in the ongoing friction between India and Pakistan. It was feared that either country might nuke the other. Our team met every morning for a few hours to plan our day and talk about what was going on, and one day we had some big security honcho in to discuss this new development. He told us that if we saw a dark cloud in the east, we were supposed to make our way as fast as we could to the American Embassy. I was glad that they had given me a compass, because I never would have known which way was east.

So I wasn't supposed to be going out to Chicken Street; I was supposed to be in my room praying, but that felt like house arrest. I know the team leaders were only trying to protect me. They figured that if anyone in our group got injured, it would be me. They thought I was too friendly and didn't have an appropriate level of fear about our situation. And that was true. I just wasn't afraid, not of Afghanistan or of any of the things that I'd been through before I came to Afghanistan. I felt fear for what might happen to other people, but I had no fear for myself.

I finally got busted for my Chicken Street excursions. Toward the end of our stay, there were some other people in the group who decided they had heard so much about this famous place called Chicken Street that they just had to go before they left, even if security was tight. They went around asking if anyone on the rest of the team wanted to join them; of course, I did. We arrived at Chicken Street one day flanked by our translators and drivers, the women from the team wrapped like mummies in our shawls, the men trying to blend in with native scarves and hats. Then one of the shopkeepers ran out of his store, crying, "Miss Debbie!" Many of the others poked their heads out to wave, big smiles on their faces.

"Well, I guess we know what you've been up to!" one of the other members of the group said. And then they gave up trying to contain me.

"There!" Roshanna pointed at a cracked window covered with a dingy lace curtain. "I think that's the place."

Daud swerved over to the sidewalk so suddenly that I nearly fell into Roshanna's lap. I sat back up again and inspected the window. There was a big, faded photograph of a woman with Catwoman makeup and barrel curls piled on top of her head. There was also a mannequin head wearing a poufy blond wig, flanked by a couple of mismatched vases with red plastic roses on the ledge just inside. "It looks dark," I said. "Maybe it's not open."

Roshanna shook her head. "Everything in Kabul is dark, Debbie. These ladies only turn on their generator if they absolutely have to."

So I took a few moments to cover my head for the short trip from the car to the door of the shop. It seemed as if it was the only door on the street that was closed; the day was balmy and other shopkeepers were letting the warm breeze inside. Then Roshanna reached out for the handle, and I got ready to walk inside my first Afghan beauty salon.

As the days passed by, I had become fonder and fonder of Roshanna—who was calling me Mom by this time—and Daud and my other Afghan friends. The idea of leaving them was killing me. And it wasn't even just them: it seemed as if I had fallen in love with the Afghan people as a whole—with their friendliness, their humor, their hospitality, and their courage. I wanted to think of some way I could come back and actually do something that would help them. And I was starting to get an idea.

When I moved to the Mustafa, it became much easier for all the Westerners who were pining for haircuts to find me. The Mustafa has an ever-shifting clientele of reporters, aid workers, and travelers—some people say spies and smugglers, too—and most seemed to be delighted that there was a hairdresser on the grounds. Again, my door was papered with notes begging for appointments. Again, I spent hours trimming while the hair piled up on the floor. One day an Afghan woman who had been living in Canada for the last twenty-five years stopped in. She was part of a medical-humanitarian team like mine, and she was also checking on some property that one of her uncles had owned but abandoned during the Taliban years. Unlike so many of the other people coming in from the West, she was swamped with memories of the Kabul she had seen as a young woman, when the last king was in power, in the early 1970s. She told me he had been trying to push Afghanistan into the twentieth century and had set off a chain reaction of fury in the more conservative countryside as well as among the city's most traditional clerics.

"People wore miniskirts out on Chicken Street!" she said. "Can you imagine anyone wearing a miniskirt in

Kabul now?" She told me that, back in the 1970s, there were dozens of beauty salons in the city and that they did a thriving business. "Afghan women have always been meticulous about their hair and makeup," she declared. "Even underneath those dreadful burqas."

When this woman left, Roshanna explained that beauty salons were among the many things banned by the Taliban—along with music, dancing, pictures of people or other living things, white shoes, flying kites, and growing grapes. "When I was a little girl, my mother took me often to the salon of my cousin," Roshanna reminisced. "While she worked on the ladies, she would let me pour the tea and sweep up the hair from the floor." Sometimes the hairdresser and her mother would sing old songs together, and they'd ask Roshanna to sing along and she would, even though she was too shy to sing around people anywhere else. This hairdresser hadn't really set out to defy the Taliban, Roshanna said, but one of her best customers' daughters was getting married and wanted just a little of the glitter and glamour that these occasions usually inspired. So the hairdresser obliged. She kept the lights low and gave the daughter the kind of modest, under-the-radar makeover that she thought would keep them both out of trouble. But word got out somehow.

"Two days later, she finds the windows of her shop all broken," Roshanna said mournfully. "Everything inside is destroyed or stolen. And her husband loses his job then, too."

I suddenly realized that I hadn't seen an Afghan beauty salon yet and asked Roshanna if she and Daud could take me to one. They agreed, but it took us at least a week to find a storefront salon that was actually open for business. We had been told that many hairdressers were working again, but they were only operating salons in their homes, still too afraid of public scrutiny to hang up a sign or post the telltale prom-queen photo. In the last few days, we had seen several places that looked like they might be salons, only to find them empty. But someone had told Roshanna about this salon, so we set out to find it—and it was no easy task, since most of Kabul's streets didn't even have names at that time. I couldn't see inside the salon as we approached, and I was afraid it might be another of the empty shells. But when Roshanna opened the door, I smelled perm solution. I felt a little bad about making Daud wait outside and told Roshanna, but she shook her head briskly. "No man comes inside here," she said. "This is not allowed in our salons because the women have no head coverings."

"But Daud and the other Afghan men see you without your head covered at the guesthouse."

"It's different at the guesthouse—like being in a little piece of America," she replied. "And for salons, it is very strict here. If the husband of the woman who owns this salon saw Daud inside, he would beat him or maybe even kill him."

I looked at her incredulously.

"It's true, Debbie," she said. "That's why the curtain hangs inside the door, so that even when the door is open no man can look in and see the women."

"No man can come in?"

"Not even the beautician's husband," Roshanna said. "It's a place only for women."

Roshanna pulled me into a small vestibule, shut the door, and then lifted a pink curtain that hung before the entrance to the room. I had a new sense of curiosity about the salon and wondered if it was going to be different from salons back in the States. Inside, it was smaller and darker than the salons at home, not much bigger than a bathroom. The view out to the street—or in from the street—was blocked by the lace curtains, and there was only one small, broken mirror instead of a wall of mirrors. Instead of a counter, there was a rough wooden plank. I thought I saw blue salon capes hanging from pegs on a wall and then realized that they were burqas, which had been removed when the women came in the door. But aside from those differences, I felt the same warm, welcoming atmosphere that I'd spent most of my life in. There were women's voices, women's laughter—and that feeling of women relaxing with one another, laying hands on one another, telling one another the details of their lives and news of the lives around them. I wondered if this was the real reason the Taliban had been so opposed to beauty salons. Not because they made women look like whores or were fronts for brothels, as the Taliban claimed, but because they gave women their own space where they were free from the control of men.

All conversation stopped as we walked into the tiny room. Two hairdressers turned to greet us. One was young and thin with deepset, dark eyes; the other, older woman had frizzy, chin-length hair. The hairdressers and their one customer greeted us with a startled if courteous "salaam aleichem"—the standard greeting, meaning "peace be with you"—when they noticed that I was a foreigner. Then Roshanna spoke with them for a few minutes. "They are sisters," she said. "Nadia is the young one and Raksar is the other. Their family house is behind this building." When she explained that I was an American hairdresser who wanted to see what Afghan salons were like, the two women broke into delighted smiles. Their lone customer stood up immediately and insisted that I sit down while Raksar finished styling her hair. Nadia brought me tea. A couple of little girls who had been playing near the lace curtains came to stand and stare at me.

Before she left to get the tea, I noticed that Nadia had been sorting a box of sticks and rubber bands. I asked Roshanna what these were for. "She uses those to give the perm," Roshanna replied, seeming surprised at the question. I asked Nadia to describe how she usually carried out this procedure. Aside from using sticks and rubber bands instead of perm rods, her approach was pretty much the same as mine except for the final stage. She told me that they just sent their customers home after they rolled them up in perm solution. The processing stopped when the hair was dry, and then the customers returned the next day to be rinsed off. No wonder Raksar had such frizzy hair—she'd probably had a bunch of these perms! The older hairdresser spoke rapidly to Roshanna for a few minutes. "She says she started this salon when the Russians were here," Roshanna said. "She had to close it down during the Taliban years. She had to bury her mirror and other supplies in her yard."

"How long has she been open again?"

"She says just for two months. At first, her husband forbids her because he wants her to stay all the time inside and help his mother. But he has no job now, so he agrees."

"Is it hard to get supplies?"

Raksar waved her hand proudly at the few combs, brushes, and scissors on the wooden plank. They were far from salon quality. The scissors looked like something you'd use to shear sheep. The combs looked like the sheep had been chewing on them.

As I talked to the two women, I realized it wasn't just that their supplies were meager; they also didn't seem to have more than the most rudimentary hairdressing skills. I asked where they had been trained, and they both shrugged. Raksar had been trained by a friend during the 1980s, and then she'd taught Nadia what she knew. Neither of them knew how to do highlights. Even without training, though, they were making pretty good money. Raksar brought in about eighty dollars a month, at least twice as much as the average salary in Afghanistan. Nadia was making less but expected her income to grow—just doing the makeup for a big wedding would greatly expand her family's finances. Besides, she told me through Roshanna, it was hard to find jobs anywhere else. She had worked briefly as a cook in a guesthouse, but her male coworkers had made crass comments about her and she'd quit.

Then Nadia said something to Raksar, and they both smiled impishly. Roshanna clapped her hands and started to laugh. "They want to know if you would like to try some of the traditional Afghan salon services," she said. "They want to share these with you, because they say you are their sister from America."

"Sure," I said, slipping off my head scarf. The two women froze in place and stared at my short, spiked hair. Both reached out gingerly to touch it. They said something to Roshanna—their voices full of wonder—and I looked up at her and raised my eyebrows.

"They say you look like a cat," she said. *"Pashak."*

"Meow!" Raksar said.

I felt a little bad about leaving Daud outside for this long, but I leaned back in the chair and prepared to relax. I sat up again when I saw Nadia approach with a long thread wrapped around her fingers. She gently pushed my head back again, then proceeded to thread my face. She ripped out most of my eyebrows and removed a mustache that I didn't even realize I had. I opened my eyes once when the pain almost made me

73

scream to see Nadia frowning just over my forehead, the thread taut between her mouth and hands. Roshanna was leaning against the wall, laughing. When Nadia was finished, I sat up and ran my hand over my face. I was sure that I would feel blood trickling down.

Then Raksar offered to show me how she did Afghan-style makeup, the kind that she'd do for someone who would be a guest at a wedding. Again, I agreed: I figured I wouldn't really know enough about Afghan salons if I didn't try all their services myself. So she lacquered me with pale base makeup, put about four brilliant curves of shadow over my eyes, darkened my eyebrows and drew the ends so that they flicked upward near my hairline, and gave me big, red lips. The kohl was the worst part. She licked the stick, dipped it in powder, blew on it lightly, stuck it in the corners of each of my eyes, and coated my inner lids with kohl. I couldn't help but wonder how many other eyes that stick had blackened. Eyes streaming, I finally stood and felt around for my head scarf. They led me over to the mirror, and I peered at myself. It was as if someone else—maybe someone in a Mardi Gras mask—was looking back at me.

But I thanked the sisters over and over, using my little bit of Dari. *"Tashakur, tashakur,"* I said, bowing and holding their hands. We did three quick little air kisses on the cheeks, then I stumbled blindly back outside, where Daud gasped with admiration. My eyes leaked black kohl for the next three days, prompting

74

all the Westerners who had been living in Kabul for a long time to ask me how I'd managed to get myself invited to an Afghan wedding so quickly.

But aside from my weepy eyes, I was excited. It seemed that I had discovered the one thing I could do to help the Afghans—and only I, out of all the talented and dedicated Westerners I'd met here, could do it. I knew that I could help the Afghan women run better salons and make more money. I knew from my own experience as a hairdresser back home that a salon is a good business for a woman—especially if she has a bad husband.

Unfortunately, I knew this all too well. I was still married to such a mean man that Afghanistan, then considered by many people to be the most dangerous place on earth, felt like paradise. All the time I had been married to him, my only salvation was that he had no idea how much money I made. I stashed it away, saving up for my freedom. I figured that the salon business would be even better for women in Afghanistan, where the men aren't allowed to step inside the salons. They'd never see the cash changing hands or be able to tell the women how to run things. I asked Roshanna to tell me about other businesses that employed women. She told me about women she knew who wove carpets, sold eggs, worked in guest-houses and tailor shops and other places. Every one of these businesses was run by the woman's father or husband or brother or distant uncle. I figured I could come back to Afghanistan with several suitcases of good hair care products and supplies, then hang around in the salons for a couple of weeks. I could teach the women whatever I knew and show them how to expand their services and make more money. I could also teach them the sanitation principles I'd learned in beauty school. I figured if someone was going to cry at a wedding, she could do it out of sentiment and not because of bacteria-laden kohl.

When I mentioned my idea to an American friend who had been working for a nonprofit in Kabul for several years, he didn't smirk. He thought I wasn't thinking big enough! He told me that he thought I should open a beauty school in Kabul, and he said he'd try to help.

When I mentioned my idea—now expanded to a school—to Roshanna, she threw her arms around me. "I want to be in your first class," she said. "My father wants me to quit working for NGOs because some of the Afghan men make trouble for me. But if I have my own salon, I'll be okay."

With the idea for the beauty school, it seemed that all my dreams came together. I'd never been satisfied to be only a beautician, even though that's a fine life. I'd always wanted to be part of something bigger and more meaningful—something that gave me the feeling I was helping to save the world.

Of course, I love beauty salons. When I was seven years old, my mother opened her first salon right next to our house. I thought it was the most wonderful place on earth, with its sleek blond furniture and gold mirrors and that long row of hair dryers, like fat little spaceships getting ready to blast toward the moon. I thought the beauticians were the most gorgeous women on earth, all dressed up in their green hot pants and white go-go boots. I couldn't wait until the day I could wear that uniform, too.

It was the 1960s in Holland, Michigan, and all the ladies who came in had big, frosted hair, with a little additional elevation from their hairpieces. Usually, my mother let me help by handing out magazines and folding towels and pouring coffee. Lots of times she just wanted me to wander the salon because I kept the customers entertained with my nonstop chatter. But I loved to help, so she gradually eased me into the business. I started by helping her fix up the hairpieces— I'd hold them on the mannequin heads while she put curlers in them, then walk the heads across the salon and set them on a couple of boxes under the hair dryers. Later, I'd hold the hairpieces down while my mother ratted them into nice, big puffs. Then she started letting me help with hair that was actually attached to someone's head. When the ladies came in for a wash, set, and style, I'd stand behind them and work the bobby pins out of their hair. It's not like anything actually happened when I took the pins out— their hair would pretty much stay put because they used so much spray.

The whole point back then was for them to leave the salon with their hair lacquered up into big beehives and come back two weeks later looking exactly the way they did when they left. We sold them silk pillowcases so their hair didn't get too messed up while they slept, but a lot of them took extra precautions to preserve their beehives—they'd wrap wads and wads of toilet paper around their hair before they'd go to sleep to hold it in place. When my mother started letting me wash their hair, they'd keep telling me to scrub harder and longer. "Draw blood," they'd say. I think it was because they hadn't been able to scratch their heads in two weeks. After my mother set their hair in big plastic rollers and let them fry under the dryers, I'd get to unwrap them. I loved that feeling of the hot, smooth hair against my fingers, so stiff from the setting lotion that the curls stood in place until my mother came to comb them out.

When I was fifteen, I went to beauty school because I figured that I could put myself through college by doing hair. But by that time, I didn't want to be a hairdresser when I grew up. I saw how hard my mother worked and how tired she was at night, and besides, I had caught a glimpse of a life that seemed like a lot more fun. I wanted to do something in the world of music. My mother had made me take piano lessons ever since I was five years old. She wanted me to take ballet lessons, too, but that lasted only a day; I was too big, couldn't balance myself on one leg or two, and couldn't fit into a tutu. But I loved music and stuck with it. In high school, I played piano, organ, guitar, and trumpet. I had so much wind that I could blast louder than any of the boys on my trumpet. I liked to sing, too, so I enrolled at John Brown College in Arkansas as a vocal performance major. But when I got there and stood among all those other, really good singers, I knew I wasn't cut out for that. I also developed nodules on my vocal cords. When I sang Italian opera, I sounded like James Brown singing Italian opera.

So I returned to Michigan and worked in my mother's salon. I married my college sweetheart, and we had two beautiful boys, Noah and Zachary. But my husband and I were both young and stupid, and we soon got restless. I remember sitting in my mother's living room when I was twenty-six and crying, asking her what was wrong with me. I had everything a woman was supposed to want—a sweet husband, children, a good job, a nice house and car, but I was miserable. I guess it's no surprise that I was soon a single mom.

Then one day I heard one of the salon customers say that a medium-security prison was opening up in the area. I had been wondering what it would be like to work someplace that actually offered health insurance and other benefits, and this customer told me that both the pay and the benefits were great. So I applied for a job at the prison and planned to do hair on the side. Since I hadn't finished my bachelor's degree, the only job I was qualified for was prison guard. How bad could it be? I thought.

It was pretty bad.

Actually, I didn't mind it at first. I had two months of on-the-job training, and I got along well with both the other guards and the inmates. I told the inmates right away that I wasn't there to punish them or make their lives harder—they'd already made their own lives hard enough. I told them that my job was to make them follow the rules. I treated them with respect, and I got respect back from them. I think they also appreciated the fact that I refused to butch up just because I was working in a prison. I wore my makeup and perfume, styled my hair with some nice long extensions, and had scarlet dragon-lady nails. One time, a fight broke out in one of the stairwells, and I called for assistance. All of us guards carried radios, not guns—since there were more inmates than guards, rioting inmates could easily use your own gun on you. As I waited for backup, I yelled at the brawling prisoners, "I'm not going to break a nail to stop this fight!" It turned into a major melee. Three guards got gashes in their heads, and a bunch of prisoners were sent to solitary. Later, one of the prisoners who had been involved winced when he heard I'd been there.

"I didn't know you were there, Miss Debbie," he said. "You didn't get hurt, did you?" I told him that I was fine but that I would have killed him if one of my nails had gotten broken.

But after a few months, I was on compassion overload. I was just too much of a bleeding heart to work in the prison. I thought that lots of the inmates were really nice people—some of the nicest people I've ever met in my life—and that some of the guards were just bullies who used their power to abuse. I didn't want to become like them, but I could feel myself changing. I didn't like the way my mouth was starting to sound. And I think other people could sense that I was changing, too. One day I walked past the cell of a lifer who had never spoken a word to anyone in the whole time I had been there. He usually just whistled all day, as beautifully as a songbird. He put his face against the bars.

"This is not a place for you, Miss Debbie," he whispered. "You don't want to turn out like the rest of them."

About a year after I started working at the prison, I was driving to work in the rain and dreading it. I was working second shift and weekends, never seeing my children, and I felt like I was selling my soul to the devil for health insurance and paid vacations. I walked into the warden's office after roll call and quit. On my last day, the prisoners lined up to say good-bye. Some of them were crying. "Good luck, Miss Debbie," they said. "You're going to have a good life now."

But I didn't know how to find that good life. I was working in my mother's salon again but was often depressed and wondering why I wasn't happy. I decided that I needed more fun. I'd gotten married and had children so early that I'd never done the high-energy dating and partying most of my friends had been through, so I decided to became the best party girl in Holland, Michigan. Whenever I do something,

I do it to the extreme, so in a couple of months I knew every club in the area and every person on every barstool. Soon that wasn't enough, and I bought a sailboat—even though I didn't know how to sail and had no intention of learning—just so I could keep it docked at the bars on Lake Michigan, in Saugatuck. People from all over partied on my boat every weekend, and the good times were always wherever I was. When I was by myself, though, reality would sink in. I was out partying so much that I wasn't being a good mom. Most of these people weren't real friends anyway—they just liked my boat.

So I thought about getting religion. I had never been an atheist to begin with, but I didn't have much of a faith structure or community to deepen my spiritual life. So I went and found a Christian church to join. Not just any church, either—this one was a full-gospel, be healed, and hallelujah kind of church. Soon it consumed all the time that I used to spend being lonely and depressed. It gave me an opportunity to use my creativity and a little bit of my musical talent, too. I forgot my disappointment that I was never going to sing Aïda on the stage of the Metropolitan Opera and became the star of the church's drama department. I wrote plays, directed them, and acted in them. They weren't stodgy productions, either—I loved *Saturday Night Live* and *Mad TV* and put as much of that kind of humor into the church plays as I could.

Even though some things about the church made me uneasy, I met people there who opened my eyes to a whole new way of looking at the world. I had always liked to travel, but I'd quickly lose interest in whatever tourist destination my friends talked me into and wind up spending time in an area that most tourists shunned. When I went to Jamaica, I was bored with riding Jet Skis and drinking margaritas on the beach of a walled-off hotel, so I grabbed a bus into town. I wound up meeting a twenty-year-old mother with five kids who invited me to her home, where we ate soup made out of not much more than fish bones. I spent the week visiting her, bringing diapers and groceries. That was where I felt content. At the church, I met a retired man named Herb Stewart, who was traveling the world working on humanitarian projects of one kind or another. He invited me to go with him to India for a month.

I had been known around town as Crazy Deb for a while. As in Crazy Deb with all the weird hairstyles and the long nails and the showgirl makeup. Crazy Deb with the boat and the all-night parties. Crazy Deb who worked in the prison. As in "I'm getting my hair cut next week—you know, by Crazy Deb." Now I became Crazy Deb because I started to travel around the world to work on humanitarian projects. That first time in India, Herb and I traveled from village to village helping people put in new wells. In one of the towns, I heard that the people had been suffering from a terrible famine. I got to know one of the families, and they told me that the worst time was during the three-month dry season. I asked them what would help, and they said rice. So I found someone with a truck and got him to drive me to a market in an area where the drought wasn't so bad, and we filled the truck with rice. How could I buy for just one family? Back at the village, we dumped the rice on a concrete slab and called people over using a bullhorn. For about a hundred dollars, I was able to feed the people in this village for three months.

In the middle of all this, I wound up getting married to a traveling preacher associated with the church. I knew his personality and mine were very different, but I wanted to be married again. I liked being married. I thought that, since he was such a religious man and since I was headed in that direction, it would work out. But shortly after the wedding, he went from being intense and brooding to being just plain mean—and insanely jealous. If I went out to the grocery store and came home fifteen minutes later than he expected, he'd be waiting at the front door fuming and follow me through the house to question me. He seemed to think I'd been off having an affair in those fifteen minutes. At first, I would try to tell him that this wasn't true, but I realized it didn't do any good to protest. So one day I tried to leave the house when he started shouting. He grabbed me by my hair and pulled me back inside, slamming me against the wall. I pushed him away and lunged toward the door, but that just made him angrier. He slapped me across the face, hard.

After that, I tried not to do any of the things that set

him off, even as I hated myself for having gotten into this situation. My mother had raised me to be a strong woman; how could this have happened? It was a tense household. My boys tried to spend as much time as possible with their grandparents. I managed to keep my husband from erupting into violence by acting like a docile, obedient wife. Then one day after church, he and I and a friend of his went to McDonald's for breakfast. His friend and I laughed over some story, and I remember thinking that this was the most fun I'd had in months. But when we got home, my husband went crazy.

"I saw the way you were looking at him," he shouted at me, spitting his fury all over my face. "You're nothing more than a whore." He chased me into our bedroom, where he backhanded me across the face and knocked me over. I hit my head on the foot of the bed. When I opened my eyes, I saw my kids and my mother standing at the door. She had just brought them back from an overnight. I remember thinking to myself how awful this was not just because he had attacked me but because my kids and mother had had to see it. Then my tiny, little mother stepped between us, and my husband shoved her.

That did it. I was so angry that I managed to push him out of the house, and then I called 911. When the police arrived, my husband was standing on the lawn shouting so loudly that all the neighbors came out to watch. I packed suitcases for me and the kids, and walked outside with my face averted, like a gangster leaving the courthouse. My mother drove us to her place.

I wanted to stay there and never return, but my husband started to harass my mother—as if she didn't have enough on her hands, taking care of my father, who had dementia and was dying of congestive heart failure. My husband called her at home, he called her at work, he'd show up in his car and block her in the driveway, demanding that she tell me to talk to him. I finally realized I couldn't stay with my mother because my husband wouldn't leave her alone, so I left my kids with their father and moved back home. I figured I'd bide my time while I saved money and made plans to get away. For about five minutes I thought that the church might help me out. I met with some of the leaders and told them what was going on. But though they said they were sorry about what I was going through, they told me it wouldn't be right for me to leave him. After all, he hadn't committed adultery. I really wished he had.

Then I heard about an organization that was giving disaster relief training in Chicago. I told my husband that I wanted to take a course, and to my amazement, he agreed to let me go. He thought the training would give me something to do if I traveled with him to third-world countries. So in August 2001, I drove to Chicago for two weeks of training with the Care for All Foundation. I learned what to do in a fire, earthquake, landslide, flood, hurricane, and bomb attack. I learned how to decontaminate myself if chemical weapons were used. I learned how to care for infants with malnutrition and how to protect people from illnesses caused by contaminated water. I learned about the real crises going on in different parts of the world. For the first time, I learned where Afghanistan was. On our last day, we were tested with a mock crisis. In retrospect, it was eerie: it was just three weeks before the 9/11 attacks in New York and Washington, and we were being presented with the scenario of Chicago being attacked by terrorists using suicide bombs and chemical weapons. We had to work in teams, set up tents, triage the victims and carry them to the proper locations, even set aside the people who were going to die no matter what you did. It was all very realistic—and frightening.

Then the terrorists crashed the planes into the World Trade Center and the Pentagon. One day I found a message on our voice mail asking me if I would join a disaster relief team that was headed to New York. I said yes without even consulting my husband. I left as soon as I could.

The next two weeks were among the hardest in my life. I was one of the many people taking care of the firemen who were reconstructing the collapsed World Trade Center and carrying away the bodies—often, bodies of their own colleagues. I did massage therapy and trauma counseling. I held them while they cried and washed their stinking, burned feet when they finally took their boots off after hours of climbing over hot rubble. I helped out in a dozen other ways, too. Sometimes I would have to go and hide in the Porta-John to cry, because I didn't want to break down in front of them. My husband called me about seventy times a day on my cell phone, and I finally had to shut it off. The whole time I was there, I was afraid he'd find out that I was touching other men and come after me. When the Discovery Channel came in to film the relief effort, I hid under a massage table until they left so that my husband wouldn't see me around the firemen.

At home again, I sank back into dread. I couldn't stop watching television coverage of Afghanistan and the Taliban. I was especially struck by the footage of the Taliban executing women in Kabul's Ghazi sports stadium. I read book after book about Afghanistan, and I felt like I was leading a life that was nearly as contained as those of the women there. Then I heard that CFAF was sending a team to Kabul the following year. I called them every day, telling them how much I wanted to go. When they finally told me that I could go, my husband heard about it and forbade me. I locked up my passport and my tickets in my mother's safe so he couldn't get at them. There was nothing anyone could have done to stop me. I knew that, for the first time in my life, I was going to the right place at the right time.

The day my friends came to take me to the airport, my husband leaned against the wall as I carried my suitcase out the door. "I hope you die in Afghanistan," he said.

"I'd rather die than live here with you," I replied. A door in my heart opened, and the tiny piece of him left inside tumbled out. I flew to Afghanistan, where my heart would soon fill with new people to love.

Chapter 3

A large woman whose head bristled with high-lighting foils tapped a tapered blue nail on Roshanna's face. "Is that your little Afghan friend?" she asked.

"Let me see!" Another woman reached for the pile of pictures balanced on the first woman's knee.

I congratulated myself for having the good sense to have had duplicates made of the pictures from my trip and continued sectioning another woman's hair for a cut. I didn't have time to sort out the pictures again. I had a perm coming in the door in just a few minutes.

My customers back in the States had waited until I returned from Afghanistan to make their appointments, so I was swamped with work in those first few months at home. I told my stories and showed my pictures over and over. And I kept talking about going back there to help the Afghan beauticians. My idea at that point was to set up a teaching salon, where I would provide services to Western customers and hire Afghan hairdressers as apprentices. My customers at home didn't snicker at this idea or tell me it was too dangerous. They were as excited about it as I was.

But I had no idea how I'd actually go about doing something like this. I'd never even set up my own salon in the States. I'd always worked in my mom's. If I was going to set up a teaching salon in Afghanistan, I'd need to rent a space, of course—and I'd heard stories from the NGOs about how rents were beginning to soar as landlords figured they could get New York prices from Westerners, even in Kabul's bombed-out neighborhoods. Then I thought about the salon I'd visited where they were using ten-year-old perm solution and scissors the size of hedge clippers. I would need to bring a lot of hair care products and equipment over to Kabul, especially if I wanted to send my trainees back out into their world with some good supplies of their own.

"Do you think I could get donations of this stuff from some of the hair care companies?" I wondered out loud. Then I thought, What the heck? I picked up a bottle of Paul Mitchell styling gel, looked on the back, and found an 800 number. When someone answered, I asked if they had a department that handled requests for donations. I bounced from one person to another and finally got an answering machine. I rolled my eyes at my customers but left a long message about who I was and how the Taliban had closed all the hair salons in Afghanistan and how the women were now trying to open them up again and what I wanted to do for them. The recording said to leave a detailed message, but I doubt they expected anything like these details.

But two days later, the phone in the salon rang. One of the other girls answered and then waved it at me.

"Who is it?" I yelled over the noise of a blow dryer. I was right in the middle of smoothing someone who had about ten pounds of long, red, curly hair, and I didn't want to give it a chance to frizz up. "Can you take a message?"

"He says he wants to talk to you in person."

So I left half this woman's hair pinned to her head and went to answer the phone. "Hey, Ms. International Hairdresser," the voice on the other end said. "This is J.P."

"Who?"

"John Paul DeJoria, the owner of Paul Mitchell. So, tell me about this beauty school or teaching salon or whatever it is that you want to start in Afghanistan."

So right there in the salon, with one of the customers' kids crying and another customer who was a little deaf talking too loudly and the door opening and closing, I told him about my idea. He didn't need much convincing that it was a good plan. He told me to call his general manager, Luke Jacobellis. "Just ask Luke for whatever you want," he said. After I hung up, I went tearing back into the middle of the salon screaming. The place was in an uproar for days.

I found a quiet spot and called Luke later that afternoon, after I'd finished with the rest of my customers. "How much product do you think you'll need?" he asked.

"I don't really know," I told him. "Enough to last a couple of years, but I'm not even sure how much that is in a country where you never know if you're going to have water or electricity. I've only been there a month."

He told me to make a wish list, so I pulled out a catalog of Paul Mitchell products, telling him—oh, how about a dozen of this, three dozen of that, four dozen if you can spare it. We made a pretty sizable list, with shampoos, conditioners, gel, sprays, color, and perm solution as well as color capes and hand mirrors— basically, everything they sold. I was well familiar with Paul Mitchell products, because my mom had used them in her salon for years. I kept remembering all those frizzy perms I had seen back in Kabul and thinking of products that would make the Afghan women's hair healthier. Just before we hung up, Luke started rattling off the names of a lot of other companies in the beauty industry that I should call. Takara Belmont for salon furniture, Redken for more hair product, Orly and O.P.I. for nail care products, and so on. Almost all of them were eager to donate.

About three weeks after I talked to Luke, a semi-truck full of Paul Mitchell products pulled up outside my house. The driver looked confused when he knocked on my door. He assumed he was dropping off his load at a warehouse or at least the back end of a very big store. "Do you have anyone to unload this stuff?" he said, jerking his thumb at the huge truck that was fuming at the bottom of my driveway.

"Just me," I said.

He looked me over and sighed. "You don't happen to have a forklift, do you?"

"Just a wheelbarrow."

I moved the cars, the snow blower, and the lawn mower out of the garage. Then, together, we moved all ten thousand boxes out of the truck into the garage as my husband watched from the living room. I'm not sure if it really was ten thousand boxes, but it felt like that many or more. They completely filled our two-and-a-half-car garage. As the truck finally pulled away, I stared at all the boxes. It was a little bit more than I could fit in my suitcases, even if I paid for over-weight.

Over the next few months, more trucks arrived, bringing salon stations and chairs, combs, blow dryers, hand mirrors, perm rods, and other basic supplies, but I had these delivered to a storage unit. My husband had started to taunt me about the hair care products in the garage. He said that if I tried to leave him, he'd burn down the garage with everything inside it. Then where would my so-called Kabul beauty school be? He also told me that, if I wasn't careful, he'd leave the front door open and let my dogs run into traffic. So I bided my time. I tried not to cross him, but I secretly rented an apartment and found a lawyer.

I still had no idea how I was going to get everything to Kabul. Then one day I called another of the companies that Luke had suggested to ask for a product donation. To my amazement, this person said that someone else had already called her about donating supplies to a beauty school in Afghanistan. I asked for the phone number of this person and followed up with a call. And that was when I first heard about the legendary Mary MacMakin, an American who has been living in Afghanistan for nearly forty years.

In 1996, Mary had started a small nonprofit called PARSA to help Afghan women who were widowed during the wars and had been forced into begging—a new and cruel development, because Afghans had practically no history of begging. Mary is one of the heroes of Afghanistan, and *Vogue* magazine did an article about her back in 2001. The New York hairstylist Terri Grauel was assigned to do Mary's hair for the photo shoot, and they had kept in contact. After the Taliban fell, Mary saw that Afghan beauticians were hastening to open up storefront salons again but were hindered by limited resources and skills that had gotten rusty. She suggested to Terri that American hairdressers could help Afghan women become successful business owners by opening up a beauty school. So Terri and some associates galvanized the New York beauty industry to launch and support a school. *Vogue* and Estée Lauder kicked in big cash donations, and then other companies directed a flow of money and products to the project. It was going to be called the Beauty Without Borders Kabul Beauty School, and it would be run as one of PARSA's programs.

I was actually relieved to find out that someone else with more clout and connections was working on the idea. I had been doing all I could in Holland but realized deep down that I probably couldn't do such a huge thing all on my own. I quickly joined forces with the PARSA group and pledged the half million dollars' worth of beauty products in my garage and storage unit to the school. They were planning to open in July 2003 inside the Afghan Ministry of Women's Affairs compound, a location Mary had recommended because she thought the women would be safe there. She knew there were still plenty of people in Kabul who agreed with the Taliban that beauty salons—and anything that made women stand out or stand on their own—were an abomination. I volunteered to be one of the instructors at the school, along with a handful of other Western beauticians.

The PARSA project was putting together a shipping container of beauty supplies that would be leaving the East Coast for Kabul in December. I had to get my stuff there well before then. A local salon owner had a friend who owned a shipping company, and he volunteered his trucks and time to move everything from the storage unit. Now all I had to do was get the stuff out of my garage and into the storage unit. The only problem was that it wasn't my garage anymore, because I had finally left my husband.

One cloudy day, my sons, Noah and Zach—at that point, both in their late teens—got together a bunch of their friends and rented a big U-Haul moving truck. My girlfriends and I followed in our cars with wheelbarrows hanging out of the trunks. When we backed the truck up to the garage, my husband came outside and told me he had a court order preventing me from removing anything from the property. He called the police when we ignored him, and squad cars pulled up a few minutes later. Despite the rain that began to fall, neighbors ambled over to get a better view of the excitement.

Two police officers walked up, but I was like a madwoman; I wasn't about to let anything stop me. "This is my stuff, and I'm moving it!" I shrieked. "You have three options: you can shoot me, arrest me, or leave me alone." They backed off and stood there watching as my sons and our friends moved all the hair care products into the truck. And that was it—the last big hurdle before I left for Afghanistan early in 2003 to meet the shipping container.

Well, there was the beginning of the war in Iraq. I guess most people would consider that a bigger hurdle.

The shipping container was supposed to arrive in Kabul in late January. I was planning to meet it there and help unload its contents at the Women's Ministry. I told all my customers to hurry up and make their appointments two days before I was supposed to leave or else they'd have to wait three weeks until I got back. They streamed in, many of them bringing donations to offset my expenses or baked goods that I could sell at the salon to raise money. I had lots of festive farewell gatherings with friends, as well as many weepy moments with my mom and kids. And then came the first letdown: it turned out that the container hadn't even left port. The departure date had been postponed because of heightened activity around the Middle East—including, I later learned, the maneuvering that U.S. and British forces were doing before their invasion of Iraq in March. So instead of flying to Kabul, I wound up flying to New York for a week of special training in makeup application at M.A.C. Cosmetics, which had donated about thirty thousand dollars' worth of makeup to the school.

In mid-February, I heard that the shipping container had finally left the United States, and I got all fired up to go again. But a week before I was supposed to fly out in early March, I got the news that the ship carrying our container was stuck in the Suez Canal. Again, it was sidelined by war preparations.

By that time, I was wild to leave Holland. I had already said good-bye too many times to my family and friends, and I didn't have any customers scheduled until late April. I had heard that relief organizations in Jordan were expecting an onslaught of refugees from Iraq. So I offered my services to one of the organizations there and left for Jordan in late March. A few days after I arrived, I heard that our shipping container wasn't stuck in the Suez Canal anymore but had already been dropped off in Kabul. And off I went to join it and the other women who shared my dream.

My driver uttered a long moan of frustration. The main road from the Kabul airport was so clogged with cars that we had progressed only about ten feet in ten minutes. He finally drove over the strip of dirt in front of some stores selling car parts, so close that I could have reached out my window and grabbed a fan belt. Then he aimed the car down a side street filled with pedestrians. He didn't slow at the sight of all those people on foot; he sped along the street like a down-hill skier in a slalom race, skidding around the pedestrians as if they were poles along a course. After thumping against the door once too often, I groped around for my seat belt, but it had been neatly snipped off.

When I arrived in Kabul in March 2003, I couldn't believe how much things had changed since the nearly one year since I had been there. Even though parts of the city still looked like ancient ruins, new buildings—fancy buildings with curved porticos and mirrored glass windows and some sort of sparkly stuff set into colored stucco—were going up all over. Where before the streets had been teeming with people, bicycles, produce wagons, donkeys, and water buffalo, they were now clogged with those as well as cars, SUVs, and tanks. There were rotaries at intersections, presumably to slow the traffic, but there seemed to be no agreement about whether the flow should go clockwise or counterclockwise, so the drivers did both. As a result, there was always a dense knot of overheating cars clogging each rotary. The roads weren't much better than they had been the year before—still mostly dirt, with huge ruts and piles of rubble to dodge—but the cars and SUVs raced along them as if they were fleeing the apocalypse. There seemed to be no traffic rules whatsoever. Two lanes might quickly become three, with rogue cars darting around the others if they saw an opening. When I arrived at Mary MacMakin's PARSA house on Plumber Street, I felt as if my entire body had been shaken apart and then achingly realigned.

The PARSA house had a living room decorated in the basic Afghan style, which means a nice rug— almost always red—on the floor and long, flat cushions called *toushak*s around the walls. There were also some beat-up tables made of dark wood, but that was about it. Mary had a few bedrooms upstairs for her steady stream of guests, and these were divided internally with plywood partitions. I threw my suitcase onto the toushak in my sleeping area and started to go back downstairs.

Then I noticed an open door leading to the top floor. On top of the house, there was a flat space that fluttered with clothes hanging from lines. Off to the side were clay pots of herbs. I pushed the clothes aside and found I could look right down onto Plumber Street. I expected it to be full of men marching around with plungers and plumb bobs, but it looked like all the other streets—crowded and lively, with some buildings that looked as if they were either in the process of being built or in the process of being torn down. It was hard to tell which. I could also see into the courtyards on either side of Mary's house. In one, a woman and children were tucking little plants into long, neat furrows in the yard outside their front door. They made a peaceful contrast to the ever-present sounds of traffic, construction, and demolition.

Downstairs, I finally got to meet Mary. She was a tall woman in her seventies with dark, determined eyes and a cap of slate gray hair, and she was chattering to a group of Afghan women in Dari faster than I could speak English. She seemed to be managing the details of about fifty different projects at once. She was sweet and gracious and dignified, and also outraged about something going on somewhere in the country. This is the way she still is, every time I see her. She told me she hadn't seen the new school and salon in the Women's Ministry but had been told that the space was almost ready for us. In a little while, she wheeled a bicycle out the door and rode off with her head uncovered into the traffic. I already knew that she was brave, that she had been imprisoned by the Taliban but they had failed to break her spirit. Still, riding a bicycle off into that traffic took another kind of guts.

The next morning, I had a joyful reunion with Roshanna and Daud outside the Women's Ministry. I arrived there with some of the other people who were involved with the beauty school, including Patricia O'Connor, a consultant from New York, and Noor, a young Afghan-Australian man who had been hired by Beauty Without Borders to stay in Kabul full-time to manage the program between visits by the instructors.

Near the gate, two men with machine guns approached us, but they were friendly and waved us into the compound right away.

The sight of machine guns wasn't even alarming to me anymore. On our way there, we'd passed one compound after another with little clusters of uniformed men and their guns in front. Some looked serious and glared at every car that passed. Some were in animated conversations with friends and waved their arms around while the guns dangled at their waists. Some looked as if they might fall asleep standing up. One of them actually was asleep in a green plastic lawn chair, his gun balanced precariously across his knees. There was a feeling of great optimism in Kabul, and I felt no danger on the streets. All those guns just seemed like manly accessories, not weapons.

When I saw the outside of the building that would house our school and salon, I got tears in my eyes because it was so beautiful. It was a low building built from a sort of caramel-colored marble on a side of the compound where someone obviously intended gardens: there was a big, circular flower bed made of stone as well as three narrow, rectangular ones. There were also three pine trees near our building, which immediately made the setting seem incredibly lush— there weren't many trees left standing in Kabul because the Taliban had cut them all down just in case anyone wanted to hide or shoot from behind them. The windows looked as if they were newly installed, and they had gracefully curved mullions of some kind of golden brown wood. The front door was made of this same wood.

When we went inside, however, we discovered that the building was not even close to being done—certainly not ready for the shipping container full of beauty supplies we were supposed to start moving into it the next day! There were the whitewashed walls I seemed to see in every Afghan building, but they were dirty and stained in many places. The overhead lights were in, but the switches weren't—in fact, there were holes in many parts of the walls with long wires dangling out. The floors were still just rough concrete, and none of the closets, cupboards, and tables we had requested had been built. And it didn't look like any of this work was in progress, either: instead of tools, there were some old bikes and a wheelbarrow stored in the room. Noor went to find the workmen who were supposed to be finishing up the school while the rest of us tried to figure out where we could move the beauty supplies. Most of the stuff could stay inside the shipping container until the next team of hairdressers arrived in a few months. However, there were some things—especially the hair color products—that would be ruined if they baked inside the shipping container for that long. We were also afraid the makeup might melt.

It turned out that Mary had space on the third floor of the PARSA house. Even though unloading the hair color products and makeup at Mary's meant that we would ultimately have to move them twice, this was our only choice. It also meant that someone would have the onerous job of removing almost everything from the shipping container and sorting through the products to figure out what had to be moved and then jamming the rest back into the shipping container. I offered to do this—I figured that I was the one who knew the products best—but I would obviously need lots of help. Roshanna had the solution right away. "You must hire men from the mosque," she said.

I was confused. "Why would the mullahs want to help me? I didn't think any of them liked the idea of beauty salons."

"Not the mullahs," Roshanna said, putting her hands over her mouth to laugh. "Lots of men wait outside the mosque for work. You'll see."

Noor and Patricia had to go somewhere, so Roshanna and I started walking to the mosque, where Noor would meet us later. I don't think I had ever walked so far before in Kabul, and I was loving it. It was hard to walk, though. I was wearing low-heeled sandals, and the sidewalks were as rough as a mountain trail, so I often found myself pitching to the side. Roshanna was in high heels and managed it gracefully. It was also hard not to stop and stare into the windows of the stores and peer into open doorways as we passed. Roshanna would wait patiently, but then I'd realize I had been looking too long and hurry along.

But there was so much to look at! I was also getting an eye-to-eye view of the people on the streets as I'd never had before and was struck by the many different looks of the Afghan people. I think Americans tend to think of Afghans as uniformly dark-haired, dark-eyed, and wrapped in turbans. Many Americans think Afghans are Arabs, just because both are mostly Muslims, but this is not true. Afghanistan was the original melting pot. Its geographic location made it a central thoroughfare on the Silk Road from Asia to the rest of the world, and—contrary to its distinction today as one of the most remote and isolated countries in the world—ancient peoples crisscrossed it again and again. Some came to trade, some came to conquer, and all left their mark. Most Afghans have Turkish or Persian roots, but many other ethnicities abound, too. As we walked along the streets, I saw so many faces that looked purely Asian that I pulled Roshanna's arm and asked if there was an immigrant community of Chinese in Kabul. She shook her head. "Those are people of the Hazara tribe," she said. "They came after the invasion of Genghis Khan."

"And that was—"

"Eight hundred years ago."

I nodded my head at another man with Asian features who was arranging a pile of rugs outside a store. "So, he is Hazara, too?"

"No, he is an Uzbek. Also some Mongol background, but you can tell the difference because of his embroidered hat. Also, many Uzbeks make and sell the carpets that you see here. They are all brothers."

As we kept walking, I tried to pick individuals out

of the stream of men coming toward us on foot and bicycles, looking for differences in their features and clothes. It seemed that lots of them were dressed in tan or gray shalwar kameezes, often with Western suit jackets over them. Then we passed a man in a long, brown robe with a little beard and fair skin. He wore a tan wool hat with a roll of fabric at the bottom and something like a ruffle above it. "What's his tribe?"

Roshanna glanced at him. "He is clearly Tajik. You see the hat, which they all wear. Massoud was a Tajik, so when you see all the pictures of him, he will be wearing this hat."

"Massoud—"

"Our great hero, Ahmed Shah Massoud, the leader in driving the Russians out. He was attacked by two Arabs just before your 9/11 and died a few days later."

We passed two other men, who stared at me as I tried not to stare at them. I was already used to people staring at me, because I was taller than any of the Afghan women I had seen so far and taller than many of the men, too. Plus, my hair was now blond and spiky and refused to stay hidden under a scarf. It seemed there was always a tuft of it sticking out. People also stared at me because I didn't conduct myself like a typical Afghan woman. Most of them kept their focus either on the street or on some space in the distance—anyplace that wouldn't cause them to make eye contact with the men. Everything about me was different from these women. I felt as if I might as well be wearing a big, striped Uncle Sam hat.

"Roshanna!" I pulled her arm and inclined my head back toward the two men. "Those men are very light-skinned, and they both have blue eyes. Are they Americans or Europeans wearing Afghan clothes?"

"No, Debbie!" She was clearly amused. "They are Nuristanis, from the mountains in the north. They say they are the descendants of Alexander the Great. Some of them have hair like yours." She tucked a stray piece inside my scarf. "Blond like it is this time and also red, like last time."

"What tribe are you from? And what about Daud?" This was all so odd to me, because I'd never thought of them as anything but Afghan.

"We are both Pashtun," she said. "We are the largest group in Afghanistan and also often the leaders. We drove out the British in the last century. The king before the Russians invaded was Pashtun, and so is President Karzai. So also were the Taliban." She made a face at that.

When we finally arrived at the mosque, Noor was waiting for us in the van, stuck in the four-deep line of temporarily parked cars. There was a stand selling kebabs wrapped in flatbread and lots of people had pulled over to buy. The mosque itself was an old building with a blue dome. It was pockmarked, as most of the buildings in Kabul were, with bullet holes as well as bigger chunks that had been knocked out by bombs. There was a big traffic rotary in front of the mosque, and all around the outside, dozens—maybe hundreds—of men sat on their haunches, some just

106

talking to one another, some fiddling with their prayer beads, some watching the cars that went past with eager eyes. Most of them looked as if they had just come down from the mountains, with their rough clothes and large, bulky turbans. Some of the turbans had pieces of cloth hanging down, which whipped in the breeze of the passing cars. "Many are from the countryside," Roshanna told me. "Their villages were bombed, so there is not work there. Or they are farmers and their crops fail because of the drought, so they come here to make money."

When Noor got out of the van, we walked over to the closest group of men. Noor told them that we were looking for about ten workers to move boxes, and half of the men jumped to their feet. A crowd of them followed us across the street. Roshanna and I climbed back into the van, and then all the men who had followed us dove for the entrance of the van. A knot of them got stuck in the door, all arms flailing and faces straining and turbans flying; then one of them managed to grab the back of the passenger seat and pull himself through. About five more tumbled into the van after him, and then another pushing, writhing knot formed in the door. Noor was outside shouting, pulling men away. Finally, another few men got into the van and Noor slammed the door shut; then we headed off to find the shipping container. The men who had made it inside crowded on one side, so they didn't have to sit near us women. They spoke to one another softly and nodded at me courteously.

The shipping container was lodged at the back of a hospital compound, along with several containers of medical supplies. Noor had to go off to take care of some other things, leaving me and Roshanna alone with the men. Then a man came out of the hospital with a battery-operated tool, and he worked on the big bolts that held the door closed. The outer door was soon cranked open to reveal a big sheet of plywood. When the men pried that aside, there were all the boxes of our beauty products. Two thousand cubic feet of them.

I went to reach for one of the uppermost boxes, and the men rushed forward with outstretched arms and shocked looks on their faces. Roshanna started to laugh. "They're not used to seeing a woman work this way," she said.

"We're all going to have to work this way." I tipped the box, and it suddenly slid out of my arms, spilling bottles of shampoo all over the ground. The men started picking up the bottles, then addressed a question to Roshanna. They talked back and forth for a few minutes, and she laughed again. "They want to know why you didn't just wash your hair back in the United States!"

Then Roshanna had to leave, and the men and I were on our own. Since I had to look inside every box because they weren't marked, I tried to do as much sorting inside the shipping container as I could so we'd have less to move back in later. I kept digging my way toward the back of the container. When I'd find hair color or makeup, I'd toss it to the man in back of me, and he'd toss it to the man in back of him—the chain extended to the ground outside, where one of the men made an orderly arrangement of boxes. The first time I threw a box, it hit the man behind me in the chest and almost knocked him over. I think he figured that a woman wouldn't really be able to toss it that far.

Soon, though, the men got used to working side by side with me. By then they were tossing boxes to me from the top of the load, up near the roof, and I was doing my best not to fall over. We finally finished sorting and repacked the container, with the boxes that had to be moved to Mary's near the door. At the end of the day, I gave each of the men some samples of shampoo and conditioner. They must have compared products after they left, because when they came back the next day it seemed they all had developed preferences for one scent or another and wanted new samples. Then friends from an NGO loaned me their cars and drivers. It was about a forty-five-minute drive from the shipping container to Mary's house, and we had to make fifteen trips, but we managed to move all the boxes of hair color and makeup to her third floor in one day. It was a good thing, too, because that evening it began to rain.

When it first started, everyone in Kabul was thrilled. There had been a drought for seven years, and it had baked the city streets into hard clay, which the thousands of cars and water buffalo and walkers ground into fine grit. Early in those first few rainless mornings of this trip, the skies had been clear. But after just a few hours of traffic, the dust and diesel fumes drifted upward like a yellow fog, hiding the sun, the mountains, even the highest buildings. I was as happy as anyone about the rain, because I had developed the worst cough of my life thanks to the dust. I hacked and hacked all night long, waking people on the other side of the wooden partitions in our bedroom on Mary's second floor. But the rain only seemed to make things more miserable. The streets turned into mud, and the sewers alongside them overflowed with fecal matter. It was impossible to go anywhere without becoming covered with mud. Whenever it stopped raining for a day, the streets dried out, and the dust was a bigger problem than before. My cough became worse and worse.

And I worried that the rain was going to postpone the biggest item on our agenda: a meeting with prospective students for the school. We had decided that the first women we wanted to reach out to were hairdressers who were already in business. We wanted to help them become more successful. Since there wasn't yet a reliable mail system in the city, Noor had spent several days before I arrived wandering around, looking for beauty salons. He knocked on the door of every salon and delivered hundreds of invitations to a meeting at Mary's house. Since public transportation was unreliable even on dry days, we weren't sure how many women would be able to make it through the mud and the rain. And we didn't know if we sought would be able to break away husbands and fathers for this unusual and cious occasion: a gathering of hairdressers.

I stood on Mary's roof and peered down to the street below. Against the mud, there was a puddle of blue that shifted and shook with excitement. Hairdressers had arrived for the meeting! Most of them were in blue burqas, but a few were in pale yellow ones—and some were in ordinary street clothes with dark scarves. I spotted several more burqas streaming purposefully down the street toward the house to join the others. I ran down Mary's stairs, overjoyed.

Some thirty women filed into the house as Mary and I greeted them at the door. They settled themselves on the toushaks in the living room, then rolled the fronts of their burqas up so that the cloth framed their faces like heavy curtains. Some of the women had babies, which they jiggled in their arms to keep them quiet. I went around the room with a platter of baked goods. One of the younger women was stunning, with huge green eyes and brown hair and about the loveliest smile I'd ever seen. She took a small cake and put her hand on my arm.

"Thank you," she said in a voice about an octave lower than I expected. "Thank you."

"What is your name?" I tried to remember the words in Dari. *"Namet chest?"*

"Baseera." She repeated it slowly so that I'd catch

syllables and the roll of the *r* at the end. Leera."

I tried to replicate the music of her voice, and she laughed. "Good," she said.

She had a face that looked as if it liked to laugh. I was ready to admit her into our first class right then and there.

Mary and I handed out a number to each of the women and took their pictures with the numbers, so that we'd know later who we were talking about. We explained to them that in-depth interviews with Noor would follow and that not all of them would be part of the first class of twenty. Since their faces weren't covered anymore, Noor couldn't come in the room. So Mary translated as I welcomed them to the meeting. I explained who I was and what our plans were for the school, then told them I needed to ask them some questions so that we would know how best to design the school to serve them. But first, I said, I'd like them to tell me a little about themselves.

This was like removing a cork from a bottle. Their stories started to pour out at once. Mary got the women to settle down and tell their stories one at a time, then quickly translated.

One woman who looked as if she were my age but was much younger—I was starting to notice how common this was—said she had worked as a hairdresser before the Taliban and had just started again in the last year. She said that she had been wearing the burqa for fifteen years. When she first took it off, the sun was so blinding that it took her three days to be able to walk around without shielding her eyes from the light.

Another woman said she had not been allowed out of her home in eight years. She said that she was depressed and very bored, and that she had come to this meeting without telling her husband. She thought there was a chance her husband might let her come to beauty school if he knew how much money she could make. She had been cutting her daughters' hair at home, and then her daughters' teachers' after they admired her work.

I pointed to Baseera, who was looking at me with wide eyes. "Can you tell us your story?" I asked.

She nodded, and Mary began to translate. "This young lady has been a hairdresser for eight years. Even during the time of the Taliban, she still made money working on hair."

In fact, Baseera was the sole support of her family during those years, because her husband lost his government job when the Taliban took over. She had customers who were wives of the Taliban, and they would come to her house for wedding hair and makeup even though it was forbidden. Their husbands would drop them off and pretend that they were just visiting. The women would leave Baseera's house with their hair and makeup hidden under their burqas and their manicures hidden by gloves. Then she got a warning that the Taliban were going to raid her house. She broke her mirrors into pieces and buried them and her other supplies in her yard because it was too dangerous to throw them in the garbage. When the Taliban came, she had to let them in, and they tore her house apart. They beat her husband and put her in jail for two days. Tears flowed down her cheeks as she told this story, and she wiped them away with the hem of her burqa. I had to put my arms around her and hold her. She was twenty-nine years old, but she seemed more like a child. One who both laughed and cried easily.

Then Mary prompted the next woman to speak, and the stories continued. I figured that the women had averaged about ten years as hairdressers. Now I wanted to know how they did things and what they actually knew, so that we'd know how to design the school's curriculum. So I started pointing to different women and asking questions. How long do you leave a perm solution in? Do you work on women with lice? How do you handle hair that has henna in it? Do you reuse a comb if you've dropped it? At this point, the attitude in the room shifted. While the women had been happy to tell their stories, they now seemed anxious that they might appear ignorant. If I had understood Afghan culture better, I would never have put them on the spot like that. I would have questioned the women in private. I didn't realize that I was toying with their pride in their work, and some of the women got angry. These most often turned out to be the women who knew the least while acting as if they knew the most. Still, I wish I'd handled it differently.

By the end of the meeting, though, everyone seemed

to be excited about the school. I was probably more excited than anyone, knowing how much these women were going to be learning and how it would change their businesses. I thought of the boxes of wonderful products we had just moved and could imagine the women trying them out for the first time—breathing in all those exotic fragrances, rubbing the silky conditioners through their fingers. The women began to leave, pulling their burqas or scarves back over their heads. Many of them kissed me on their way out the door. Just as Baseera was kissing me good-bye, Roshanna arrived, and the two of them spoke for a minute.

"I want to know more about this one," I told Roshanna. "Can you ask her to stay a few minutes longer?"

So the three of us settled on Mary's toushaks, and Roshanna began asking questions. "She comes from Mazar-e Sharif, in the north of Afghanistan," she began. Then she listened and translated while I held Baseera's hand, because she had started to cry again.

Baseera said that, in the late 1970s, the war against Russia was raging near Mazar. Bombs had fallen near the children's school. Her father was a progressive thinker and wanted Baseera's two older sisters to stay in school—she herself was only three years old at the time—so he moved the whole family to Kabul, where Baseera's mother's brother lived. The father found a nice house for them. He performed what is called a *garroul,* meaning that he gave the owner a large sum of money for the house; after five years, the family could either get some of the money back or keep the house. After they were settled in Kabul, the father went back to Mazar to conduct a final piece of business, but he never returned. Baseera's anguished mother waited for months to hear from him and finally had to assume that he was killed either by the Russians or by the mujahideen, even though no one ever found his body. She took a job cleaning a school, and eventually, all the girls were students there. In five years, the terms of the garroul were up, and Baseera's mother decided they should take the money and move to a house that wasn't as nice. Her wages were meager, and the family was becoming poorer and more ragged. Her brother said that he would take care of collecting the money for her. This role was expected of him as the oldest male relative. But when Baseera's mother asked him for the money, her greedy brother refused to give it to her and ordered her out of his home. So the family now had no house and no money.

By the time Baseera was eight, she was still going to school but couldn't live at home. She stayed at the house of one of her teachers and did the housekeeping there, because her mother couldn't afford to feed her. Baseera missed her mother terribly and saw her only on Fridays, but the teacher was kind, as if Baseera were one of her own daughters. Soon Baseera decided that she wanted to be a teacher, too.

But when she was twelve, her mother engaged her to

a twenty-nine-year-old government clerk. Her mother was afraid that, because she had no husband and no money, people might assume bad things about her daughters, maybe even accuse them of being prostitutes. There were also rumors floating around Kabul that men were trying to snatch young girls and sell them in other countries. Baseera didn't understand any of this. Her cousins teased her that she was engaged to an old man, but she was still playing with dolls and paid no attention. Even at her engagement party, she raced around the room and tumbled with the other children in her fancy velvet dress. When her husband to be bent down and gave her a gold ring, she thought this was just another game.

Over the next two years, her betrothed stopped by and gave her presents, but she still paid him no attention. Then one day, she felt a terrible pain in her back and lay down at her mother's house. When she stood up, blood streamed down her legs. She called her mother and screamed that she was dying. No, her mother told her after running into the room—this meant that it was now time for her to be married. So when she was fourteen, Baseera was married to the man who gave her the gold ring. She remembered it as a terrible day. The beautician threaded her eyebrows, and she cried from the pain of it, and then she continued to cry with fear of what would come. Her mother had told her only that her husband would do something to her after the wedding that would make her bleed some more. I later learned that mothers didn't tell their daughters about the details of the wedding night because they wanted the girls to appear innocent of any knowledge of sex. Sheer terror was a good indication of virginity. Baseera said she cried so much before the wedding that the beautician had to keep applying her makeup over and over, because her tears kept washing it away. Later that night, men from her family and the mullah signed the nika-khat in another room while Baseera sat in her old teacher's lap. The teacher said she was sorry that Baseera had to marry and quit school. Baseera would have made a fine teacher, she said.

When her mother shooed her into a room with her husband later that night, Baseera pressed herself in the corner and shrieked. Her false eyelashes washed away, and she pulled the big, lacquered curls from her hair in despair. Her husband stayed away from her for three days, but on the fourth he insisted. The bloody cloth was presented later to his mother.

When Baseera was nine months pregnant with her first child, there was still war in the country, but not between the mujahideen and the Russians—now the mujahideen factions were fighting with one another. Many people were fleeing Kabul, and her husband thought they should go, too. He said that they could get space on a bus leaving the city, so she agreed. But her labor pains began before they could board the bus, and she and her husband and sister-in-law went to a hospital. It was closed and all the staff was gone—and there were no lights because the power had been off for days—but it was still crowded with people hoping to find someone left who could care for them. Baseera had her first baby on the cement floor of the dark hospital. She didn't cry out. Instead, she bit her wrist when the pain was bad and pinched her sister-in-law, who was the one who wound up delivering the baby. It was a girl. Her husband was happy about this, even though neither she nor anyone else in the family was.

Baseera had another daughter during the civil war and yet another during the reign of the Taliban. Her labor pains for the third came after the 11:00 P.M. curfew, and everyone was afraid to take her to the hospital without official permission. But she hurt so much that she had to walk, so she went outside. Her family brought toushaks out of the house and laid them down on the sidewalk, and she had her third girl near her front steps. She had finally had a boy only a few months ago. She wanted to come to beauty school because she didn't know anything about cutting or coloring hair. And she never wanted to wind up like her mother, so poor that she'd have to send her children to live with someone else.

By this time, all three of us were crying and had streaks of smudged makeup all over our cheeks and hands. This was the first time I had heard one of these sad Afghan stories in such detail. Roshanna's family had certainly had a hard time, as had every Afghan family. But they had triumphed and stayed together, and she had a good job. Baseera's story broke my heart. No wonder she seemed like a sorrowful child. It was almost as if she was still the bewildered girl of fourteen who wasn't ready to be an adult.

That night I was more determined than ever to make this school work for Baseera and others like her. My sole concern was continuity. I worried that there was only Noor to watch over the school when the American hairdressers weren't there. Not only did he know little about hairdressing, but he wouldn't even be allowed to walk into the school once it opened. There just wasn't anyone in Kabul who was qualified to run the school on a daily basis. As I went to bed that night, I wondered if I would be able to take a longer chunk of time—say six months—away from my own customers to work here. I wondered if I could stand being away from my mother and sons for that long or if I could ever learn to get around Kabul with the same ease that Mary did. I had my doubts about whether I was up to this. Still, I felt that someone from the team would eventually have to stay in Kabul to keep the school going.

"Wake up!"

I opened my eyes to see Mary bending over me. The last thing I remembered was the mullah rousing me at 4:30 in the morning with the call to prayer, after I finally fell asleep on one of the toushaks in her living room. My cough had gotten so much worse during the night that the force of it was shaking the wooden partitions in my bedroom. I'd tried to muffle it so that I wouldn't wake everyone else up, but I could hear sighs and people tossing in their blankets all around me. So I finally went downstairs, hoping to get a few solid hours of sleep. I was scheduled to leave in a few days, but I was afraid the airlines wouldn't even permit me to get on a plane. Concern over the spread of SARS was at its height, and I heard that the airlines were putting people into quarantine if they had bad coughs. I was already sad about leaving Afghanistan but didn't want to stay here—or in Pakistan—in some back room filled with SARS suspects.

"Wake up, Debbie," Mary said again as my eyes closed. "I have something I want to show you."

The light coming in the windows was dim, and there wasn't much noise yet from the street. I knew it had to be really early if the noise from the street hadn't begun. "What time is it?"

"Put your clothes on." Mary's voice trailed behind her as she went outside. "You need some fresh air."

Before I knew it, we were in a taxi headed out of the city. When I asked her what we were doing, she shook her head mysteriously. One of her Afghan helpers—a boy named Achtar, whose arm had been mangled in an accident—was sitting in front with the driver, and he just smiled at me. The taxi went so far out of town that it finally left all the kebab stands, gas stations, and melon wagons behind, and started up a mountain road. It stopped, and we got out. I couldn't see why we were stopping, because there was nothing there but the mountain and the road. Then Mary and Achtar started off on a little path through the rocks, and I followed them. We walked and walked, and finally came to a rock bridge over a stream, and everything was green beneath us. Farther downstream, young girls carried buckets of water on their heads. I saw a village in the distance. Some men walked toward us on the path, and they exchanged sharp words with Mary. I asked her what they said. "Taliban territory," she replied. We walked past fields and over more bridges. Again, men walked past us and said something to Mary, and again she snapped back at them. When I asked her what they said, she shrugged. "Taliban territory." We finally came to an old, old city where a narrow street wound between walled compounds.

I was really a mess. I hadn't had my morning coffee, my head wasn't covered, and my sweater was so short that it didn't even cover my butt. I was just so wrong for this place, but Mary kept on going as if this was the most natural thing in the world. Then we got to Achtar's house, which was a hut made from sun-dried mud bricks.

"He made the bricks himself," Mary said, and Achtar pointed out the bits of straw glinting in the bricks. "He also built the hut himself," she continued. "He's very proud of this, because his family used to live in a tent." Achtar ushered us inside, where his father sat on the carpet waiting for us. He looked as if he were a thousand years old, with a chest-length white beard, a black turban with a bolt of blue plaid cloth wrapped around it, and indistinct gray eyes that drifted around the room. I realized that he was blind.

Achtar's mother came into the room carrying a big pot of tea. She was tiny, not much bigger than the boy. I was half afraid that I'd get dysentery from the tea, but it would have been impolite to refuse it. So I drank the tea while Mary talked and talked. It was like a dream, sitting there with the boy and the tiny woman and the blind man, and I could feel the cool, clean mountain air settling my cough. I was struck by the idea that beyond the war-torn buildings and the sad stories of the people who had survived the bombs, there was something magical about Afghanistan. I wondered again if I could live here myself, as Mary did. I wondered if I could be as sure-footed among these people.

There was one more dreamlike place that I visited before leaving. Westerners had started to whisper of an Irish pub—the first bar in the post-Taliban era—that had opened in Kabul, and a few of us went to try to find it. We drove around the neighborhood where it was reputed to be without seeing any signs of a bar; then finally someone decided that the gate with the really big cluster of buff-looking guys with machine guns and no turbans had to be the place. They checked our passports, searched us, made us sign our names on a sheet, and then they opened the gate. When we stepped inside, it was as if we had jumped four thousand miles. There were tables with umbrellas and gardens. Inside the building there were a bar to lean against, pool tables, and dartboards. The place was crowded with people from all over the world; I was sure I could hear a different language at every table.

You couldn't actually buy liquor, no doubt because the proprietors had promised the authorities that they wouldn't sell alcohol. What you could buy were coupons, and then you traded the coupons in for drinks. We had a lot of fun that night, getting away for a few hours from the dusty, crowded, complicated Kabul just outside the gate.

We went back two days later, and it was all gone. The guards had disappeared, the gates were locked, and we could see only a dark, empty building through a crack in the wall. I heard later that they had gotten a bomb threat and decided the money they could make providing Westerners with an escape wasn't worth the danger.

Chapter 4

The women watched me with solemn eyes as I approached the easel and painted a big red circle on a piece of paper. "Red," I announced.

Anisa translated this into Dari, and they all nodded.

"Pretty easy so far, huh?" I added. "I bet you could have told me that yourselves!" After Anisa translated; the twenty women in pale blue uniforms all laughed. Roshanna gave me a thumbs-up sign from the back of the group.

After an agonizing wait of five months, I was finally back in Kabul to teach color theory, which was my part of the Beauty Without Borders curriculum. I was so excited to return that it was all I could do to stop grinning. Anisa was an Afghan-Canadian hairdresser who was one of the other volunteers. We were both still pinching ourselves that we were helping to launch this amazing project.

I took a deep breath and painted blue and yellow circles a foot below and to the left and right of the red one, as if the three balls were tucked inside the angles of a triangle. Then I mixed colors to make an orange circle between the red and yellow circles, a green circle between the yellow and blue circles, and a violet circle between the blue and red circles. I painted black lines connecting the red and green circles, the yellow and violet circles, and the orange and blue circles. It looked as if I was painting a sort of blobby, multicolored daisy. But with my three jars of primary colors, I planned to explain how they could turn a brunette into a redhead with blond highlights. Or green highlights, whatever the customer wanted.

I had been in town for only a few days. Noor had picked me up at the airport and apologized right away that there wasn't a room reserved for me. But I wasn't worried about that. I told him just to drive to the beauty school and I'd find a room in the nearest guest-house. Sure enough, we found one just down the street from the Women's Ministry. It was in a big, clean white house with bunnies and a rooster running around in the yard. There was no hot water when I went to take a shower that night, but really, I hadn't expected it.

The next morning I walked to the beauty school,

and it was just as lovely as I'd hoped it would be. The walls were a creamy white, and there were colorful pictures and shining arrays of product everywhere. There was the music of women's voices, women's laughter—the sounds of women taking care of one another—that is just part of a salon and beauty school. To me, these sounds are a sensory feast—like stepping into a hot bath or opening the door of an oven where cookies are baking—that always makes me feel good. One of the Afghan-American hairdressers was demonstrating scissor techniques on a student's hair, and they all looked up with big smiles as I came in. Roshanna broke away from the group and threw her arms around my neck. All twenty students were dressed in blue uniforms. They looked so different from the nervous, burqa-cloaked gathering we had seen in that first meeting back at Mary's house. I looked to see if Baseera was among them but found out later that Noor hadn't picked her for this class.

I told the women how much I was looking forward to working with all of them, then stayed in the background to watch. In the afternoon, I worked in the salon with some of the other hairdressers, and the students watched me. There was a funny moment when one of the women who worked in the ministry came in for a haircut. When I pulled out a blow dryer after I finished cutting, she gasped as if I had pulled a gun on her. She had never seen a blow dryer before and had no idea why I was pointing it at her head. When I turned it on and hot air blasted out, she screamed and jumped out of the chair.

A few days later, I gathered the class for our first session and handed out small color wheels for each of the students to consult. As Anisa translated, I painted my own version of a color wheel and started to go through the basics of color theory. I talked about primary colors, secondary colors, and complementary colors. I explained that complementary colors are opposite each other on the color wheel. I pointed to the colors I had painted on my easel—red was opposite green, orange was opposite blue, and so on. They nodded.

"Does anyone have any idea what this has to do with hair?" I asked.

They were polite but clueless. "No," several replied meekly.

"Anyone want to make a guess?" I looked around the room. "Roshanna?"

She made a little face, clearly regretting that she had ever befriended me.

I explained that underneath everyone's primary hair color, there is a contributing pigment. Someone's hair might be black, but when you bleach it you often find that orange is the contributing pigment underneath. So if you want to change someone's hair color, you have to take that underlying pigment into account and counteract it by selecting a color from the other side of the wheel. If orange is a contributing pigment but the client doesn't want orange hair, you'd pick a hair color with a blue base—like blond—to counteract the orange. To demonstrate this, I smeared some blue paint over my orange circle and showed them how the smear turned brown. "See that?" I asked. "I've used the complementary color to get rid of the orange. Understand?"

Oh yes, they all assured me sweetly. They understood.

That afternoon at an Internet café, I sent an e-mail to my friends in Michigan telling them about my first class. As I looked at the date on the e-mail, I had such an odd combination of feelings. It was September 11, two years after the terrorists' attacks on New York and Washington, D.C. That was the event that made the world suddenly take notice of Afghanistan and realize that Osama bin Laden and other extremists had a stranglehold on the country. That was the event that triggered America's invasion to drive out the Taliban. And of course, that was the event that had wound up propelling me and the other Beauty Without Borders volunteers to Afghanistan. I knew that September 11 was a day of public mourning back in America, but it was an ordinary day in Kabul. As I looked out the window, cars honked and maneuvered around one another, shopkeepers arranged their wares, and pedestrians hurried along, wrapping their faces against the wind and the dust. Still, I felt a new burst of determination. I wanted to make sure that the beauty school—and the new chance that it offered the women of Afghanistan—would be one of the good things to come out of September 11.

The next day, I thought I'd start the class by reviewing what we'd covered the day before. I picked up a lock of a young woman's long brown hair, and said, "What do you do if you want to turn her into a blonde? What are some of the things you have to think about?" No one even tried to answer. Instead, they fidgeted, their kohl-rimmed eyes darting toward the door, toward the row of mannequin heads, toward the salon capes hanging on the wall. Anywhere but at me. Even Roshanna ducked behind one of the other girls when I looked her way. I tried some of the other concepts we had talked about the day before. The color wheel? Contributing pigments? Mixing red and yellow to make orange? They all just looked at me as if I had suddenly decided to give them the formula to build a rocket. By the end of the day, I was tired and frustrated. I was starting to doubt my ability to teach.

On the third day, it was the same impasse all over again. I stood in front of them for hours talking about color theory, but they just didn't get it. And they had to get it, or else they'd never be able to color someone's hair properly. By the end of the day, they looked miserable, and I'm sure that I looked miserable, too. I decided maybe we'd just try doing some color together, using a board of hair swatches that one of the manufacturers had supplied. However, I couldn't find it. I finally looked at the girls and clicked my scissors in the air.

"We're just going to have to make swatches out of your hair!" I announced. When Anisa translated this, they all shrieked and put their hands over their heads. Long hair was still a really big deal in Afghanistan. The long-haired girls felt like the romantic heroines from the Bollywood movies from India that they all watched, and their husbands often demanded that they keep their hair long. Even their parents wanted them to keep it long, because long hair made unmarried girls more marriageable. But I swooped around them with my scissors and snipped away small strands for a new swatch board. I got about ten swatches alone from one girl who had hair down to her butt. There was so much shrieking and laughter that one of the ministry guards finally knocked on the door. I made a face at the students and opened the door, thinking that the guards were going to want to march me out to the street for making too much noise. "You make *us* happy with all that laughter!" they said, smiling apologetically. "But please not so loud. People are asking what goes on in here."

That night I lay on my miserable bed at the guesthouse and cried. I had been so excited about starting this beauty school, but now I felt as if all I was doing was torturing the students. What I was telling them seemed so simple to me—it had always seemed simple to me—but they were still clueless. I knew they weren't stupid. We had carefully interviewed them to make sure we picked hairdressers who would really be able to make use of what they learned and make their own businesses stronger. And they had caught on to the other concepts quickly. So it seemed that this was my failure—my big, fat Afghanistan failure—and I didn't know what to do about it. Then Val and Suraya started pounding on my door.

When I had gotten my room at this guesthouse five days earlier, I saw that it was full of Afghans who had been living in Europe, America, or Australia. They had returned for various reasons—some to work for NGOs, some to look for family property that had been abandoned during the wars, some to visit old friends. I was thrilled to find myself in the midst of them, thinking this was the best of all possible combinations: Afghans who also spoke English. But it turned out that most of them had very little interest in speaking to me. They were caught up in the excitement and heartbreak of rediscovering Kabul, and they were eager to use their native tongue again, not English. I'm sure I would have been the same way, but it made it hard for me to make friends. I was terribly lonely there until I saw someone else who looked as out of place as I felt. That was Val, a Serbian-American photographer and husband of a gorgeous Afghan-American journalist named Suraya. The three of us became instant, indispensable friends.

"After three days of class, they just look at me like I'm speaking Greek," I told them. "I don't think I'm going to be able to teach them anything!"

"You have to be patient, Debbie," Suraya said.

"It's been three days already!"

"More patient than that. These women have been so traumatized. They've fled war after war after war, and they're still surrounded by chaos. And lots of them haven't even been out of their houses for years."

"I know that," I said. "That's why I thought they'd be so ready to learn something new."

"Yes, but they haven't had to learn anything new in ages. You know, it's like a car—if you haven't driven it in five years, it's not going to start up right away. That's what their brains are like."

"Yeah, well, I'm not a freaking mechanic. I don't know how to get them started again."

"Didn't you do disaster relief training?" Val asked. "Doesn't some kind of short-term memory loss come with post-traumatic stress?"

After we hung around and ate some dinner, I thought back to my disaster relief training in 2001, before I'd even known where Afghanistan was on the map. All of a sudden, it seemed so obvious to me that these women—and maybe everyone in Afghanistan—had post-traumatic stress syndrome. It might be true that I was a lousy teacher, but they'd been through so much and were still going through so much that it had to be hard to concentrate on new things. It would be hard even if they were working with someone who'd been teaching all her life. So I bucked up and determined to try again.

And the next day, I had a breakthrough. I was trying one more time to get across the idea of the contributing pigment as something you had to counteract in order to get the color right. They were all looking at me with courteous incomprehension—blank if benign stares—and I was groping around for an analogy. "Think of it as Satan!" I finally said, pointing at a patch of orange paint. "It's this evil thing in the hair that you have to fight. You have to use the opposite color to keep it from taking over."

And suddenly, one of the students got an aha! look on her face. This was Topekai, a young woman with dark, intelligent eyes and a quick, decisive manner. I pulled Anisa closer and asked Topekai one question after another to make sure she really understood. I was so excited that I kissed her on both cheeks—twice—and led her back to the rest of the class, hugging her so tightly that she could hardly walk.

"Tell her to teach them," I told Anisa. "She'll know how to put it in the words that they'll all understand." I explained the contributing color concept again, and Anisa translated. Topekai—blushing with pride but speaking in a strong, clear voice—explained it in her own words. Then another two girls said they understood. I broke the class into small groups so that those three students could work with the rest of them. Finally, everyone got it. After that, the color class was a huge success. I'd whip questions at them—like "You've got a woman who's a natural level four and she wants to be a warm eight, so what do you do?"—and they'd whip the answers right back at me. When we got to the foiling part of the class—my own Achilles' heel—I gave them a demonstration, then left to have a cigarette. When I came back, they had their mannequins perfectly foiled. Each little folded packet was like origami, a work of art.

After that, it was pure joy for me to come to the school every day and work with the students. Their diligence amazed me. I knew that most were juggling children and often abusive husbands and mothers-in-law, that they lived in homes without water or electricity or any of the amenities Westerners take for granted, that they braved sneers and skepticism from people who believed women should stay at home. But they showed up on time every day, incredibly focused on making better lives for themselves. Their skills progressed rapidly, and I knew they'd leave at the end of the term with everything they needed to run successful businesses.

It was also a joy to be there because I could see that they were having fun gossiping and giggling and fussing with one another's hair. At the end of the day, they'd often turn on a tiny radio and try to find some music. If they did, they'd show me how they danced at weddings. Some of them told me this was the first time they'd really had fun in years. The beauty school and salon were like a hothouse, and these girls were like flowers that had been stunted and stepped on— but still, never broken. Now they were bursting into bloom before my eyes. It was fun to be around them. And as they talked and either Roshanna or a translator told me what they were saying, I learned even more about Afghanistan—sad stuff as well as funny stuff. One day, Topekai and two of the other girls were talking back and forth as they were practicing on their mannequins with perm rods. I wasn't really listening since I still didn't speak much Dari, but I kept hearing odd English-sounding words. Had they really said "*Titanic*" and "Leonardo DiCaprio"?

Finally, I asked Roshanna what they were laughing about. "We were remembering how the Taliban weren't just hard on beauticians," she said. "Sometimes barbers got in trouble, too!"

It seemed that, even though such things were strictly forbidden, foreign movies still made their way into Afghanistan under the Taliban's radar. The movie *Titanic* was an especially big hit on this underground circuit, and the Afghans were quite smitten with its stars. The men coveted the look of Leonardo DiCaprio's hair in that movie. As I recall, it was sort of long on top and hung to the middle of his cheeks. However, that style ran counter to the look that the Taliban had decreed proper for a Muslim man—short hair, long beard. Finally, one cagey barber figured out how to profit from the new trend. He popularized a cut that had some of the DiCaprio length on top but not so much that it couldn't be tucked under a prayer cap. One of his customers blew it, though—he took off his prayer cap, his long, DiCaprio locks fell out, and someone ratted to the Taliban. They started checking under other prayer caps to see if there were any more blasphemous haircuts in Kabul, then traced it all back to the barber. They threw him in jail for a few days. Truly a prisoner of fashion!

• • •

We stood on the street outside the red door, sniffing the air. "It doesn't smell like a restaurant to me," I said.

"Two people swore to me that they served food," Val said. "Let's go in and find out. If they offer us a massage instead of wonton soup, we'll leave."

The sign on the building said that this was a Chinese restaurant, but that meant nothing. Most restaurants that catered to Westerners—meaning they sold alcohol and had mixed-gender dining—didn't put up signs for fear of drawing hostile attention. Many of the places that claimed to be Chinese restaurants were actually brothels. But Val and Suraya and I had a craving for Chinese food, so we pushed the door open and went in. There were actually tables inside with people sitting at them. This was a good sign, even though the waitresses were serving drinks in skirts that were slit all the way up to their thighs. This is just not a look one sees in Kabul. Someone at another table leaned over and told us that they used to wear miniskirts but it caused too much of a ruckus outside, with Afghan men crowding around trying to look into the door. "Men were falling off bicycles!" the person at the next table said. This is the way people in Kabul always seem to describe the public reaction to women who stand out too much.

As we picked at our food, I was telling Val and Suraya that I thought the original Beauty Without Borders plan was flawed. We had planned to fly foreign

136

hairdressers over to Afghanistan each time the school was in session, but doing so was really expensive. I think we had spent more than $25,000 on airfare alone for the first class, and who knew how long we'd be able to get funding? After my sputtering start at the beginning of the color class, I had also been thinking that it would be better if we trained Afghan hairdressers to be teachers, rather than bring in Westerners and go through all the complicated translations—sometimes having to explain terms for which there were no words in Dari. I had seen for myself that the Afghan hairdressers were able to put the important concepts into terms the other students understood. And while the Western hairdressers could show the Afghan students some snazzy new styles and techniques, the fact was that the Afghan clientele weren't much interested in that kind of stuff. I also told them that I thought one person from the beauty school needed to be in Kabul all the time to maintain continuity with our local supporters and our hosts at the Women's Ministry. That person couldn't be Mary MacMakin, because she was too busy with other PARSA projects. And it couldn't be Noor, because he couldn't even walk inside the school when the students were there.

"Would you want to stay here all the time, then?" Suraya asked me.

"I've been thinking about it," I said. "But it would be hard to be here on my own. And it would be hard being away from my mother and my kids all the time."

"You need a husband." Val said this as casually as if he were offering me another egg roll.

"I just got rid of a husband," I reminded him. "I don't think I want another one quite yet."

"He's right, Debbie! You do need a husband," Suraya exclaimed. "It's very hard for a woman to live alone here, even a Western woman. You need a husband to support you while you support the school."

I rolled my eyes. "If you haven't noticed, I'm not so good at picking husbands."

"No problem," Suraya said. "Marriages are arranged in this country. We'll just have to find the right man for you."

"I thought only first marriages were arranged."

She smiled. "This will be your first marriage in Afghanistan."

So then we had a long, silly discussion about the kind of man I should marry. We agreed it wouldn't do to marry one of the Westerners. They either were in Afghanistan for a short period of time or were missionaries who had been here for twenty years with wives and children, or they were alcoholics working for one of the embassies or big NGOs. It would be hard to find the right kind of Afghan man, too, because most of them wanted a wife who would be subservient and make his dinners and serve him tea and rub his mother's feet. We just couldn't see any of that happening. But at the end of the night, Suraya vowed she was going to find me a husband. And even though it all seemed like a big joke, it also made a weird kind of sense to me. Afghanistan was great when I was with the students or my friends, but when they went home, I was lonely. It's a very family-oriented culture, but I wasn't part of a family. I wasn't part of a big NGO, either, where people live together in big compounds and become sort of like family. I wanted to stay in Afghanistan, at least for a longer stretch of time than the few weeks when school was in session. But I wasn't sure I could do it alone.

The girl couldn't have been older than fifteen. She had a filthy blue scarf around her hair that dwindled into ragged shreds on her shoulders. She had an open sore on her cheek. She reached out to put her arms around my neck, and I forgot every warning I'd heard about the prisoners having lice. "Help me," she whispered as she hugged me. "Please help me."

I turned to Suraya. "Why is she here?" I asked.

After a brief conversation, Suraya translated. "She was married to an old man who beat her, and she ran away. Her parents reported her to the police for breaking her wedding vows."

Oh my God, I thought. If I had been an Afghan woman, I would have been put in prison for leaving my abusive husband.

Suraya wanted to write an article about women in Afghan prisons. Because I had spent time working at a prison in the United States, the women's minister had arranged for the two of us to visit the Kabul Welayat, a women's prison. I had heard so many terrible stories about this place that I was a little nervous about going. I had ongoing struggles with my health—the "Kabul cough" that I always seemed to get from the dust, plus constant problems with my stomach—and people had warned me that I should be careful about picking up new ailments in the prison. I had thought about doing something with the women's hair there, but then everyone warned me about lice. I couldn't bear the idea of lice. So I packed up a big box of gift bags, which Paul Mitchell had donated months before. I had passed dozens of these bags out to my customers, as well as to church groups and schools back in Michigan. They had stuffed them with health and beauty samples, hair ribbons, and all sorts of fun, girlie stuff. I took enough for the guards, too, so that they would be less tempted to steal from the prisoners.

The prison guard who escorted us was a huge woman with breasts the size of watermelons. Before she took us inside, she pointed to my purse. I handed it over with a smile that I hoped would charm our way through another hour of bureaucratic hassles. She ignored me and turned my purse upside down, emptied it on a counter, then picked up two bottles of fingernail polish. She looked closely at them and set them on a shelf behind her. Soon, Suraya and I were following her down a hallway that became darker and danker with every step. When we stopped in a room to see the first group of prisoners, I gasped.

Despite how bad the stories about the prison had been, I was unprepared for the horror. It was one of the worst days of my life, and I've had some really bad ones. The prison was a dark, old building with long, damp hallways, and there were about five women crowded into each small cell. Robbers and murderers back at the prison where I'd worked in Michigan had better cells. Some of the women were trying to sew on old, broken-down machines. Some of them had their children living in the cells with them, dirty children who stared at us with eyes that had gone dead.

The big guard ordered the women to line up for the gift bags, which now seemed like a hideously bad joke. As each one stood in front of me, my heart broke all over again. They had sores and scratches on their skin, their hair was greasy and matted, and their eyes were as dull as those of dead animals. I'll tell you, I have visited leper colonies in India where the people looked better. Suraya was taking notes and translating, and I kept asking her why each woman had been imprisoned.

One of them was there because she had been raped.

One was there because she had been raped and her husband had killed the rapist. He was also in prison, but her term was longer.

Several young girls were there because they had tried to run away with their boyfriends.

One was there because she became pregnant with her boyfriend before her parents were able to marry her off to someone else.

One was there because she had tried to kill her

brother-in-law. Her husband had died, and she had remained in her father-in-law's house with the rest of her husband's family. But her brother-in-law beat her son and raped her. Finally, she poured gasoline over him while he slept and set him on fire, but he didn't die. His father came to her in prison and asked why she had done this. When she told him, he went and shot his son dead in his hospital bed.

The stories were all horrible, but the young girl weeping in my ear—imprisoned because she had fled her abusive husband—did me in. I cried and cried, until I embarrassed Suraya.

When I got back to the school, I was still crying. All the students came crowding around. "What's wrong, Debbie?" Roshanna said, throwing her arms around me. I told them that it was the brave women of Afghanistan—standing strong through wars and forced marriages and so many different forms of confinement—who had inspired me to leave my troubled marriage back in Michigan. I told them that I owed my freedom to them. I told them that I would love them and Afghanistan forever for that. By the time I finished, many of them were crying, too. I think I actually became real to the students then. They didn't just see me as another do-gooding American but rather as one of them.

The visit to the prison also showed me how rare and precious the beauty school was. Here our students, in their blue uniforms, with their new skills and growing professionalism, had hopes for the future. But they could just as easily have been suffering in prison, hidden and without hope. In fact, they could still wind up there. Women were still getting sent to prison for having boyfriends or leaving abusive husbands.

Things were going well at school, but life at the guesthouse was getting worse and worse. That stupid rooster I'd thought gave the place such a nice touch when I first moved in? He woke me up every damn morning, usually right after I had fallen back asleep after the mullah woke me up. I glared at the rooster every time I saw him. One day I had the guesthouse guards—called *chowkidors*—hold him down while I painted his toenails red. Also, the water never seemed to be hot at the guesthouse when I wanted to take a shower. I finally took my things over to the beauty school early one Saturday morning, when there was no one there but me and the ministry chowkidors, because I knew there would be hot water. But just as I was lathering up, I saw a scorpion in the shower and started to scream. One of the chowkidors came flying in the door with his machine gun ready, thinking that someone had attacked me. I was trying to cover myself with a towel while he was shouting in Dari and looking for my intruder—until he saw that it was a scorpion. He sank against the wall laughing. Then he picked up a bottle of shampoo and squashed the scorpion.

The cold water and the rooster were only minor annoyances, though. The man who ran the guesthouse was a nasty old guy who was forcing his fifteen-year-old daughter to marry a man in his forties. The groom-to-be was very rich. He had figured out how to skim a layer of fat from all the reconstruction money flowing into Afghanistan, and he was reputedly now worth millions. It was kind of like the Gold Rush in Kabul right then. If you had a good idea for gouging, you could make a fortune. The old man who owned the guesthouse was greedy and wanted to attach himself to this rich man, even though his plan was making his daughter miserable. I used to find her crying in the bathroom all the time, and she'd tell me that she wanted to go to school, not marry. It made me sick.

The guesthouse had also become party central for Afghans who had been living in the West, and that was getting old. There was always a crowd of people in the living room, dancing or eating or sitting on tou-shaks talking away, passing around platters of rice or chunks of hashish rolled in sugar. Most of them didn't want to be bothered talking to me. That left me stuck with either the owner—and he was always trying to maneuver me or one of the other women into a corner—or one of his friends. And lots of them were as creepy as he was. One Friday night, there was an especially big bash. I dressed up and came downstairs. I tried to have fun—and mind you, I'm not usually the type who doesn't know how to have fun. But the west-ernized Afghans were as cliquey as ever. The old man was drunk and even more disgusting than usual.

I talked for a while to his one friend who wasn't as

much of a pig as the rest of them. This was Ali, a sandy-haired Afghan in his mid-forties who had been living in Germany. I was never quite sure how he made a living, but he always had nice clothes and plenty of money. He seemed to know everyone in town—when I needed to figure out how to get something for the beauty school, Ali usually knew what to do. He was charming and handsome, but maybe a little too charming for my mood. I finally said goodbye to him, left the guesthouse, and took a taxi over to visit Roshanna. When I came back later that night, the party was still going. Val and Suraya had joined the throng, but I just waved to them as I stepped over a drunk Afghan man who was passed out near the stairs and went up to my room.

A week later, someone pounded on my door. I was in my pajamas and was reading in bed, so I just called out, "Who is it?"

"It's us," Suraya shouted. "We found you a husband!"

"Where?"

"We met him at the party last Friday and then we spent a day with him. Come on down!"

"He's an Afghan?"

"Yes! Come and meet him."

I put my book down. "He'd better not be that guy who was passed out at the bottom of the stairs."

I could hear them whispering outside the door, and then Suraya laughed. "He might have been that guy, but he's standing up now."

"Forget it," I said.

"He's perfect for you," Suraya insisted. "Put something sexy on and get out here!"

So I got out of bed and got dressed, then walked down the stairs to meet Samer Mohammad Abdul Khan.

I recognized him immediately as the guy who had been passed out near the stairs. He didn't look much more appealing to me now that he was upright. He had black hair, a little black mustache, and a jagged scar on one cheek. With the scar and his dark, dark sunglasses, he looked like a member of the Colombian mafia. He was wearing a black shalwar kameez, too, and I wondered whether he could be a progressive thinker if he wore such traditional clothes. When Suraya announced that we were leaving, Samer—or Sam, as she called him—turned and walked out the door in front of me. I wasn't impressed that he was leaving me in his wake, but at least it gave me a chance to check out his ass. It looked okay, but in those baggy clothes it was hard to tell.

I didn't even get to say hello. We climbed into Sam's car—also black—and Ali sat in the front with him, with Val and Suraya and me in the back. Suraya introduced me to Sam as his new wife; Ali introduced Sam to me as my new husband. They all laughed uproariously. It was as if I were in a car full of drunks. In about fifteen minutes, we arrived at a Turkish restaurant. Sam pointed to a table at the back of the restaurant and said something to the waiters; soon they came with wooden screens that they arranged around the table. All the marital conspirators shuffled chairs around and made sure I was sitting right across from Sam. He took off his sunglasses, and I suddenly had a flicker of interest. He had warm brown eyes that reminded me somehow of my dad's. He kept his eyes averted from me. I suddenly realized he was shy.

And then the negotiations began.

"I'm standing in for Debbie's mother," Suraya said. "Sam, what are your thoughts about a dowry?"

He smiled and said something, but Suraya shook her head emphatically. "What did he say?" I asked Ali.

"He offers two camels."

Suraya started to tear into Sam in Dari.

"What's she saying now?" I asked.

"She is saying that you are her beloved daughter and she wants gold," Ali replied. "Plenty of gold. Also a house and a car."

Sam threw up his hands as if fending off a physical attack. The waiters arrived with pizza, and Sam handed a piece of pizza to Suraya. Then he went on for a long time in Dari. "He says he will give gold, land, and car, no problem," Ali told me. Then he said something to Suraya and Sam. The whole table looked at me and laughed.

"What are you saying?" I shouted.

"Ali is a bad man." Suraya patted my arm. "He said that I will have to settle for less because you are not a virgin."

It went on like this for an hour. I got to know most

of the essentials. Sam had a well-drilling business based in Kabul, but he and his family had been living in Saudi Arabia for the last twenty-seven years. He was one of the Uzbek mujahideen who had fought with General Dostum—an infamous Afghan warlord—against the Russian occupiers during the war. He spoke fluent Arabic, Dari, Turkish, Uzbek, and Pashto, less fluent Hindi, and a smattering of Malaysian, Indonesian, and English. He'd gotten his start in business by selling pajamas to pilgrims in Mecca. He was ten years younger than I.

When we finished dinner, Sam asked if we wanted to come over for tea. So we all piled back in his car and went to his house, where Sam sat on a toushak as far as possible away from me. The four of them kept going on and on with the negotiations for my dowry. No one was even asking me about what I wanted, and I decided to pipe in. "I don't know if you know how marriages work in the West, but I wouldn't have any other kind," I told Sam. "I want a partner in business and life and a lover. I'm not going to stay in the house and serve you tea."

"I see this kind of wife on television, and I want one," Sam said through Suraya. "I don't want a woman who doesn't leave the house."

"I'm not doing your laundry, and I'm not cooking or cleaning. I want to make enough money so that I can pay to have that kind of stuff done."

"And I'm not going to go to the bazaar with you or run errands for you. I'll hire someone to do that."

"You better not want babies. That factory is closed."

He winced. "How can I want babies when I have seven daughters?"

Suraya jumped in to explain that, oh yeah, he had a wife and seven children back in Saudi Arabia. In most places, that would be a pretty big deal breaker. "You're nuts," I told her, but then she gave me the rest of the story. It had been an arranged marriage to someone he'd never met. He didn't even know her name until ten days after the wedding. He didn't love her but couldn't divorce her because she would be forever shamed and maybe even destitute, since wives who have been divorced usually can't go back to their parents—and in that culture, she certainly couldn't go out and get a job. She had refused to leave Saudi Arabia, where she lived with his parents. They had given him the go-ahead to pick up a second wife. To his way of thinking, he was available. To my way of thinking, another wife and seven children and a gun-toting past with a warlord was just a little too much baggage.

Then Sam looked directly at me for the first time all night. "If you're not serious about this, don't play with my heart."

"I just met you!" I said.

"You're not serious?" he asked, through Suraya.

"I don't know!"

He went upstairs to his room and came back with a package. It was a bolt of lavender silk with embroidered daisies and lots of sequins. This was a courtship ritual that I'd never heard of—I guess the groom's family is supposed to give the bride's family fabric for her wedding dress. But I hadn't a clue about it then. I sat there with this god-awful gaudy stuff in my lap trying to figure out what I was supposed to do with it, but Suraya cried, "Mrs. Sam!"

A week later, Val, Suraya, and I decided we'd had it with the old man's guesthouse. We had stomach problems all the time and thought it might have been the food the old man was serving us—probably kebabs fashioned from the goats who grazed the medical waste and other garbage outside the hospital every day. And Suraya had had a run-in with one of his chowkidors. The guesthouse did our laundry—that was part of the deal—but it was understood that the ladies would wash their own underwear. Suraya had all sorts of lacy underthings that she'd washed and hung outside to dry under a blanket, so that no one would see them. But she caught one of the chowkidors under the blanket, sniffing her stuff. When we mentioned to Sam that we wanted to leave—he was now hanging around the guesthouse every day—he invited us to move into the house he was renting. So Val and Suraya moved into one room, and I moved into another. And suddenly, Sam and I were nearly constant companions.

Not that we were able to spend much time alone. The whole concept of dating hadn't hit Afghanistan yet. Maybe people dated back in the days of the king, but the practice seemed to have died along with that era. Sam and I were almost always surrounded by Suraya, Val, Ali, Noor, and a friendly diamond smuggler whom we'd met at the old man's guesthouse. If I was seen alone with Sam or any man, people would assume that I was a prostitute. So we went on lots of picnics or out to the Turkish restaurant with Val and Suraya. And when we did, there was always this joking about Sam and me getting married. Val and Suraya pretended to be in ongoing negotiations, because the family of an Afghan bride usually spends months hammering down the details of the dowry. We had a lot of fun with these negotiations. I laughed so loud once when Suraya and Sam were haggling at the Turkish restaurant that Sam was embarrassed. He went over to a table full of staring Afghans and told them I was a general with the international peace-keeping forces, so they'd understand that I was supposed to act badly.

But everyone acted as if Sam and I were engaged, although I still wondered if they were serious. Every day, Sam would show up at the Women's Ministry to visit me outside, under the chowkidors' watchful eyes. Every evening, we'd be together but surrounded by the cast of characters who hung out at his place—he'd decided to turn it into a regular guesthouse, so there were more people who had rented rooms. Every once in a while we'd manage to sneak a few minutes alone, but it was sort of frustrating since he couldn't speak English and I couldn't speak Dari. I'd creep into his office when no one was around, but lots of times I just wound up watching him play Spider Solitaire on his computer. I thought he was cute. I thought he must have a good sense of humor, because he had a hearty laugh and the Afghans all seemed to be laughing with him. I didn't think there was a hidden ugly side to him, because I saw him both when he was out with friends and when he was doing business in his office. His mood didn't seem to change much. I liked him more all the time, even if I wasn't in love with him.

But everyone else talked as if we were getting married right away. I went along with it. One day, Ali told me he was starting the paperwork for us to get married, and he took me to a building to get my picture and fingerprints taken. A few days later, Val and Suraya told me to get dressed, that we were going to see the judge about the marriage. Sam dressed in a dark shalwar kameez. I was in a pink embroidered dress and pink shawl that Suraya had given me because she thought none of my clothes were nice enough. Ali came along, too. We all drove to a dirty, old three-story building and walked down a long hallway. It was dark inside, because the power wasn't working that day. I peered into the rooms we were passing, and it seemed there were men drinking tea in all of them, some squatting on the floor. We finally got to the room with the judge and sat on a broken couch with so little stuffing that our butts almost touched the floor. A man with a gray turban and gray beard sat at a table—this was the judge, I gathered—and two men sat on either side of him drinking tea. They all darted curious looks at me.

When we finally walked up to the judge, he scanned each of the papers Ali set in front of him slowly, running his finger over the print as he read. He looked back and forth from me to the photograph we'd taken a few days earlier. He said something to one of the men sitting next to him, and that man shook his head. Then the judge said to me—through Suraya—"We've never had a foreigner here before."

I nodded my head solemnly. I felt shockingly pink in this dark, drab room.

"You are single?"

"Yes."

"How do we know you are single? You need to get a paper from the American Embassy saying that you're single."

"They have no idea whether or not I'm single!"

The judge fished a cigarette out of his pocket. "Well, we need some sort of proof."

I had a thought and dug in my purse for my passport. I pointed to where my visa read "single entry," meaning that I was allowed to enter the country once. "It says single right here."

The judge confirmed this with Suraya, then tapped the table with his cigarette. "A woman cannot divorce a man in Afghanistan. Did you know that?"

"That's not a problem," I said. "If I don't like him, I'll just leave him."

I don't know if Suraya translated this properly, but

the judge seemed to accept it. He said, "All right, then. Repeat this after me."

And as I was repeating after him, I realized that he was reading the nika-khat—the legal document that made us man and wife. I wondered how it was possible that I was marrying someone to whom I couldn't even talk, but I kept repeating the judge's words anyway. In a few minutes, it was signed. There was nothing said about "Now you can kiss the bride." Instead, Sam and I turned slowly to the long hallway outside the room, married only twenty days after we met. We had already planned a party that night to celebrate birthdays for Val, Suraya, and me—we were all born around the same date—so we stopped to buy the traditional candies that are handed out at a wedding. We also stopped at the school and told the students, who were thrilled. Roshanna hugged me with such force that she just about knocked me over. "Now, you are really Afghan." Sam started referring to Val and Suraya as his father- and mother-in-law.

I was thinking, worst-case scenario: I'll just go back to America and never tell anyone that I got married. The problem with that was that I'd never be able to return to Afghanistan.

I wanted to keep our marriage a secret, at least for a while. I didn't want to tell my family or friends in Michigan that I had gotten married again, since most of my relationships didn't have even the life span of a goldfish. And I didn't want word to get around in Kabul. There were lots of reporters buzzing around because we were getting ready to graduate our first class from the beauty school. I certainly didn't want my mother and grandmother and sons to read that I had gotten married in a newspaper or see it on television.

So things stayed pretty much as they were, at least on the outside. I shared a room with another woman, and Sam stayed in his room. When we'd get together with the whole group in his living room or out at a restaurant, we'd content ourselves with longing gazes. We met in his room a few times when the house was empty for delightfully furtive sex. But even though I was enjoying this precipitous plunge into marriage, I was still planning to go back to Michigan a month after the first class graduated. Now, however, I figured that I would return to Kabul more regularly, even when school was not in session. Maybe I'd alternate two months of Afghanistan—and marriage—with three months of my old life at home.

Frankly, I didn't have a lot of time to think about whether I had married another freak. Graduation was approaching. All of the beauty school organizers wanted to make it the biggest party for a group of women that Afghanistan had ever seen. I volunteered to plan it, figuring it wouldn't take me much more than three days to set everything up.

Wrong.

It took me two full days to find a location that could handle two hundred people, including media. We wanted to invite every politician and dignitary in town, but these people wouldn't go anywhere unless their security was assured. I inspected one place after another, but there was always a problem—too small, too dirty, bad neighborhood, or too expensive. I finally realized that the Turkish restaurant—the place where Val and Suraya had hammered out the details of my so-called dowry—might work. Sam and Suraya came along with me to negotiate things, and then all I had to do was invite people.

Back in Holland, Michigan, this wouldn't have been a big deal. But back in Holland, Michigan, I wouldn't have been inviting the president of the country to come to a party. We figured we'd invite all the most important people in the city, but I didn't run in that crowd—I didn't even know their names. So I made a guest list that looked something like this:

President Karzai and his people
Foreign affairs minister and his people
Women's minister and people
Women's hajj minister (the Islamic women's
    minister—very important)
Transportation minister
Head of the U.S. international peacekeeping forces
American, British, Canadian, Dutch, German, and
    Turkish ambassadors and people
General Khatol Mohammed Zai, the only female
    general in Afghanistan's army

If I were in Holland, Michigan, I would have tracked down the addresses of these people and mailed the invitations. But there was no postal system in Afghanistan; there wasn't a way of looking up their addresses. Among Sam, Roshanna, and Suraya, we finally came up with a rough map of the city showing the compounds where most of these people might be contacted. So I set out one day, dressed in my most conservative clothes and wrapped as tightly as an overseas package, to deliver handwritten invitations. At each place, I was greeted by armed guards who wouldn't consider letting me in without an appointment. And I must have seemed suspicious to them, since I didn't even know the names of some of the dignitaries I was inviting. I left the invitations with the guards but at least thought to ask for the phone number of each dignitary's assistant.

After three days, no one had called to RSVP. I called all the assistants and found out that none of them had received the invitations. So I wrapped myself up again and went out to redeliver them. Two days before the party, I tried calling around to find out who was coming, but the entire city's phone system was down. So I had to go from compound to compound one more time, requesting quick meetings with the assistants to get a head count. I finally returned to the beauty school victorious. It seemed that we would have a tremendous turnout, with some of the biggest names in Kabul in attendance. The girls were so excited that I considered taking their scissors away from them.

On the big day, the beauty school was pandemonium, with all twenty students as well as the hairdressers getting ready for the party. Everyone was running around in pink and green curlers, doing one another's makeup, settling their false eyelashes in place. Anytime new people walked in they could hardly breathe for the hair spray and powder. I did my own makeup quickly and ran out before the others, just to make sure everything was ready at the Turkish restaurant—and found that nothing was ready. So in my full party regalia—I'm talking a pink-and-gold Punjabi outfit, gold high heels, hair as tall as Marge Simpson's, and eyelashes like butterflies—I started moving tables. I'd finally gotten them all into place when the security officer for the Dutch ambassador arrived. He took one look around and told me it was no good. The tables were too close to the windows, and important people don't sit by windows because someone might take a shot at them. Even if I moved the tables to the other side of the room—which I did—he wasn't happy with the place. There was no back entrance, in case the ambassadors and their party wanted a quick exit. The buildings on either side of the restaurant were too close and too high, making it too easy for a shooter to station himself above and wait for a good target to come along. And where were the security guards?

Well, where were the damn security guards? Sam arrived in time to find me screaming at the owner of the restaurant. I thought he had promised to bring in extra security for the event, but he thought I was doing it. And if the place wasn't ringed with guards, none of the dignitaries would get out of their cars. Fortunately, Sam was a friend of the head of the Turkish peace-keeping forces, who obligingly sent over thirty soldiers. They arrived just minutes before the guests. The musicians started to play, we began to serve drinks—not with alcohol, of course—and just when I was starting to panic that the students had been kidnapped, they swept into the room looking like a parade of 1950s debutantes. It was a dazzling celebration. Halfway through, General Zai asked if she could make a speech. "My sisters, I salute you!" she cried from the center of the room. "Tonight I stand here proud to call you my sisters because through your hard work and perseverance, we can create a brighter, more beautiful future for Afghanistan!"

It was a wonderful night. As I looked around the room, I was particularly happy to see all these men and women mingling in this pleasant way. Outside the old man's guesthouse, I hadn't really seen any mixed-gender crowds. After about half the guests left, I felt like dancing. I pulled a few of the students by the hands and told them that we should dance to celebrate this great achievement, but they all backed away. And these were the ones who danced like harem girls after work at the beauty school! Finally, I took Topekai's hands and asked her to dance.

Topekai had been my breakthrough student—the first one to grasp color concepts—and she was different from most of the women in that first class in other ways, too. Her family had been poor, and, like many others, they'd fled to Pakistan to get away from the wars. But her husband's brother had emigrated earlier to America and was dutiful about sending money, so they never suffered the kind of grinding poverty that many of my other students had. When they returned to Afghanistan, her brother-in-law sent enough money for her husband to start a business selling wood for home heating. Topekai's was a loving husband who helped out with the children and even washed the family's clothes when she put in long hours at school. Topekai had always seemed so strong and calmly determined that I assumed she wasn't as bound by the culture's restrictions as the rest of them. When I asked her to dance, she looked at her husband gravely, and he nodded. So we danced, but modestly. Even so, a quiet circle of watchers formed around us and her cheeks grew pink.

If I'd known then what I know now, I never would have asked her to dance. It was a cultural faux pas. If Suraya had been standing nearby, she would have quickly told me I was stepping over a very substantial line. Topekai's husband had not consented because he approved of his wife dancing in front of other men; in fact, he was terribly shamed by this. He had consented only because he didn't want to embarrass me and because I had helped his wife gain the skills she needed to run a successful business at a time when his own business was struggling.

But I didn't figure this out until much later. That night, I was only full of deliriously high hopes. I stayed late and did my best to charm all the dignitaries. The American Embassy had called earlier in the day to offer their regrets because there had been some sort of terrorist threat against Americans. I never gave a thought to my own safety. I kept exchanging glances with my handsome stranger of a husband. I looked forward to the next few days, when all the other Americans would go home, when the media would go away, when we could finally sample our new life together in privacy. I was so happy that I didn't even realize my feet were bleeding until I got home and pried off my gold high heels.

Chapter 5

I stepped through the doorway of the charred house, angling my shoulders to keep from getting soot all over my clothes. There were no interior walls, only shapes that were jagged and sharp against the gloom. The November air was cold and heavy with smoke. I shone the beam of a flashlight through a hole that went all the way to the attic. As I did, I stepped on something that crunched and then skidded from under my foot. My mother bent down to pick it up. It was one of my old dolls.

"Don't worry, honey!" she said, as if I were still six years old. "We can probably get it cleaned up again." She tried to rub the soot off its face, but I could see that its cheeks were cracked.

The destruction made me feel as if I were still in Afghanistan, not back in Michigan. Only a few weeks ago, I had gone with an Afghan-American friend to look at the house his family had abandoned during the wars. There were huge rocket holes, even in the interior walls, and rats skittered away from us in every room. It was hard to recognize it as a home—it could have been any old wrecked building—but my friend told me it had once been one of the finest houses in Kabul. As we moved from room to room, he pointed out where the dining room table had been where they had eaten their last meal together. He showed me where his father had kept a beautiful old cupboard from Nuristan to store his coin collection. It was all gone. I couldn't imagine that kind of loss then, but now I was beginning to understand how you feel when your family home goes up in smoke. There weren't even any visual clues of our old life together. Where was my father's chair? He had died more than a year ago, but my mother always kept his chair in the same spot. Where was the cupboard where we stored the Christmas ornaments?

This was only a few days after the graduation and a week after my marriage to Sam. We had hardly had time to get to know each other as husband and wife when I received my mother's e-mail about the fire and left for Michigan the next day.

My mother had already moved into the cottage on the shore of Lake Macatawa that I'd rented after my divorce from the preacher. This was my dream house, a little blue bungalow with a front porch and a view of ducks paddling by. All it lacked was a white picket fence. It was a perfect place for my mother and sons and me to put ourselves together again after the trauma of the fire. My mother was especially fragile. I went back to work with her in a few days, and I could see it was all she could do not to cry in front of the customers. She jumped every time there was a loud noise and kept forgetting what she was doing. The fire had burned up all her pretty clothes, and she trudged around in other people's bulky sweaters and pants for weeks.

Even though I hardly knew Sam at this point, I missed him terribly. He and I would call each other and use up all the words we knew in each other's language in about a minute. *Hello, I love you, I miss you, good-bye, see you soon!* When we had to say more than that, I'd call Suraya, she'd call Sam, and we'd work out a three-way call with translation. It seemed that Sam missed me as much as I missed him. He had gone back to Saudi Arabia to work out some problems in his family's business. By the time he finished with that it was hajj season, the time of year when hundreds of thousands of devout Muslims make a pilgrimage to Mecca. It was impossible for him to get a plane back to Kabul then, because all of the flights had been booked for months. He was stuck with his family—his parents, his brothers and their families, and his other wife and children.

Through Suraya, he told me he thought about me all

the time. "I've never loved a woman before," he said. "This love thing is very bad. It gives me a pain in the chest." But sometimes during these calls, I could hear children crying in the background. Sometimes I could hear a woman shouting. It made me nervous all over again that I had married a man with another wife and children. It made me feel like his mistress, not his wife. It was not a good feeling.

He hadn't yet told his family about me, Sam explained. I was a combination of three things his parents hated: American, Christian, and a hairdresser. And he didn't want to make life any worse for his first wife than it was. His parents thought she was worthless because she hadn't produced a son for him, and they treated her like a servant. They might be even crueler to her if they started to hope that a second wife might bear him a son. Already, he said that his family was suspicious about the phone calls. They could hear my voice coming over the line from across the room. Sam told them he was carrying on some kind of negotiation with the American Embassy back in Kabul.

My mother was getting a little suspicious about all the phone calls, too. Once, a friend of Sam's who spoke pretty good English called and left a message that I should call my husband the next morning. "What's he talking about?" my mother asked.

I cast about for a reasonable-sounding lie. "The words for 'husband' and 'friend' are the same in Dari," I said. "So Afghans usually think they're the same in English, too."

I could have told her all about the marriage right then, but I didn't. I still didn't want anyone to know about it. I wasn't sure if I had made the greatest mistake of my life—or rather, yet another greatest mistake of my life—by marrying him. And besides, I was starting to feel pretty comfortable back in Michigan. I missed Sam, but it was great to be around my family and friends again. My kids were doing well, and I was living in my dream house. My customers had started returning to the salon in droves when they heard I was back, so I had money. I asked my customers how long I could be away without them giving up on me and finding a new stylist. They told me they could manage without me for about two months. Before I knew it, three months went by. I thought this was the perfect arrangement: three months in the States with my cottage and my loved ones, two months in Afghanistan with my secret husband and continued involvement with the beauty school.

But toward the end of my stay, I started to get anxious about going back to Afghanistan. If one of the beauty school organizers didn't return soon, I was afraid that all our hard work to raise money, build the school, and stock it with products would help only the twenty girls who had just graduated. I knew there were hundreds more who wanted to attend our school. They had been hanging around and begging for a spot in the next class. I also knew that nice new buildings in Kabul didn't stay unoccupied long, no matter whom they belonged to. Noor was telling me that there was no money left in Kabul for our expenses and that there was some grumbling inside the Women's Ministry about unpaid bills. The other organizers were telling me there was no more money in New York. Someone had to go back and make sure we held on to the school until we found more funding. It seemed obvious that that someone was going to be me. I finally broke the news to my mother, who just smiled. "We all figured you were going to go back right away," she said.

So I put a FOR SALE sign on my car and struck a deal with my ex-husband to get paid for my portion of our house. With that money plus donations from customers, I went on a shopping spree for the beauty school. I bought a lot of the items that we would need for the second class, like more color, peroxide, perm rods, combs and brushes, spray bottles, foils, and a few mannequin heads. I packed nearly one whole suitcase with the kind of stuff I had pined for in Kabul, like deodorant, tampons, Wet Ones, and duct tape. I packed another suitcase full of wax—forty-five pounds of it—knowing it would be a big hit among Afghan brides and Westerners who wanted to go hairless. I was hoping we could do enough business in the school salon during after-class hours to keep the bills paid, at least until other funding came through. Most of my old clothes weren't suitably modest for Afghanistan, where women's clothes have to cover butts and arms, so I left them behind. I packed the collection of stuffed frogs that my dad had given me over the years, as well as my favorite pillow, a couple of bottles of tequila, and some margarita mix. All the essentials.

I got off the plane in Islamabad, Pakistan, and faced a familiar sea of humanity. It was a dark sea, as it seemed to be mostly men with dark jackets, capped here and there by off-white turbans and some white prayer caps. After some jostling, the crowd funneled into long lines going through customs. I emerged on the other side, enlisted two men to grab my six suit-cases, then proceeded into the waiting area. I scanned lots of bearded faces, then finally found the one I was looking for. It was the friendly diamond smuggler from the nasty old man's guesthouse in Kabul, waiting for me with a book of poetry tucked under his arm.

It might seem odd for me to have become pals with a smuggler, but in the war years lots of Afghans were smuggling one thing or another, just to survive. Neither Sam nor I had known him long, but we had grown very fond of him during my last stay in Kabul. He had been a rich diamond smuggler then. He would come to the guesthouse with a cake and expensive whiskey at least once a week to celebrate his birthday. After a few glasses of whiskey, he'd croon Afghan love ballads all night. Val and Suraya had briefly considered marrying me off to him, but he already had three wives and didn't speak a lick of English. He had two houses in Pakistan—one in Islamabad and one in Peshawar—but he was otherwise reduced in circumstances now because one of his diamond shipments had been confiscated in Iran. Still, he was lavish in his attentiveness while I stayed in Islamabad. He was the typical Afghan host, who treats a guest—and especially the wife of a friend—like a cherished sister. He took me to a beautiful old guesthouse, insisted upon paying all the bills. He assigned a handsome man who spoke English to be my babysitter until I decided how I was going to get to Kabul. I don't think Fahim, my babysitter, had spent much time alone with a woman before, and he became sort of smitten with me. He still calls me after he's had a few drinks.

After a few days of checking out airfares to Kabul, I decided to go by land. Even though I had sold my car—I wouldn't get the money from the house for a while—I didn't have much money left after having bought my plane ticket to Pakistan and all the supplies for the beauty school. In fact, I had a mere three hundred dollars to get me to Kabul. I had gotten a plane ticket into Islamabad, thinking it would be cheaper to fly there and then take one of the special flights for people working with NGOs into Kabul. This would cost only one hundred dollars, and I qualified as a volunteer for PARSA, which was registered as an NGO. But then I found out that I could take only forty-four pounds of luggage on the NGO flight. I had at least ten times that amount. It would cost me hundreds of dollars to take a regular flight and hundreds more to pay for overweight luggage. I finally realized the only way I could get me, my wax, my curlers, my stuffed frogs, and my tequila to Kabul was by car.

Driving from Pakistan to Afghanistan might sound easy, but it meant that I had to travel over the Khyber Pass. This is a narrow groove through the Hindu Kush mountains that has been used by travelers for centuries, but it's so far from the centers of government in any country that it has always had a reputation for being wild and lawless. It can be dangerous for anyone to travel the pass, but especially so for an American woman traveling without a husband. The diamond smuggler spent several days lining up an escort for me. While he was in Peshawar taking care of this, Fahim—my handsome babysitter—escorted me out for shopping and lunch. One day when we were sitting in a restaurant, Fahim got a call on his cell phone. After a few minutes of conversation, he told me that the diamond smuggler—he called him Hajji, the honorary title for anyone who had made the hajj pilgrimage to Mecca—said that we had to hurry up and leave.

"Did he find someone to take me to the pass?"

Fahim shook his head. "Hajji's wife needs grapes. We must go to the market."

I turned this over in my head. I had met a few of Hajji's wives, and there were a number of other women living in the house, too. Solid, able-bodied women. "What, are their legs broken?" I asked.

He shook his head. "No, no, no. They must not leave the house."

I was stunned by this. Here I had traveled halfway around the world by myself and was getting ready to make my way through the Khyber Pass, which is widely considered one of the most dangerous places in the world. Yet Hajji's wife called him all the way in Peshawar and then he called Fahim all the way back in Islamabad to go to the market to get her some grapes. I wondered what these people must think of me.

The diamond smuggler finally drove me to Peshawar, which is about thirty-five miles from the border of Afghanistan. He left me in the care of someone I truly loathed, an old Talib I had had the displeasure of meeting back in Kabul. He distinguished himself by groping both women and men whenever he could. If Sam and I wanted to mess with any of our friends, we'd make sure they wound up standing next to him at a party. Not only was he promiscuous in Kabul, but he drank like a fish, too. But here in Peshawar, he was pious and strict with everyone in his household. He welcomed me into his mansion, which was one of the biggest houses I've ever seen. Then he pointed to a woman wrapped in a dark shawl who was hovering in the background. "Look at my old wife," he said, stroking his beard. He always stroked his beard in a creepy sort of way. "I need nice young one, maybe American like you."

I stood in the living room awkwardly and removed my head scarf. As soon as he left the room, one of his wives came and threw it back over my head. I'd never been in a home where the women had to be covered even while they were inside.

I was hoping to leave the next day, but every day the old Talib kept saying, "Tomorrow, tomorrow." So I wound up spending a lot of time with the women of the house. Some of them were as creepy as the old man. His sister kept snatching things out of my suitcase and pretending that they were gifts for her. She got my travel reading light and a pair of shoes that way. But the rest of the women were just sad. Their lives were so boring: they'd cook, clean, and spend the rest of their time sitting in the women's section of the house and painting their hands and feet with henna. By the time I left, I was covered with so much henna that I felt like a circus freak. When they thought no one could hear them, they'd ask me how they could get out of Pakistan. One of his daughters told me she had been forced to marry a man who lived in London and came back to see her only every two years, just to get her pregnant. Another daughter told me how much she wanted to continue her education, just like her brother. If her father didn't force her to marry, she had hopes of getting a medical degree. But even if she got the degree, she said, he'd never let her leave the house. It made me sick that she already knew she had no future other than the inside of a house.

One of the old man's pompous brothers was always trying to get me into a debate about Eastern versus Western culture. "Our women are happy," he insisted. "Look at them. They have no stress, no tension like women in the West."

This was the only time someone had ever tried to argue this kind of issue with me. I didn't want to challenge him in his family's house. But I thought to myself, Hey, buddy, your wife just put a note in my pocket telling me how miserable she is! The only reason she stays is that you keep her in a gilded cage.

Finally, the old man told me he had arranged my trip through the Khyber Pass. He said his son-in-law would take me, but at a fairly steep price. I wanted to call Sam and ask if the price was fair or if I should bargain with them, but the old man wouldn't let me. I had a feeling that he didn't want me talking to Sam, who would be furious at this most un-Afghan-like treatment of a guest. Even the down-on-his-luck diamond smuggler on his worst day wouldn't have thought of charging me. So I told the old man this arrangement would be fine, because I would have done just about anything to get out of his house.

The next day the son-in-law drove a big white car to the front of the house and shouted for the servants to load my six suitcases. They took them from my room before I was able to pack my favorite pillow, so I came outside with it tucked under my arm. He told me to wear my black veil ninja-style, with only my eyes showing, and warned me not to speak for the next eight hours. I wasn't to let anyone see that I was a foreigner. So we started toward the Khyber Pass. The traffic got thicker and the roads steeper and bumpier, and the mountains seemed to glower around us.

We passed one of the brightly painted jingle trucks

that I so loved. These are semis that are more like ice-cream trucks, with every surface painted, mirrored, tasseled, and embellished in one way or another so that they can deliver their sheets of insulation or boom boxes or whatever with a sort of carnival style. This one was turned over on the side of the road. The son-in-law was sweating, even though the snow was swirling outside. "Don't talk," he said. "Don't even look at anyone. This is where the Taliban is protected, where the opium sellers are protected, where the bandits live. There is no law here. Not Afghan law, not Pakistani law." We drove through a place where the pass narrowed to about forty feet, then eased into a crowded section of the road that was lined with stores. I saw machine guns hanging in one window, grenades lined up in another. I figured you could probably buy a nuclear bomb there if you had enough money. And then we came to the actual border.

I had been anticipating something that looked like the border between the United States and Canada—a nice booth where they ask you what your business is and how long you plan to stay. But I'd never seen anything like this border aside from disaster movies, in which people are fleeing a flood or volcanic eruption with everything they own on their backs or on the backs of the donkeys they've got tied to their waists. We had to park the car and get out. As I sank into the mud in my high heels—because no one had told me I was going to have to walk—a tiny boy with a wheelbarrow made his way to us through the crowd. We put all my suitcases in the wheelbarrow, and then the boy tied ropes around them to keep them in place. The son-in-law strode ahead of me, and I had to work hard to keep up, still clutching my pillow. With every step, my feet sank up to my ankles. I had to really tug to get them loose, hoping all the while that my shoes didn't fall off. I was afraid that if I bent down to pick up a shoe, the crowd would trample me. I was also afraid that, if I took my eyes off the son-in-law, I'd lose him among all the dark jackets and turbans.

Finally, we came to a checkpoint, where an officer asked for my passport. I handed it over silently, and he raised his eyebrows when he looked at it. "You are not allowed to come here without an armed guard!" he announced. "It is very dangerous."

"But I'm already here."

"You should have an armed guard."

"Pardon me." I kept my eyes down. "Next time, I will observe the rules."

He waved the passport at me. "Is this really you?"

I nodded, still covered in a black veil with only my eyes showing. He stamped my passport, and I stumbled forward into Afghanistan.

The son-in-law had disappeared, but I managed to find a taxi to take me down to Kabul. It already had three men in it, but the driver obligingly loaded up my suitcases and told the men in the back to move over. I leaned into the car door with my head and face covered for the next five hours, never saying a word. I was dying to go to the bathroom, too, and gestured to the driver that I had to pull over. He finally stopped at a miserable roadside facility. Aside from a little collision with another car, the trip proceeded uneventfully. No bandits, no snipers, no Taliban hunting us in their white jeeps. As we drove into Kabul and I started to see some things that were familiar to me, I whipped off my veil and lit a cigarette. The looks on those men's faces! I just had to laugh.

The taxi dropped me off at Sam's guesthouse. I wasn't sure who would be there, but soon Ali appeared in the doorway, dressed just like a casual-Fridays professional in the United States. He came rushing out to help me with my bags. Afghan men are not used to women throwing their arms around them, but I figured Ali was pretty well westernized. After my ordeal on the pass, I couldn't help it. But he returned my hug, then helped me get settled. He went into the kitchen and made me tea, then came out with the tea and an assortment of biscuits on one of the beautiful turquoise plates from the tiny village of Istalif, high above Kabul. We sat and talked until the sun started to set.

"It's good that you're back," he said. The light brown of his eyes was very much like that of the tea warming my hand. "The house feels like a home now."

I smiled. "It feels like home to me, too."

"Would you like to call your husband?" He punched some numbers into his cell phone and then grinned as Sam answered. I couldn't hear his actual words from across the room and wouldn't have understood them anyway, but I heard Sam's unmistakably jaunty tone. Ali handed me the cell phone and watched as Sam and I went through our list of words. Then I told Ali to ask Sam when he would be back. I heard a flurry of words at the other end, and Ali shook his head. Sam still hadn't been able to book a flight back to Kabul, although he'd gone to the airport every day and stood in line, hoping that one of the pilgrims had opted to stay longer and give up his seat. But there were about thirty thousand hajjis trying to return and only one flight each day. His prospects of coming back to me soon were dim.

"Salaam aleichem!" I said to a startled woman pounding the keys of an old typewriter. Then I handed her a sample of styling gel and made my way down the hall to the next office.

I made a point of circulating through the Women's Ministry soon after my return, showing one and all that I was back and that I was getting ready to reopen the school. Then Noor and I spent two days interviewing women for the next class. One of the first to walk in the door was Baseera, still in her burqa. I didn't recognize her until she folded it back over her hair and I saw those gorgeous green eyes. "Welcome back to Afghanistan," she said in English, very proud of herself.

I was thrilled to see her again. I told Noor right away that I already knew her story. "As far as I'm concerned, she's in this class," I said.

The rest of the women who streamed in ranged in age from fourteen to forty-eight. I eliminated some of them immediately. There were a handful of really sweet girls under eighteen, but I told them right away that we wouldn't even consider them. I said that they should go back to an academic school and get all the education they could. They all looked at me with huge, tragic, kohl-smeared eyes, and I kept begging Noor to explain that I was trying to do them a favor. I was ready to refuse an eighteen-year-old for the same reason, but she began sobbing. She started to tell her story, so shy that she talked with her veil held over her mouth. Her father had been killed by the Taliban, and her brother was in charge of the family, she told us. She couldn't read or write because her brother hadn't permitted her to go to regular school, but he had given her permission to go to beauty school. I decided right away that I would take her, even if she didn't match the profile of the woman we had agreed would profit most from the school. I didn't care if she had no skills going into this or if she turned out to be the worst hairdresser in town. It mattered only that she was breaking my heart, and that this was the sole way I had to help her.

There were so many compelling stories. There always are. The next girl was about twenty. Her mother was dead, and her father's legs had been blown off by a land mine. She was now the sole support of her family. How could I not take her, too?

We finally picked twenty-seven women for the

second class, which would begin in a month, at the end of March 2004. We told all the women we interviewed that we would put a list of names for the class on the door to the school. I figured I would be able to hide in the back of the school that day—there was lots of cleaning to do anyway—and would not have to face the disappointment of those who didn't get in. But then Noor walked into the school, and all fifty women rushed in behind him. It was a crowd of strong emotions. Some of them were dancing with elation, and the others either wept or followed me around, still trying to make their cases in a language I couldn't understand. I would have taken all of them if we'd had the money. They all clearly needed this opportunity. But I didn't even know if we had enough money for the twenty-seven we had just picked.

I felt terrible by the time I finally got home that evening. Those sad faces haunted me. All I wanted to do was get in my bed with a book and a margarita or two. But when I opened the door, I saw a young girl—maybe fourteen years old—sitting on the couch. She jumped to her feet when I walked in, knocking over a cup of tea that had been balanced on the arm of the couch. She immediately bent down over the spill and swabbed it with her scarf. At the same time, Ali rushed downstairs. He looked uneasy for a second but then walked across the room to take the box I was carrying.

"This is my niece," he said. "This is Hama."

"Tell her not to worry about the tea."

"Come," he called to the girl. She walked over and

stood next to him, her head slightly bent and her pretty chestnut hair falling out of a barrette into her face. She peered up at me through the curls and smiled, then reached out and shook my hand. She was tiny, and her hand was tiny, too, with fingernails the size of teardrops.

"Let me paint those nails!" I pretended to stroke a brush over her fingernails, and she laughed.

"She wanted to join your class, but you didn't accept her," Ali said reproachfully. "I told you she would be coming to the interview day."

I didn't remember that, but I shook my head anyway. "She's too young, Ali. She should be in school."

"She's twenty years old," he said. "Her father is too sick to work, and her mother is sick, too. I've been looking out for her, but she wants to go to your school."

"She's not twenty!"

"Yes, twenty," he said, but he wouldn't look me in the eye.

I held the girl's chin in my hand. "How old?" I asked. I had learned at least this much Dari doing the interviews for the school.

Hama stretched out the five fingers of one hand, then the other, then the first again. I shook my head. "Fifteen is too young, Ali. Tell her to go to school."

She looked back and forth between us, then grabbed my hand. Her bright little face crumpled up, and she started to cry. "Please," she said. "Please beauty school."

I ran my fingers through her hair and straightened her barrette, then dabbed the tears away with my wrist. She was so young that I wouldn't have been surprised if she still played with dolls, if she had such things. Still, I couldn't insist that she spend three more years growing up. She seemed so desperate that I wondered if three more years of being young were even an option for her.

So I told her, "Maybe."

After I lit my cigarette, I waved the match around in the air to put it out, but it continued to flame. So I touched it to a bead of sweat that had formed on the side of my margarita glass and watched it fizzle. I lifted the glass to nibble a crust of salt from the edge, then caught sight of Sam looking at me from across the room. The contempt in his eyes was unmistakable.

"Don't think I'm going to give up my cocktails just because you went and got religion," I muttered to myself as he strode from the room.

Sam had finally returned to Kabul. He had argued so energetically at the airport in Saudi Arabia that they'd decided to let him ride in the cockpit. We had a joyful reunion, but the stress of the next few weeks all but destroyed that joy. First of all, he had come back from Saudi Arabia different from the man I had married. He was a party guy when I met him, always the first to hoist a glass and crack a joke. But he had been overexposed to all those pilgrims back in Mecca. He was now praying five times a day and scowling if he saw me drink or smoke. It was kind of scary, but Roshanna assured me that all the hajjis came back like this and that it wouldn't last long. Then there were other, huge problems. While he was gone, his partner in the well-drilling business had drained the money out of their checking account and left the country. Thieves had stolen some of his construction equipment, and three of his workers had been kidnapped. He was trying to salvage his business at the same time that I was trying to reopen the school. The cultural expectations each of us had brought into the marriage soon became huge hurdles. I knew we were going to be able to work through these differing expectations only with a lot of patience, but neither of us had much. We were expending our patience elsewhere.

I had really been looking forward to having Sam as an ally while I struggled to prepare for the second class. He had always been a staunch supporter of the school but was now so testy that he wasn't much help. And it was getting harder and harder to go to the Women's Ministry every day. The minister's assistant kept asking me if my funding had arrived. I kept assuring her that it was coming any day now. She questioned why it was taking so long, but fortunately, she didn't push me too hard. In the meantime, Topekai and three of my best students from the first class came every day to help me. I was grateful for their assistance and their companionship, but I also felt terrible that I couldn't pay them. They kept saying, "No problem, no problem," but I knew they were all desperate for a salary. I intended to hire them as teachers once I got funding, but there was still no word from New York about new donations—and no money, either.

In desperation, I asked one of the Western women who worked for an NGO in Kabul to spread the word that I was doing hair in the beauty school salon. Customers started to straggle in. That helped me give a little money to Topekai and the girls, but it certainly wouldn't be enough to run the school once the new class started. The girls could see that I was worried, and I could often hear them talk about me in soft voices. One day they all came into the school carrying big, overstuffed bags and wearing proud looks on their faces. They sat me down at one of the styling stations, then started pulling out beautifully embroidered napkins, aprons, and pillowcases—all their own work, which they did at home in the evenings. "You sell these," Topekai said. "Use the money for the beauty school." I started to cry. Here I had come to Afghanistan to help them, but I was so poor that they were selling their needlework to help me.

My only consolation in this difficult time was Hama, who always seemed to be hanging around the house when I got home from work. She was the only one there with a smile for me, because Sam was still frantic about his business and the kidnapped workers. Their relatives showed up at the house every couple of days to see if we had heard anything, but we hadn't. Sam called all sorts of officials, but no one really seemed to care about these men. The house was also full of other people, and it was starting to make me crazy. Ali had a room there and had somehow assumed responsibility for renting out the other rooms. He even had a family of seven in one of them. The rest were men who partied into the night. I didn't like the way they looked at Hama. She didn't like it, either. When the men started drinking, she clung to my side—I couldn't even go to the bathroom without her coming along. I'd finally take her into my room to get her away from the men. She'd sit on my lap and put her arms around my neck, as if she were a tiny, frightened child. She even smelled like fear. I'd coax her off my lap, and we'd play games and paint our toc-nails, anything to forget the men.

But it was hard to forget the men. When I wasn't inside the beauty school, all I saw were men. Since this was the first time that I wasn't living with West-erners—and particularly Western women—I was starting to feel painfully isolated. I'd walk to the Women's Ministry every day, aware that I was one of the few women on the street. It seemed as if the other women who were outside were like leaves, blowing quickly without notice. Topekai and the other girls always got rides to work, and they'd leave promptly at 3:30, well before sunset. I'd often stay longer to cut someone's hair or to clean up. If I left when it was starting to get dark, I'd soon realize that I was the only woman on the streets. The men noticed pretty quickly, too, and they'd stare at me as I passed.

I grumbled about this in the mornings to Topekai. "I'm starting to think of this place as Manistan, not Afghanistan," I told her. "There's way too much testosterone in the air."

She peered at me with her dark, keen eyes. "Don't understand."

"This—" I waved my arms at the world outside our doors. "This is Manistan, not Afghanistan."

"Yes!" Comprehension broke over her face like light spilling in the window. "Very much Manistan!"

Then one night I said good night to the Women's Ministry chowkidors, walked half a block, and was surrounded by five young men. They tried a few words in French, then English, but I just ignored them and kept walking with my head down. Then two of them grabbed my arms, and they all crowded in closer. I looked around to see if there was anyone to help me, but no one else was on the sidewalks just then. There were only cars, the beams from their headlights wide and fuzzy in the dust. No one was going to come to my rescue. Still, this was the kind of situation I had trained for at the prison back in the States, and I broke their holds pretty easily. Then they started to shout and push me toward one of the compound gates, and I knew I had to act quickly or I'd be in real trouble. I sent all my anger down my arm and into my fist, and I punched one of them in the solar plexus and sent him sprawling. And I yelled—I yelled all the bad words in Dari that my students liked to teach me. My attackers backed away and then stopped. One of them laughed.

I didn't want to give them time to regroup, so I barreled toward them. They turned and ran around the corner, missing the sight of me tripping over a loose stone and falling into the sewer.

When I got home, Sam and Ali looked at my torn skirt and the bruise on my face and the shit on my shoes and asked what had happened. Then they grabbed their guns—they all had guns—and bolted out the door. I think it might have been therapeutic for Sam to have a target for all his frustration, but I was relieved that they never found the guys.

Then, all of a sudden, the funding for the beauty school fell into place. A journalist came to interview me, and after I told her about my money woes, she suggested that I try a German NGO that funded educational projects for women. They responded right away, offering to fund the next two classes. Not only was it enough to pay for the teachers' salaries as well as meals and transportation for them and the students, but it also provided each student a stipend while she attended.

I ran to Sam's office, where he was sitting at his desk, holding his cell phone in his fist. "I've got the money!" I said. But his phone rang, and he turned his back to me while he yelled at someone in Arabic. So I went into the living room, where Hama was looking at one of my salon magazines, and I danced her around the room.

There was a big notice taped across the main door to the beauty school, blocking my entry. I leaned forward to read it, but it was written in Dari. As I started to straighten up, I felt something at the back of my head and turned slowly to see the Women's Ministry chowkidor with his machine gun pointed right at me. He lowered the gun a little and licked his lips. He was only about nineteen, a sweet boy who had always been eager to try out his few words of English when I passed by. Now he couldn't remember any of them and stammered out a few sentences in Dari.

"He says that he is sorry, but he will have to shoot you if you go into the school," said one of my new students who spoke English. All the other students and teachers were standing together with doleful faces, as if they were waiting for a funeral. Baseera was peeking out of her burqa crying. Only Hama stayed by my side.

"Tell him I have to get my stuff out of there." I folded my arms and dug my high heels into the sod.

Then someone from the ministry shouted across the compound, and the student translated. "They say you may leave now."

"I'm not leaving until I get my stuff."

"They say that everything inside belongs to the ministry."

"These things were donated to the beauty school, and I am not going to leave them here!" I shouted across the compound. A crowd started to gather. Other ministry employees, people who were just walking down the sidewalk, the woman who usually sat on the street in the middle of traffic begging—everyone wanted to get a look at this American woman who was causing such a commotion. Then they all became silent as a door opened at the far end of the courtyard and the minister's assistant started to make her way toward me.

I was actually prepared for this showdown. The day after I had found out about my new funding, Roshanna and I had gone to the Women's Ministry to tell the minister's assistant the good news. I watched her face as Roshanna talked, expecting it to brighten up a little. Instead, she responded sharply and at length. Roshanna's smile trembled. "The minister is upset that it has taken you five months to begin the second class," Roshanna translated.

There was another flurry of sharp words from the assistant, then Roshanna nodded. "The minister doesn't understand why there has been a problem with money, since the beauty school received so much publicity."

Another flurry, and then Roshanna took a deep breath. "And the minister has received complaints that there was too much laughing inside the school. Also, people have complained that they have been able to look inside and see the women without their head scarves."

I had tried to breach this gulf over the next few weeks. I stopped in three times to tell the minister's assistant that we had some extra room in the class. I suggested that if the ministry had any girls in mind for the school, we'd be happy to put them right into the next class. I also offered to do hair for everyone in the ministry for free. Roshanna came with me the last time. I saw her eyes widen as she caught sight of a paper on the assistant's desk. When we got outside, she whispered, "They're going to evict you! The paper said they are going to take the building back and keep all of your products!"

I called and visited everyone I knew, looking for someone who had enough clout to plead our case successfully to the Women's Ministry. One of my customers was an Afghan-American woman who had both political and family power in Kabul. She went to work on her network of contacts. When she called me back, I was sure it was to tell me that she'd found the right string to pull. But her voice was full of regret. "You're lost," she said. "They're taking everything."

"We paid for that building, and we're supposed to have it for two years. They signed an agreement!"

She sighed. "Whatever you do now, do it very fast."

Of course, the first thing I did was to shriek like a madwoman. Everyone in the house went running for safety. I threw myself on my bed and cried to think of all that hard work, all those wonderful products the beauty companies had donated, all the trust that the students and people at home had put in me. I cried for about an hour, or maybe six—I lost track. Then I stopped crying and took the much more satisfying path of anger. My parents had raised me to be a strong woman—a fighter—and I was going to be strong about this. "Over my dead fucking body will they take this school," I told my pillow.

It was Friday, the beginning of the weekend in Afghanistan, and school was supposed to begin on Saturday. So Ali and I called about five taxicabs. Sam got back from a meeting as they pulled up in front of the guesthouse, and I explained my plan to him. "You're a crazy woman!" he exclaimed. "You can't fight the Women's Ministry. They'll have you arrested." But he was a fighter, just like me. In that way, we were well matched. I explained my plan. I told him to get a truck and meet me near the ministry with some workers. So he found a truck, then swung by one of the mosques and loaded it with guys who were squatting in front waiting for jobs. All of us pulled up along the street in front of the ministry, but back far enough so that the chowkidors couldn't see us.

My plan rested on the fact that there were two doors to the beauty school. One of them was inside the ministry compound, and that was the door we usually used after passing through the gates. But there was another, small door to the school, in the compound wall, about thirty feet away from the gates. We used this door if the gates were locked or if there were too many other things going on in the compound yard. I unlocked this little door, and all of us filed silently into the school. Ali unfolded sheets and blankets on the floors, and we started piling them with bottles of shampoo, conditioner, color, and other products, then carried them out to the taxis and truck. I laid out all my scarves on the floor and filled them with nail polish and makeup, and we carried these out, too. Then I pulled my mannequin heads off the shelves and gave two to each of the men from the mosque. They wrapped their arms around them wonderingly and tiptoed outside. I had also brought my suitcases and some boxes, and we filled these up with whatever was left. By the time we finished, the only things in the beauty school were the styling stations, a television for showing videos, and the mirrors.

Sam borrowed money from everyone he knew, then went off to look for a guesthouse to rent. We wanted something suitable not only for a new location for the school but also for his business offices and our living quarters. There was no way that the beauty school would fit into our current guesthouse, and besides, we were both tired of the other people who were staying there. We liked Ali well enough but didn't like the men he had been renting rooms to. It might seem crazy for us to have picked up and moved everything like that, but frankly, Afghans did it without breaking a sweat. They had fled conflict and hardship so many times that they were really good at relocating in a hurry. Our only problem was the constant problem: money. Kabul landlords typically demand six months of rent up front, and we weren't sure we could find something in our price range so soon. If we moved the beauty school away from the ministry, it would be more expensive to operate, too. In exchange for Beauty Without Borders' having spent some fifty thousand dollars to build the school inside the compound, the ministry paid for our electricity, water, heat, and security.

On Saturday morning, little Hama—I had decided to let her into the class—and I walked to the Women's Ministry arm in arm as if nothing were amiss. Baseera, Topekai, and my other students and teachers were already there waiting for me, crowded around the door with big smiles. If they noticed that the place had been cleaned out, they didn't mention it. And it didn't really matter that we didn't have any products to work with, because I wanted to have a first-day orientation anyway. I talked about the goals of the program. I talked about my expectations. I told them there were lots of women who wanted to get into this program, so I wouldn't tolerate stealing or unexcused tardiness or absenteeism. I told them that I would be giving each of them a kit with everything she needed for the whole three months, and that this kit could not leave the building. We had had problems in the first class with the girls losing or breaking things, and we just couldn't afford it. I got so wrapped up with my vision of how this second class was going to run that I almost forgot the crisis looming just outside the door.

Now the crisis was under way. The minister's assistant was standing right in front of me, frosty but polite. We did the formal greeting—three kisses on the cheeks—because you don't skip that in Afghanistan, even with your worst enemy. Then she started ranting and raving in Dari. The student who was translating couldn't keep up with her. All of us just stared as this woman went on and on, working herself into a lather and gesturing with such force that she almost toppled off her high heels. She was addressing the crowd as well as me. All of a sudden, everyone looked at me and gasped.

"What did she say?" I asked my horrified student.

"She says that you are not a good teacher, and that the ministry will open its own school here. She says you have been stealing from both the foreign beauty corporations and the Afghans. She says"—my student started to sob—"she says that she is going to drag you out of the compound by your hair and that you will be arrested and thrown out of the country."

The assistant swung around then and glared at me. "Why is it that I seem to care more about these women than you do, even though I'm an American and you're Afghan?" I said to her, tears streaming. She stepped forward as if she were going to slap me.

Suddenly, Sam was standing next to me. I felt as if the cavalry had just arrived! He held a hurried conversation with my students to find out what was going on, then coaxed me out to the street. I was hysterical, but he was calm. He lit a cigarette for each of us, then we went to see just about everyone in Kabul who could do anything about this, from government officials to Mary MacMakin. In the end, so many complaints were lodged against the Women's Ministry that they caved in. They eventually gave us back all our stuff, and I apologized for any cultural insensitivity on my part that might have contributed to the dispute.

Bottom line, the Women's Ministry wanted our building, our supplies, and control over the school. They kept the building, and I've never set foot in it again.

Sam had come to the ministry initially to tell me that he had found us a new location. It was a roomy stucco guesthouse called the Peacock Manor, with a small outbuilding near the street that would be perfect for the beauty school. It was going to take $22,000 to prepay six months' rent, but we put together our money with some from Noor and Ali and signed a contract for a year. We were pretty confident that we could eventually fill its rooms with paying guests and make good on the investment. Both Sam and I and Ali planned to take rooms there ourselves.

Before we moved in, Sam and I went to inspect the building we wanted to use for the school. I picked up an old shoe that was lying in the rubble on the floor and threw it into a little room at the back. A woman with big, startled eyes peered out from behind its door. She was broad-shouldered and sturdy, with the kind of wide, high-cheekboned face that reminded me of American Indians. She was very dirty, her face and arms smudged, her shapeless tunic torn and stained. I thought she was homeless, but Sam questioned her sharply and discovered that she came with the compound. Kind of like the sinks and the toilets.

"His name Shaz." Sam never got his gender pronouns right. "He make good cleaner for school and guesthouse."

"How much do I have to pay her?"

"Eighty dollar a month, probably." He walked off to try one of the light switches.

"Salaam aleichem," I said to Shaz. "My name is Debbie."

She just stared at me, then backed into the little room.

The next day Sam hired men from the mosque to knock out walls, put in a bathroom and plumbing for the sinks, build shelves, and help me paint. Shaz painted right along with me, and I was pleased by the energy and muscle she put into her work. But the walls were so cracked that regular paint only seemed to emphasize their flaws. I finally sent her to get a bucket of sand from a construction site across the street and dumped it in my paint. Then I mixed it around, painted a swath, and stopped to gauge the effect. I turned around to see what my helpers thought of this impromptu texturizing. The men were standing there with their mouths open and their brushes dripping midair. They seemed to think I had lost my mind, but Shaz smiled for the first time. She had several gold teeth, a startling contrast to her dirty face and drab clothes.

I nearly did lose my mind a few days later, when we were moving the salon furniture from the Women's Ministry into the school at the Peacock Manor. After getting one load of boxes inside, I heard an odd noise coming in the window and went back out to find a young cow tied to the fender of a nearby truck. It was nibbling around the edge of the front tire and mooing so loudly that I had to laugh. I didn't know why it was tied up in front of our guesthouse, but I had learned by now to expect this sort of thing in Afghanistan. I petted it for a minute, then went back inside to continue unpacking boxes. I kept hearing the cow mooing, and the sound soothed me. It was like something I'd have heard back in Michigan when I was a child and had about a million pets.

The next time I walked out to get a new box, I nearly slipped into what seemed like a street of blood. Someone had slaughtered the cow right outside the door. They were making steaks out of it just a few feet away. I didn't have the luxury of going to my room and hiding in the dark. I had to keep moving boxes the rest of the day, careful not to track blood inside or look at the little cow's head, now tilted lifelessly on top of the crumpled heap of its empty skin.

Chapter 6

I rampaged through the kitchen cupboards, then finally spotted a small tray of biscuits wrapped in a napkin. I whipped off the napkin and rushed into the living room. "Salaam aleichem," I said for the fourth or fifth time to the man who was pacing in front of the windows facing the street. He jerked around to glare at me, one end of his black turban quivering above his head, the other twisted in his hand. Then he brushed past me to stomp upstairs so that he could stare at the street from the window in his room. A few minutes later he stomped back down, went outside, and jerked the gate to the street open. He spoke to our chowkidor, who shrank back against the wall as if the black-turbaned man were breathing fire.

Then someone from the Ministry of Commerce called. "The business seminar ended late," the woman on the other end of the phone said. "Traffic is pretty bad, too, so Nahida won't be home for a while."

"What do I do about her husband?" I asked. "He's going nuts."

"Calm him down!" she said. "Get someone to explain it to him, or he'll beat her."

"He'd beat her right in front of me?"

"He's Taliban, you know—they're pretty strict with their wives."

"He's Taliban?" I felt my mouth go dry. I figured that if I didn't find a way to please this guy, I might wind up dragged behind a camel on a one-way trip to the desert. "Is there anything else you forgot to tell me about him?"

"Well, he's an opium addict, too. You want to stay away from him if he looks like he needs to go off and smoke."

When Sam and I took over the Peacock Manor Guesthouse, there were a lot of people coming in and out for parties but no paying guests. Our first real guests were a woman named Nahida and her husband, a bad-tempered, scar-faced man from the city of Herat.

Everything I knew about running a business was confined to beauty salons. I knew nothing about a business in which you were supposed to feed people and keep a clean house for them. Plus, I wanted this guesthouse to have the kinds of amenities that would make it appeal to journalists and other Westerners, so I knew it needed a lot of work. But I figured I could take my time getting it up to speed.

Then I got a phone call from an NGO based in Herat, which is far to the west of Kabul, near the border between Afghanistan and Iran. The NGO told me that a twenty-one-year-old girl named Nahida had come to them and begged them to help her become a student at the beauty school. She had heard about the school from a relative who lived in Kabul, and she was desperate to attend and then open her own salon in Herat. Her biggest obstacle was neither distance nor money; it was her husband. The NGO had scrambled to figure out a way to appease her husband and make it possible for Nahida to attend the school. They talked to her relatives in Kabul, who promised that Nahida and her husband and their child could live with them for free. The NGO also promised to send her to business management classes and help her open her salon in Herat. All this was starting to sound pretty good to her husband, who wasn't working at the time. But he was concerned about the moral atmosphere at the beauty school and the character of the people running it, so the NGO wanted me to let them stay at the Peacock Manor for a week to reassure the husband on both counts.

Talk about pressure! I had only about a week to make sure the guesthouse was running smoothly enough to accommodate guests and, especially, to assure the husband that I was showing the proper reverence for the ways Afghans did things. The guesthouse was missing a lot of things when we took over. It had beds but no pillows and blankets, pans but no glasses. Worst of all, it was missing a teapot and teacups. There's almost nothing more important to an Afghan than tea. Sam and I went out shopping for this stuff, but I had no idea what to buy. And I had no idea how to go about making tea once I got everything back to the guesthouse. I was used to boiling water and dumping in a tea bag, but I knew Afghans went through a much more elaborate process to make tea. They could all tell by the taste if it had been done right. I was really getting nervous about this week with Nahida and her husband, and the teamaking was the first big hurdle.

To make things worse, they arrived two days early. Sam and I hadn't even slept in the guesthouse yet ourselves, but we drove over to meet them. They were standing next to our chowkidor, one of the three workers who had been kidnapped. Along with the others, he had been found unharmed in a cave guarded by ten Taliban. He was so traumatized after three months of capture that he couldn't work in the well-drilling business anymore, so Sam had hired him as our guard. He was too traumatized to do that, too. Most of the time, he'd just sit at the kitchen table and cry. It appeared as if he had been crying again, because his eyes were all red and he hiccupped when he talked. Nahida's husband glowered at him, then turned to look at me as if he had already decided that I was an unfit instructor for his wife. But Nahida—a caramel-skinned girl with determined black eyes—grabbed my hands and kissed me. "Thank you for welcoming us," she said.

Sam went out to buy kebabs, rice, and nan for dinner. Nahida quickly picked the guest room with two twin beds, and she and her husband began to settle in. While they were upstairs, I tried to get the tea going. It took me a while to light the gas stove, since I had used only electric before. Then I stood there looking at the pot of water and the tin of tea, trying to figure out if I was supposed to throw the tea in the water before or after it boiled. I heard a little cough behind me, and it was Nahida, her head still tightly covered. "Let me help you!" she said, and then she took over. She did it sweetly, too, trying not to make me look like a total incompetent. Even though Sam hadn't married me for my tea-making abilities, I knew he might be ashamed if we served bad tea to the Talib. I was grateful to Nahida for her help, although as she moved around the kitchen with such practiced deliberation, I wondered at her middle-aged demeanor. It seemed as if something had completely stripped her youth from her. We didn't get a chance to talk much that first night, though. We ate and then sat in the living room watching a Bollywood movie. I turned up the volume so we couldn't hear the chowkidor weeping in the kitchen.

The next day Nahida had to attend a business seminar at the Ministry of Commerce. Sam had to go off to work, and her husband had to stay at the Peacock Manor with me while I was trying to fix up the space for the school. I tried to be polite when we were in the same room, but he turned away abruptly every time he saw me. I think he was alarmed that I had the gall to leave my head uncovered in my own house. As the day went on, he grew more and more agitated.

After the Ministry of Commerce called, I approached the husband cautiously and tried to explain the problem. He just scowled at my feeble Dari, so I phoned Sam and told him what was going on. "You talk to him," I begged, then handed the phone to the Talib. He held my phone to his ear for a few seconds, then snapped it shut and dropped it on the table. I thought he was going to hit me, but then Nahida ran in the door and began to speak to him breathlessly. He lunged for her before she was able to remove her shoes and dragged her up to their room. I phoned Sam again.

"You have to come back right now!" I shouted. "She's going to get the snot kicked out of her!"

"I'm coming, I'm coming!" Sam shouted back. "I am on our street."

I could hear the Talib yelling and Nahida screaming. It sounded as if he was breaking a chair against the wall. At that moment, Sam rushed inside and called the husband. Amazingly, he left off beating Nahida and came downstairs.

"Let's break his legs now," I whispered, but Sam ignored me. He was right: Nahida was probably the one who would suffer for it in the end. So I went upstairs and found her trembling on her bed. I pulled her into my room, and we spent the night talking.

Nahida told me that her bad luck had started when she was born into a family with four girls and only one boy. For families in a country where the girls can't get jobs, having a lot of daughters is considered a hardship. Her family never made her feel unwelcome, though. Her parents were loving if poor, and her childhood was a happy one. Then the Taliban came into power. Her family tried to keep their girls hidden, but a neighbor who wanted to curry favor whispered about their beautiful, unmarried daughters. So one day, this forty-five-year-old Talib policeman came and demanded that her parents give her to him. He wasn't even offering a dowry, and this is considered out-and-out theft in Afghanistan. His only offer was that he wouldn't kill Nahida's father if he agreed to let her marry. Nahida was only sixteen and hated the Talib, but she wanted to protect her father. She agreed to the marriage.

When the Talib brought her back to his house after the wedding, she was surprised to find out that he already had another wife, an older woman who was enraged that this young woman had to become part of her home. The first wife had borne the Talib five daughters, but he wanted Nahida because he hoped she could produce a son. Sons are much valued in Afghanistan, because when they marry they continue to live with the parents and help support them. So Nahida became a slave not only to the Talib but also to the first wife. She was an unruly slave, as she would rather take a beating than do things she didn't want to do. She refused sex with him for a while and was beaten for it every time.

"Here are the scars," she said, as if she were showing me trophies. She reached behind her to pull up her tunic, then bent over. Her back was scribbled with marks of all sizes, some merely flat and discolored, some that were barely healed. She pointed out the cigarette burns on her feet and stomach, the places no one could see.

Nahida had hoped that the Talib would tire of her rebellion and divorce her. Even though divorce was considered to be the most shameful thing that could happen to a woman, she thought it far preferable to this marriage. Then she got pregnant and had a son. To her way of thinking, this was the worst thing that could happen. Suddenly she was his favored wife, and she knew he'd never let her go. She was so miserable that she wanted to kill herself. She even poured some gasoline on her clothes one day. Self-immolation was sort of a trend among Herat's desperate housewives. But she saw her little boy staring at her and couldn't go through with it.

Then Nahida discovered that she was able to parlay

her new status to get a little more freedom. When the Taliban were driven out of power, she told her husband that she was going to get a job and that he couldn't stop her. She wandered around Herat listening for the sound of foreigners. When she heard a group of people speaking English, she followed them and convinced them to help her. She said she knew that no Afghan was going to be able to help her. She was smart and soon became both computer literate and an English speaker. She managed to save a little money by embroidering things at home and selling them to the foreigners. All she wanted now was to get away from her husband.

"I've been raped by him over and over, beaten by him and his first wife, and their children spit on me," she concluded, touching one of the scars on the bottom of her foot. "I am happy only when he's smoking his opium. I pray every night that he will die."

As that week went on, I was really afraid that Sam and I were failing the test. Nahida realized that I was hopeless in the kitchen, so she'd sneak in there and prepare a proper meal so I could carry it out and pretend I had made it. Regardless, the Talib husband was always angry about something. He quickly decided that he hated Sam, because he was a Pashtun and Sam was an Uzbek, and they had fought on opposite sides during the war. I tried everything I could think of to appease Nahida's husband, knowing that he wouldn't let her join my third class if he hated me. But nothing worked. He was always shouting at her or smoking his opium or pretending not to see me as he watched television.

Two nights before they left, I was in bed dreaming that I was falling down the stairs. I woke up because Sam was shaking me. When I opened my eyes, I saw that he was on the other side of the room looking for his gun, but I was still shaking. "Earthquake!" he said. "Get out now!" A pile of books on my nightstand slid to the floor, and the glass in the window broke with a loud pop. I screamed and clambered out of bed, more frightened than I'd ever been in my life. It was cold and dark, and the floor was shuddering under my feet. I could hear people outside shouting and crying, and I was sure the house was going to come crashing down on our heads any minute. I was already imagining us buried in the rubble with the weeping chowkidor trying to dig us out with a spoon. I rushed into the dark hallway and collided with someone, then slid down the steps and ran out the front door.

A group of us gathered in the front yard, waiting to see what would happen next. With a long, grinding moan and then a crash, a corner of the house next door collapsed. But as we waited and shivered and listened to the people shouting up and down the street, the shaking stopped. I managed to stop crying—I had been wailing, even though I had made it out safely— and gradually everyone started to laugh and talk, in the way that you do when you realize you're not going to die. Then we looked at one another, and I almost died of embarrassment. Nahida and her husband were both fully dressed, up to his turban and her head scarf. Sam and I were standing there in our underwear, with miles of naked goose-bumped flesh glowing in the moonlight. I squealed and tried to cover myself.

The Talib graciously turned his head the other way, and Sam went running off to look for the chowkidor. The poor man was usually afraid of everything, but he ran back in the house and came out with an armload of sheets to cover us. I guess the sight of me nearly naked scared him more than the earthquake did. We didn't want to go back in the house yet, and someone appeared with tea and biscuits. I don't even remember who it was. We sat on the grass together until five in the morning.

Somehow, this changed everything. The Talib decided to trust us. When Nahida went to her class the next day, her husband went to work with Sam and ran errands for him. When they left, the Talib told me that he had decided to let Nahida come back in three months and go to the beauty school. She was bright with happiness. She took a little amethyst ring from her hand and slid it up one of my fingers.

"So that you will think about me until I get back," she said as she kissed me good-bye.

Roshanna and I stood on the right side of the man-nequin head, and Topekai and the two other teachers stood on the left. Baseera, Hama, and the students sat demurely in green plastic lawn chairs in front of us. I made a circle with my fingers and settled it on the mannequin's hairline, just over her forehead. "We call this the 'front' of the head," I announced.

Roshanna translated this into Dari for Topekai and the teachers, and then they introduced the concept to the students in their own words. I continued moving the circle over the mannequin's head to highlight the different parts of the head: the top, crown, back, nape, and left and right sides. "You have to know the parts of the head before we can move on to perms and styling. Later on, when I tell you to 'part the hair from the crown to the nape on the right side,' you'll know what I'm talking about."

I waited as Roshanna translated this for the teachers. Finally, Topekai flashed me a bright smile, then began putting the lesson in her own words, touching the parts of the mannequin head with her long, graceful hands. The other teachers added their comments, too. As the students nodded, I whispered to Roshanna that my plan was working. As I taught the second class, I was also training my brightest students from the first class to be teachers. It was as cumbersome as a three-legged sack race, but it was working. I could see that the curriculum was really coming alive for the students and their skills were progressing rapidly. I figured that by the time we had our third or fourth class, Topekai and the other teachers might not need me and a translator at all.

All the students were paying close attention except Hama, who was looking at the cell phone in her pocket. "Leave your cell phone in your purse, please," I told her, reminding myself not to allow any more fifteen-year-olds into the beauty school. Topekai shot Hama a scornful look. I figured she was thinking the same thing.

I also made other changes during the second class. I wanted my teachers to take some responsibility beyond teaching. I figured they would better develop business skills if they learned how to be managers as well. This meant that they needed to arrive at the school early enough to make sure there was sufficient gas to run the generator when there wasn't any electricity. Since we rarely had more than four hours of city power each day, the generator was crucial. They also needed to make sure that enough water had been pumped up to the tank on the roof so we wouldn't run out in the middle of class. It seemed that the taps always went dry when the girls were practicing shampoos and then had no way of rinsing off. If it was a cold day, we also needed enough wood to keep the fire going. If we ran out of gas, water, or wood in the middle of the day, I wanted the teachers to take care of getting more by themselves.

It took them a while to settle these and other responsibilities on their own shoulders, partly because most of them didn't have much experience with making decisions. There were also cultural issues, which were hard for me to understand. It seemed to hurt their pride to have to think about mundane matters such as power and water or to make sure the floors around the stations and the product shelves were clean. They thought Shaz or some other lower-caste person should handle this. Besides, to get more gas, water, or wood, they had to go outside and talk to the chowkidor. They were embarrassed—even bright, self-assured Topekai was embarrassed—to have to talk to men outside their family. It took them a long time to decide who should be the one to go talk to him, then the person selected always had to have someone go with her. It was hard for me to be patient with them because my personality is so different. I hardly ever deliberate before taking action. I just *do,* occasionally with disastrous results.

One day I decided just to ignore the teachers when I knew the electricity was down. I sat in my room, drank my tea, even put on my headlamp and read a book. Topekai finally knocked on my door.

"*Bakh niest,* Debbie," she said apologetically. "Cannot practice cut hair."

"There hasn't been any bakh for three hours," I said. "Take care of it!"

She sighed, then pulled on her scarf and went outside to talk to the chowkidor.

By the time the third class came around that summer, the teachers had learned to keep the place running with enough gas, water, and wood. I decided they could take on even more responsibility, so I presented them with a chunk of money at the beginning of the term. They would be in charge of buying whatever the school needed, like hand soap or new towels. All I wanted them to do was keep track of the receipts.

Their skills as managers continued to grow. When the fourth class began in the fall, I told them not to call me unless the building was burning down. I told them that they could handle everything else, and they did.

I also began changing the curriculum during the second class so that the graduates could better meet the needs of their Afghan clients. When we'd designed the original beauty school curriculum for the first class in 2002, we had two weeks set aside to teach proper makeup application. It didn't take me long to see that Western ideas about makeup didn't make any sense in Afghanistan. By Afghan standards, American women wore so little makeup that we looked pretty much like men—and homely men at that. When I'd have an American customer leave the salon with a pre-party manicure, I'd hear my students muttering if she hadn't let them fix her up with elaborate hair and makeup. Without those enhancements, they thought she looked little better than one of the village women who tend chickens.

So in the second class, I focused on helping them apply Afghan-style makeup better. Sure, all the brides would still want to look like drag queens, but I figured that they could at least be more attractive and unique drag queens. I showed the second class how to use makeup to enhance each bride's best features. How to contour a chubby face and enhance the cheekbones, or how to make a big nose look smaller. How to lighten someone's skin without making it look as if she had fallen into a bucket of flour. How to coordinate makeup with the color of a dress. I used Baseera as my model one day, showing how a more customized approach made her green eyes look like jade, her coppery hair look like fire, and her lips look tender and sweet instead of garish.

I also wanted my students to feel free to experiment and explore their own ideas about beauty, but that was really a stretch for them. They thought they had to give each bride the exact same hairstyle and makeup. I thought they could distinguish themselves as beauticians—and make more money—if they deviated from the formula. So I spent a day talking about creativity. I went online, printed out copies of paintings by famous artists, and showed how they had hugely different approaches to a portrait or a still life. I made the students watch videos of fashion shows, in which the women wore blouses trimmed with moon rocks and shoes made out of toilet plungers. Okay, maybe not that but other crazy stuff. I told them creativity was about going wild in their minds. I told them that they could always rein their imaginations in once they had let them gallop around the stars.

"You're not just beauticians," I told them. "You're artists!" Then I gave each of them a "creativity" mannequin head. I told them I wanted them to fix up their mannequins with really creative—and not necessarily beautiful—makeup and hair. "I'm going to bring in a panel of judges to determine who made the most creative head," I said. "That girl will get a special prize at graduation." Roshanna translated this. The class dissolved into excited chatter before Topekai and the teachers had a chance to say anything more.

As we walked toward the market, I noticed that there were even more men staring at me than usual. Maybe I wasn't dressed modestly enough, or maybe I was swinging my arms and looking around too much and didn't appear sufficiently humble. It seemed that ragged men in turbans were lining up to scowl. Then I heard someone yelling from the archway of a building, *"Fesha! Mordagaw!"*

I didn't know what those words meant, but Sam spun around as if someone had fired a dart at him. He caught sight of the men who were doing the yelling and flung himself through the crowd. One of them disappeared, but Sam grabbed the other and slammed him against the building. He punched him, and blood smeared across the wall. I stood in the middle of the crowd screaming at him to stop. When he finally let up, some men stepped forward to lead the beaten man away. Sam strode back to me, and the crowd parted to let him pass.

"We leave now," he said, smoothing his hair back into place. He acted as if this brawl had been a minor annoyance.

"You almost knocked that guy's head off!"

"This my job." Sam scowled at the bruises welling up on his punching hand. "He call you a prostitute and me your pimp."

Now it seemed as if everyone we passed was trying

hard not to look at us. I watched Sam's back as he strode toward the car and recalled the stories he had told me about his days and nights fighting the Russians. He had killed men, although the first time had upset him so much that he'd hung around the camp and asked if he could cook instead. It was months before he could venture out again. In our life together, I had never seen any evidence of violence in him. He was hospitable to strangers, kind to the poor and weak, and gentle with me. He loved the sappy Bollywood movies, in which the stars danced around on mountaintops and sang love songs to each other. He liked the Rambo movies, too—Sylvester Stallone has a passionate following in Afghanistan—and was fond of his machine gun, but I didn't know many Afghans who didn't have guns. One of my customers at the Peacock Manor salon was the educated, elegant wife of an Afghan diplomat and politician. I knew she carried a pistol in her purse; I knew this because she shrieked one day when a student moved her purse from one station to another. "Watch out!" this woman said. "There's a gun in there." So I had never worried about Sam's life as a warrior before, but now I was a bit alarmed. Even his appearance among all these men with turbans and sandals made him seem alarming: in his black Western suit and sunglasses, he looked like a bad guy in a movie.

He turned and regarded me impassively. "I can't be at bazaar with you. Too many trouble, and maybe I have to kill someone."

So much for shopping with the mujahideen. So much for any romantic notions I had that Sam and I would explore the city together. I was terribly busy running the second class and the guesthouse, but in the moments between the busyness, I was lonely and pined for a companion. I was also eager to get out and see more of the city. I had really wanted to go to the *mandai*—the huge outdoor market near the Kabul River that goes on for blocks and blocks—because it sounded like fun. I also needed supplies, and we were passing vendors who were selling things I needed. "Can't we stop and pick up just a few things?"

"It is not possible."

"So I can't ever go to the mandai?"

"I give you my car. Maybe you take Roshanna."

Sam made good on his promise to turn his car over to me. I was a little nervous about driving it by myself, so my first time on the road was with a bunch of visiting foreigners. We followed a van all over the city because I had no idea how to get around. The van bounced through crowded streets, and we all screamed as I just barely navigated us around the wagons and donkeys and pedestrians. I attracted plenty of attention as a woman driver, too—there were women in other cars, but they almost never drove or even sat in the front seat. Men were falling off their bicycles! They were screaming at me, "I love you, mister!" The first time I heard someone say that, I thought that, despite the eyeliner and earrings and head scarf, someone thought I was a man. Then someone told me that Dari doesn't have words that make gender distinctions; *he, she,* and *it* are all the same word. That explained Sam's pronoun confusion! I quickly got used to people addressing me as "mister" or referring to me as "him."

Even though driving in Kabul was as scary as anything I'd ever done—like being on a roller coaster that shot off its track—I got a little bit better at it. I started to feel pretty cool about being one of the few women behind a wheel. The policeman who directed traffic at the rotary got used to seeing me and would hold up his hand to stop all the other cars as I passed through. Once he walked up to my car window and waved at me to stop. Then he asked if I wanted to share some of the tea he had in a thermos over on the sidewalk. I had to laugh. The traffic was backed up for a mile and getting worse by the second because of me, but this police officer was ready to pour me some tea. That's one of the things I love about Afghans. There's always time for tea.

The novelty of driving wore off pretty quickly, though. You couldn't relax for a minute, and besides, I always liked to drive with a cup of coffee and a cigarette. My cell phone often rang, too, and I'd have to grab it. A call usually meant that there was chaos at the school or the guesthouse, or that a customer had managed to make her way through the city and was waiting, desperate for me to touch up her roots before she left on vacation. One day I was managing the cell phone, coffee, and cigarette, and I just missed running into the back of a water buffalo. I decided to give up driving in Kabul.

So I asked Sam to line up a driver for me whenever I wanted to go out. I was dying to go back to the mandai, but I didn't want to go by myself. All sorts of people had told me it wasn't completely safe for me to go alone, and I didn't know enough Dari to bargain with the vendors. I wanted Afghan prices, not the high prices that I'd get as a foreigner. If Ali had been in town, I would have asked him to take me, but he was traveling. Little Hama would have been happy to come, but she hardly spoke any English and couldn't help me bargain. Finally, I convinced Roshanna— who, when she wasn't helping me teach, was trying to start her own salon—to come with me. I wore my longest, darkest skirt and dark shoes and even a burqa, hoping that no one would spot me as a foreigner.

The driver parked near the river. This is an area, by the way, where the mujahideen factions had battled it out so fiercely that the buildings on either side of the Kabul were riddled with holes. I didn't know how some of them were still standing. Roshanna and I set off arm in arm. The driver followed about twenty feet behind, making sure we were safe. We crossed a narrow bridge over the stinking river, where a few people crouched to wash their clothes. Once we reached the other side, the mandai began.

People were selling stuff from tables, from blankets spread on the ground, from wagons and wheelbar-rows, from stalls and stores. Even from their own bodies—there was one guy who had key chains hanging all over his sweater. I think some of these vendors must have been there illegally because a police officer walked around with a stick, swatting at little boys selling a few ashtrays on a towel and a man with a half-dozen lacy bras hanging from his arm. These people would dart away through the crowd, then set up somewhere else. I wanted to stop and look at everything, but Roshanna kept urging me on. "Better to move quickly," she said.

But it was impossible for me to move quickly. There were so many people that it seemed as if a huge parade had just broken up. There was so much stuff that it seemed as if an enormous warehouse had exploded and rained products. Since the burqa didn't offer much in the way of peripheral vision, I had to keep stopping so that I could turn around to see everything. Different kinds of goods were roughly grouped together. Roshanna pulled me into a side street and showed me a courtyard surrounded by three stories of shops that sold fake flowers—giant roses, long garlands of poppies, even plastic Christmas trees. We passed a row of stores that sold treadle sewing machines, all with beautiful gilded designs on the sides. We passed a row of stores that sold nothing but knives and scissors, and then a row of stores that sold nothing but baby cleanup products. Of course, there was a huge area that sold nothing but scarves.

As we were walking past a stand that had long strings of dried dates hanging from a wooden frame, I felt something poke me in the butt. I didn't think anything of it. I figured the mandai was so crowded that someone had just bumped into me by mistake. I sped up a little, but then I felt it again—this time, more like someone helping himself to a handful. "I think someone just grabbed my ass," I whispered to Roshanna. She tugged me ahead.

But then I felt it again. Definitely, someone was groping me. I turned to look behind me and saw this big, ugly man who was nearly walking on my heels. I glared at him through my little burqa window and figured that he would take this as a warning not to do it again. But as soon as I turned back around, he reached out and grabbed me again. Then I whirled around, flipped up my burqa, and punched him full in the face.

Roshanna's eyes nearly rolled back in her head. The vendors in the shops around us ran into the street in a panic. I was screaming at the top of my lungs in my best bad Dari that this guy was grabbing my ass and I wasn't going to stand for it. The guy had fallen to the ground, and everyone was crowding around trying to figure out what the problem was. I could hear Roshanna telling them in Dari that the man had been pulling my sleeve.

"He wasn't pulling my sleeve!" I said. "He was grabbing my ass, Roshanna." But it was too shameful for her to say this, so she just kept telling everyone that he was pulling my sleeve. Then she dragged me away.

"This happens often in the mandai," she told me. "Please calm down and we will go home soon."

"I thought they were forbidden to touch women who aren't their wives."

"Yes, but they do."

"You don't do anything when it happens?"

She shook her head. "Too embarrassed."

We walked for a few more minutes in silence. I was too angry now to take an interest in the carnival of goods around me. I was outraged that Roshanna and all these other women had to put up with men grabbing them in the mandai. I remembered all those women in prison who had dared to challenge the sexual order by having a boyfriend or running away from a bad husband. Why was it that the men in the market could break the rules so easily? I remembered the scars on Nahida's back and felt a new surge of rage on her behalf.

Roshanna and I stopped to buy toilet paper, and I felt a hand on my ass again. I turned around and saw that the same ugly guy had followed us there. I also saw a police officer at the edge of the crowd, so I grabbed the guy by the shirt and started to haul him over to the cop—again shouting in my bad Dari that he had grabbed my ass. The officer listened for a few seconds, then took out his stick and began to beat the guy. I watched with satisfaction, as if this one little bit of payback helped balance the scales between the men and the women. But Roshanna laid hold of my arm and marched me back toward the car.

"I'm sorry, Debbie, but I will never come to the mandai with you again," she said. No matter how often I asked her to come with me, she refused—sweetly, graciously, but emphatically refused.

Shaz—my gold-toothed housekeeper—and I were kneeling in the bathroom near the *bokari,* a wood-burning stove that kind of looks like a fancy metal garbage can. This one heated both the bathroom and the water, and I had filled the upstairs of the guesthouse with smoke trying to set myself up with a hot bath. Shaz cracked the window to let the smoke out, then she opened the little door in front of the bokari, stuffed more newspaper around the wood, and squirted some gasoline inside. I retreated to the far wall while she tossed in a lit match, then came closer as I saw the fire blaze. Smoke started to leak out again through a curve in the metal pipe that vented the bokari outside, but Shaz had a solution to that, too. She ran out of the bathroom, then came back with strips of damp cloth. She wrapped the curve of the hot pipe with the cloth, where it sizzled and then adhered over the fissures in the metal. In a few minutes, the smoke had cleared. I could take a bath without coughing to death.

This was the kind of heroic effort that kept me from giving up on Shaz. Not that she didn't work hard. She worked like an industrial machine when it came to scrubbing the floors but, still, a faulty machine—she'd scrub some parts of the floor nearly down to the foundation and miss others entirely. She'd rush through the guesthouse and leave a trail of broken cups or sometimes lamps in her wake. She was supposed to iron our clothes, but she often just seemed to forget to do it. Maybe she didn't even understand why people did such things, since she herself was so unkempt. Sam would reach into his closet and pull out one rumpled shirt after another, then ask me why we couldn't find a better cleaner. And Shaz was always, always supposed to clean up the bathrooms in the school and salon every morning. No matter how many times I told her this, I'd still see customers coming out of the bathroom with politely displeased looks on their faces.

I decided one of the problems might be that Shaz just had too much work. When we'd first moved into the Peacock Manor, her biggest job was to keep the guesthouse clean. But as the beauty school got going, the amount of work escalated. I didn't see how she could get it all done, so I told Sam to let her know that we'd try to find her an assistant. The next day Shaz showed up with an older woman who looked so much like her that I told Sam to ask if the older woman was a sister or cousin.

After a brief discussion, he turned back to me. "This his mother."

I was shocked. The other woman looked only a few years older than Shaz. "How old is she?" I gestured to Shaz.

"Twenty-five," he said.

Here I had assumed Shaz was at least fifty—older than I! "I want to know more!" I told Sam as I saw him move toward the door. "I want the whole story."

"You need ask Roshanna," he said. "Shaz not tell man all the sexy details you want to know."

So I had to wait until Roshanna stopped by the Peacock Manor later on that afternoon. Then I pulled the two of them into my room.

Shaz and her mother were Hazaras. The Taliban, who were largely Pashtun, had special contempt for Hazaras, dismissing them as ignorant folk—not much better than donkeys, meant only for the most menial jobs. While Shaz's family had stuck it out in Kabul during most of the war, they fled to the mountains when the Taliban arrived because it was rumored that the new rulers planned to massacre all the Hazaras. Shaz and her family lived in a mountain cave for a year, foraging and even stealing from farms so that they had enough to eat.

As Shaz related this part of the story, I was surprised to see her smile. It turned out that she was married to a good man then, someone she loved deeply. Her memories of those years were happy ones despite the hardships. Then her husband stumbled across a group of Taliban one day, and they killed him. When she and her family heard that the Taliban were gone, they ventured down from the mountain and found relatives who helped them for a little while. Shaz's family soon decided to marry her off to a man whose first wife had not yet borne him a son. But Shaz was never able to conceive with this man, and he divorced her. Then her family married her off to a third man, who was living in the city of Kunduz, north of Kabul, with another wife. He didn't want her to move into his house with the other wife, so she continued to live with her mother. Still, he hoped Shaz would bear him a son, and he made infrequent visits to Kabul for sex. He also tried to get her to give him money. She solved this problem by going to Gold Street and turning her savings into rings and bracelets that he overlooked. Shaz had not yet been able to conceive a child with this man, either. She dabbed at her eyes with her dirty hands as she told Roshanna that she was afraid he, too, would divorce her.

So I resolved to keep Shaz on, no matter what. After all, I was running a program that was supposed to be helping women, and I didn't want to help just the beauticians. I wanted to help poor, less-skilled women like Shaz, too, if I could.

But it seemed that her work never improved. She continued to break things. Or sometimes, things just disappeared and I was never sure if she had thrown them away because she had broken them or if someone had stolen them. I had a hard time believing that Shaz would steal from me, because she often brought me valuables I had left lying around in the wrong place. But finally, a gold ring disappeared from my bedside table and I demanded to know what had happened to it. Shaz, her mother, our chowkidor, our cook—the whole household was caught up in an uproar of accusations and counteraccusations. Finally, Sam suggested that we all go see a psychic mullah he'd heard about. The idea was that everyone who was a suspect would stand in front of the mullah and declare his or her innocence, and then he would be able to decide who was telling the truth. I was looking forward to checking out the psychic mullah, but Shaz's mother announced that she had found the ring on the floor of the beauty salon. So I never really figured out what had happened.

Then another problem developed with Shaz. One of the students came running into the salon crying with her hands folded up over her chest. I grabbed her, made her lie down, and screamed, "I think she's having a heart attack." Topekai and Baseera gathered around to talk to the girl, and she told them that Shaz had grabbed her breasts. "No," I protested. "I don't think Shaz would do something like that. Or if she did, she was just playing." But two of the other students came forward to tell me that Shaz had done the same thing to them, grabbing not only their breasts but their crotches, too. One of them lifted up her tunic so that I could see the side of one breast. There were dark bruises on it.

I called Roshanna and begged her to come over. When she arrived the next day, I sat Shaz down and told her what the students said. "This is sexual harassment," I told her. "If you were a man, they could put you in jail for this."

Roshanna translated, but Shaz shook her head as if utterly confused. "She says she does not do these things," Roshanna said. "She says the other girls tell lies about her."

I didn't know what to think. For the next few weeks, I kept asking the students if it had happened again. Several times they said yes, Shaz had grabbed them. I didn't want to believe this because it reminded me of the ugly man who'd groped me in the mandai. I thought that Shaz might be so starved for sex or affection that grabbing the other girls seemed like the only way to get it. I was trying to rationalize her behavior because I still wanted to help her. But then one day I saw Shaz come up behind one of the students while she was putting on her shoes and grab her breasts. The student clutched herself and began to cry. I flew across the room and pushed Shaz against the wall. "That's it," I said. "You're fired."

It made me miserable to fire her. It made all the teachers and even the students miserable, too. Shaz was now part of the family; she was like the bad kid whom everyone still loves. All of us moped around for a week. One of my customers who's a psychologist asked what was wrong, and I explained the situation. "Someone probably has done the same thing to her all her life," the woman said. And then Shaz came back. She hung around the front of the compound all day and looked inside mournfully every time the chowkidor opened the gate. I finally walked outside and pulled her back in. I put my arms around her, and we both cried. "Just don't ever do it again," I told her.

Somehow, being fired seemed to change her. She started remembering to clean the bathroom. She stopped breaking so many things. Her clothes and her hair were cleaner. I was relieved because I had come to love Shaz and I wanted this visual evidence that her life could improve, just as the beauticians' lives were improving.

Then one day Sam bumped into Shaz's mother as she was headed for the gate, and she dropped something on the ground. It was one of the flashlights we kept near our bed so that we could find our way to the bathroom in the middle of the night. He fired her on the spot, and none of Shaz's pleading could make him change his mind.

"If she steal small thing, one day will steal big," Sam said.

Nahida, her Talib husband, and their son returned to Kabul just before my third class began. They lived with her relatives while she absorbed everything my instructors and I could teach her. I knew Nahida was going to be one of my best students ever. I wished that she were staying with us at the Peacock Manor so that I could see more of her away from the school, but Sam and I would often invite her and her husband over for dinner. Nahida would rattle off business plans. She had so many great ideas! Her husband sat there like a big, dumb rock.

When Nahida left, we kept in touch by phone and e-mail. The salon she opened was hugely successful within months. She printed up business cards and handed them out at weddings. She distributed flyers that offered two cuts for the price of one when a customer brought a friend. She started to make a lot of money, and her husband liked this. But it didn't make him a better husband. He still beat her because she refused to have sex with him—she didn't want any more children, and he wouldn't use birth control. He beat her for a lot of things, and when he couldn't think of a reason, he beat her for being smart and young and pretty. And especially for being a woman.

When my friends back in Michigan asked what they could do for Afghanistan, I'd have a huge list of things they could do or send. And I'd always ask them to pray for Nahida, that she'd survive this marriage.

She was hiding some of her money, so her husband didn't really know how successful she was. She worked so hard and was beaten so often that even the first wife started to feel sorry for her. Then Nahida began bringing presents to the first wife—sweets for her children, perfume, a new dress if they were going to a wedding, even a new television. Over time, the two wives became like sisters. Then the first wife became pregnant and had a boy. Nahida was sure this was her ticket out of the marriage. This was what she wanted more than anything in the world. She begged the first wife to convince the husband to divorce her.

"Tell him that I am bad, tell him that I shame him by working outside the home, tell him to divorce me because I only cause trouble for him," Nahida implored her.

"I will try," the first wife promised.

The first wife began to whisper these things in the

Talib's ear. She pointed out Nahida's many failings as a wife and how people in their neighborhood laughed at him because he couldn't control her. She told him that she herself couldn't bear to live in the same house with this disrespectful upstart. The Talib took heed of what his first wife was saying. He beat Nahida even more to try to force her to become a fitting wife.

But finally, to keep peace with the first wife, he agreed to divorce Nahida. He even agreed to let Nahida take their son—"the spawn of that evil woman," according to the first wife's whispers—even though fathers almost always get to keep the children in a divorce. Nahida moved back into her parents' house, and they were overjoyed by her return. Now she has her own salon, with several employees. She exports handicrafts from the provinces, works as a translator, and speaks at women's conferences. She tells me she doesn't care if she ever marries again, and what's more, she doesn't have to.

Chapter 7

In late spring, I suddenly lost half my funding from the German NGO that had pledged to pay for the second and third classes. The NGO was sponsored by the German government, and its own funding had been cut, so the bad news rolled downhill to me. I had already accepted twenty-five girls for the next class but now had funding for only twelve and a half of them. I'm not a fund-raiser. I'm clueless about how to write up grant proposals and do all the stuff that gets projects funded. So I fell back on the only way I know how to make money. I decided that I would build up the salon business and ask Topekai and a few bright students like Baseera to put in more hours after school with our paying customers. I figured I could bankroll the next class with the salon profits, since there are precious few luxuries for Westerners living in Kabul, and they were eager for some pampering.

I put together flyers about the salon and left them in places that foreigners frequent, like the Western restaurants and the store where they buy alcohol. I also asked the customers who came in to take flyers with them and spread the word in their compounds. Lots of new people started calling to make appointments. Now I had the challenge of telling them how to get to the Peacock Manor in the absence of street signs and addresses. So my directions went something like this:

Go to the Internet café near the rotary in Shar-e-Now, the one near the emergency hospital with the red and white paint on the wall. Take a right, and you'll then be on the main street in Shar-e-Now. Before you get to the bombed-out movie theater you'll see a bright yellow building. Turn right there, then drive past the street with all the dead cows. Continue past the old warlord house, then go left at the next street. You will see a blue-and-white-striped box and a sign that says ASSA in black letters. Just ahead, there's a gray building with a lot of Afghan men hanging out in front, a tailor shop, a compound with a blue gate, and a hand-pump well on the corner. My guesthouse is the one with the blue gate. If you tell me when you're coming, I'll be the foreign woman with a yellow scarf standing on the well and talking on her cell phone. There will probably be a small crowd gathered around me.

Lots more people started to come to the salon, meaning that Topekai, Baseera, and Bahar—another bright student from the second class—were exposed to a wide range of foreigners. At first, it seemed that every Westerner who came to the salon did something to shock them.

One young woman came in and wanted a bikini wax. "She is bride?" Topekai asked me, erroneously assuming that Americans also went in for prenuptial hairlessness.

I shook my head. "She's going off for a week in Cyprus with her boyfriend."

Another woman came in the door and made a big show of unwrapping her head scarf and struggling out of her long coat. Then she pulled her shirt tightly over her belly, so that we could all see a tiny bulge. "I'm pregnant!" she shrieked joyfully.

Bahar beamed. "You husband, he is happy?" she asked.

"Oh, I'm not married," the woman replied. "I'm going it alone."

Another woman came in and introduced herself as someone on the diplomatic staff at one of the embassies. When she took off her coat, all the Afghan beauticians glanced at one another and then ducked their heads to keep from laughing. The woman was wearing a blouse that revealed her chubby midriff and a hideous miniskirt that just barely managed to stretch over her very ample bottom. Even I was shocked! As I cut this woman's hair, I could hear my girls laughing in one of the back rooms. When she left, I poked my head in the room to see what all the hilarity was about. There was Baseera with her skirt pulled up around her thighs and a pile of towels stuffed in her underwear, strutting back and forth. "I am diplomat!" she said as she sashayed around the room. "I am *big* diplomat!"

Little by little, though, my beauticians became accustomed to the foreigners' odd ways and learned to maintain straight faces and a professional demeanor. I knew this was a good thing, because if they learned to cater to the foreign crowd, they'd really be able to make good money.

However, I occasionally found myself in the awkward position of having to turn customers away because I was the only beautician they trusted to do their cuts and color, and I didn't have enough time to take care of all of them. In the States, girls go to beauty school for an entire year. Then they often work at a quick-cut place for several years before they get a job at a nice salon. They work for a few months there as shampoo girls or assistants to the experienced stylists before they have their own customers. My Afghan beauticians got only twelve weeks of beauty school and a few hours apprenticing in the salon, meaning that they weren't yet prepared to give Western customers the quality they expected. But I knew they could do a good job if they got more practice because they were highly motivated. So I really focused on making them more marketable. If a customer came in wanting a cut and highlights, I'd tell her that I'd do the cut but that I would have Bahar do the foiling—that she did it better than I did, which was true. I also decided to add more services. I had discovered an ob-gyn table way in the back of the shipping container, where I was still making weekly visits to get more supplies. I had no idea why the table was there but realized I could use it for massages, facials, and even pedicures. A Canadian massage therapist had been training Topekai and Baseera, so this was perfect. I started telling customers that we were doing massages and pedicures. The pampering side of the salon—especially the pedicures—really began to boom. In one two-week period, we worked on feet that hailed from Bosnia, Australia, London, the United States, Germany, France, Switzerland, Russia, and the Philippines.

We also started to dabble in the Afghan bride business. This was a surprising development, as I had never anticipated doing bridal makeup. That was what I was training my students to do, and the drag-queen look just wasn't my specialty anyway. But it turned out that there were a number of Afghan women who had been living in the West for years, returned to the country, and gotten engaged here. Their parents wanted them to go through the traditional Afghan engagement and wedding routine, but these girls were gagging at the idea of extreme makeup and mile-high hair. The first Westernized Afghan woman who found herself in this fix pleaded with me to do her wedding. I agreed, but I set the price high, charging $300 for her makeup and $10 for each member of her bridal party. The going rate for an Afghan bride was about $100 to $160, but I wanted to set my prices so that there would be no danger of my salon competing with those of my students. This first bride came in with all her relatives and friends, and I worked on her makeup for about five hours. I could have done it in two, but it seems that the traditional approach is to stretch it out over five hours and make it an event. At her wedding the bride told everyone that I had done her makeup, so I started to get a lot of calls from other brides in the same predicament.

Even with this extra business, I still wasn't making enough to pay all the expenses for the school. I had been getting lots of calls from men who wanted to come in but had turned them all down because men simply were not allowed inside beauty salons in Afghanistan. But I ran into so many foreign men who begged me for haircuts and even manicures that I started to feel sorry for them. Afghanistan can be really intense for foreigners who are here a long time.

They're locked up in their embassy or NGO compounds all the time, and when they leave their walls to do some outside work, they never know if their vehicle is the one that will attract a bomb. Whenever I'm out in my car and see one of the four-wheel drives belonging to a big NGO or a tank from one of the peacekeeping forces, I tell my driver to drop back a few hundred feet just in case they're targeted. So I felt sorry for these men who needed a little luxury in their lives. I also knew they could provide a good income stream. I started working on them in the late afternoons and evenings, after both the school and the regular salon were closed and all my girls had gone home.

But just as all these efforts to expand the salon business began to work, Kabul's security situation became really bad. It was election season again, only this time the stakes were even higher. Afghan men and women would be voting by secret ballot for a new president in October. There were nearly twenty candidates running, and there was a lot of strife among the different factions putting up candidates. There was also an undercurrent of suspicion in some areas that the United States was going to rig the election to create a victory for its favorite candidate, the current president, Hamid Karzai. And of course, the Taliban was opposed to the elections no matter who won. There had been an increase in kidnappings and bombings and overall violence, and the American Embassy was telling Americans to keep a low profile.

The United Nations had an alert system that applied to its own employees, but most of the NGOs and embassies in town followed their lead. Green City meant you could go just about anywhere, White City meant you could go only to a few highly secure sites outside the compound, and Red City basically meant you should figure out how to evacuate. The United Nations was on White City most of the time in those months. Even though the Peacock Manor didn't have White City security features—no concertina barbed wire on top of the compound walls, no bomb-filmed windows, no rocket barricade on top of the building— some of the foreigners still managed to sneak out to my salon.

I ignored the alerts myself. It didn't seem to me that so much fear was warranted as long as you were cautious and respected the culture. My strongest reaction to the White City alerts was annoyance, because they were bad for business. But many of my customers couldn't manage to maneuver around the White City restrictions. They called to cancel their appointments and wail that they were stuck inside their compounds. After I got a number of these calls, I had a bright idea.

"How about if we come to you?" I asked. "If you can line us up a bunch of customers, I'll take Sam's car and fill the trunk with products. Then the girls and I can do hair in your compound for an afternoon."

Before long we were making regular forays to the different NGO compounds around town. Our customers were so grateful—and so happy for the diversion—that they were giving great tips. After one of these trips, the girls were bouncing in their seats because they had made so much money in tips—and that was on top of what I would be paying them for the work they had done. I asked Baseera how much she had gotten in tips.

"Fifty dollars!" Her green eyes glowed. "My husband not make so many in two weeks!"

Sam kept looking at me while I was trying to read a book. We were in our room and the television was on, but he wasn't following the Bollywood drama. He was staring at me whenever he had the chance, even though he'd deny it when I'd catch him at it.

"What is it?" I said for about the fifth time. "Why are you looking at me?"

He sighed and tapped his pen against his mug of tea, as if it were an egg that he was trying to crack. "I need send money home," he finally said.

"Why?"

"He needs go to doctor."

"Your father?"

"No, *she*. She needs go to doctor."

"Which she? Your mother, your sister, your daughter—"

"My wife."

"Is she sick?" If I had to think of her, it was easier to think of her wasting away of a fatal illness and fading entirely from the periphery of my life.

He shook his head, then sighed again. "She is pregnant."

I felt as if I had been dropped from an airplane.

I had been working so hard that spring—school in the mornings, salon customers in the afternoons—that I wobbled across the compound back to our room every evening, hoping my dear husband would dote on me a little. I learned quickly, though, that I pretty much had to pin him in a corner and put a choke hold on him to get any affection. And that, of course, wasn't what I had in mind. To be fair to Sam, he was still having a terrible time with his business. But once the business began to improve, his behavior didn't change that much. There were cultural differences between us that were as tricky to cross as the Hindu Kush mountains. And neither of us had any idea how to do it.

We fought a lot. In fact, one of Sam's first new English words in those days was *dinosaur,* his pet name for me because he said I fought like one. Acts of affection—or rather, lack of—triggered one argument after another. For instance, we had many nights of yelling and tears because I'd come into our room and kiss him, and he'd pull away with a look of distress on his face. We finally got Roshanna to translate the problem. It turned out that I was kissing him after he'd performed his ritual cleansing for nightly prayer. He'd have to heat up some water and do it all over again.

But even when I'd remember to touch him before he cleaned up for prayer, he was pretty unresponsive. He didn't understand why I wanted to hold hands or hug or kiss or touch. He hadn't ever done any of that with his Afghan wife, and his father never did any of that with his mother. I don't think Sam had ever seen an Afghan man behave like that with a woman. Afghan men walk around the streets of Kabul holding hands with each other. They often stand talking with their arms around each other or caressing each other's arms, but you never see a man doing any of these things with a woman. Once when Sam and I were going somewhere in the car, I reached over and started to rub his arm. He reddened and pulled away. "Is not time for sex, Debbie!" he hissed.

"I don't want to have sex right now," I said, although who knows—maybe I would have if he hadn't looked as if he wanted to jump out of the car. "I just want to snuggle."

"What is this 'snuggle'?" he asked, exasperated. He really didn't get it.

And like most women, I wanted my husband to be a soul mate—not just physically affectionate but also interested in my deepest thoughts and feelings. This was pretty tough given the language barrier, but I was determined to try. I'd follow Sam around the compound with my Dari-English dictionary, trying to figure out how to say "I'm so depressed" or "I really miss my father at this time of year." Sam would listen to my tortured sentences, then just stare at me, utterly lost. He finally decided that he needed to round up some foreigners to soak up my conversational excess.

One of them was a young photographer named David, who rented a room at the Peacock Manor. Sam told David he'd pay him four dollars—about two hundred afghanis—per hour if he'd talk to me. I think the rate was even higher after sunset.

I was also going crazy because I felt so terribly confined at the Peacock Manor. At least when the school was at the Women's Ministry, I'd had to walk back and forth to the other guesthouse. Now all my activities took place within the walls of our compound. I was desperate to see other places and other faces, but I didn't really want to go out alone, either. I didn't speak Dari or know my way around town, and there were all those security alerts. I pretty much knew hairdressers were in the "soft target" category, so I had to be cautious. But Sam was not only reluctant to go anywhere with me but also reluctant to have me spend any time with the Afghans who came to the guesthouse to visit him. He'd ask me to go sit in our bedroom until they left. This caused a lot of wailing. I was sure that he was ashamed to be seen with me. I finally wailed to Roshanna about this. She said, "Oh, no, Debbie! He loves you so much that he doesn't want other men looking at you."

But no matter how many times Roshanna would smooth things over, the fighting continued. Sam often treated me more like a servant than like a wife because that was the only model he knew. I felt I had to set him straight on this one right away. When he'd ask me to make him some tea or find his shoes, I'd shoot back,

"Are your legs broken?" He told a group of our foreign friends once that it was easier to have a thousand Afghan wives than one American wife. "You tell a thousand Afghan wives to sit, and they sit," he said. "You tell one American wife to sit and she says, 'Bite my ass.'"

We could joke about these cultural differences—sometimes. And sometimes we'd yell at each other in our own tongues, and one of us would wind up sleeping in the living room. Sometimes I'd stomp outside the gates to get away—from him, from the guesthouse, from our cramped little bedroom, from Ali and David and the other guests, from everything. That was what I'd done in Holland, Michigan, if I had a fight with someone—take a nice, long walk under the stars to get my emotional equilibrium back. At least this got a strong reaction from Sam. The first time I did it, he ran after me in a panic. "Please understand this is not good place to be angry," he said, tugging me back toward the guesthouse. "Karzai controls the day, but the Taliban still controls the night."

One morning after sleeping in the living room, I decided I had had enough. I called Roshanna and told her that I was leaving Sam and asked if I could move in with her and her family. She rushed over to the guesthouse to find me packing all my stuff in my two suitcases and wrapping the things that wouldn't fit in the suitcases in my head scarves. She started to laugh when she saw the mountain of bulging scarves, but I was sitting on the floor crying, so she sat down next to me. In a few minutes, she started to cry, too. This is another thing I love about Afghans—they never let you cry alone. She tried to comfort me, but I couldn't be comforted. "I'm leaving," I sobbed. "I'm leaving Sam and the school and Afghanistan, too. I want a hot bath, and damn it, I want some bacon!"

Sam came back to the house to find the two of us sitting there weeping. He stood in the doorway and took in the scene with a look of utter shock on his face. I think he thought that something had happened to my sons or my mother. Then Roshanna took him aside. She spent about an hour with him explaining how hard both the country and this new marriage were on me. Then she came back with a basin of water. Next thing I knew, she was washing my face and combing my hair. She picked out an outfit and helped me put it on. Sam had given her money to take me to a nice restaurant, as well as the use of his car and driver. We went shopping for more head scarves, then we sat in the restaurant for hours. I realized that my biggest problem right then might not be Sam. Maybe I was missing the kind of company you can only have with a girlfriend. Roshanna and I had both been so busy— she with her new salon, I with the school and salon— that even though we worked together to train the teachers, we hadn't had fun together in ages.

I still don't know if Sam and I would have made it through this period of time if Val and Suraya, my friends from the guesthouse, hadn't returned to Kabul. They stayed with us at the Peacock Manor, and gradually, Sam's understanding of what it meant to be a Western-style husband started to improve. The four of us spent a lot of time together laughing and talking in the living room, and I noticed that Sam watched Val and imitated him. If Val rubbed Suraya's shoulder, Sam would rub my shoulder. If Val held Suraya's hand, then Sam would reach out for mine. We started to tease him about this, so he decided to get back at us by steadfastly ignoring whatever Val did one day. But when Suraya sat on Val's lap, Sam stood up and then plopped himself into my lap.

Little by little, with the help of our friends, Sam relaxed with this outspoken, emotional, independent woman he had married. And as I grew to understand the sexual culture I had married into, I stopped taking his husbandly deficits so personally—or at least I tried. I learned to love him more and more, despite his brusque ways. And difficult as our marriage was, I also knew that I would never have been able to keep the beauty school going if it hadn't been for Sam's help. I had to remind myself of that every time I felt like throwing something at him. I had to remind myself of my students' wretched pasts and of the pride and hope on their faces now. I had to remind myself that if I kept throwing things at him, we wouldn't have anything left. Already, we had no working flashlights because I had flung them all at him. So the battle between us—what he called the Afghan-American war—died down, at least for a while. We became more like the partners, sexual and otherwise, that I'd hoped we would be back when Val and Suraya were arranging this marriage.

But when Sam told me his first wife was pregnant, I fell apart. I had wanted to be in total denial about this other woman. I hadn't wanted to think about the possibility that he'd slept with her when I was in Michigan and he was back in Saudi Arabia. Now I felt as if he had cheated on me. I grabbed his mug and threw it at the wall, where it shattered into hundreds of tiny, toothlike shards. "How far along is she?" I asked him.

"Five months."

I mentally counted ahead. That meant she would be having the baby in October. If we managed to stay married, we'd celebrate our first anniversary that month. My birthday was at the end of October, too. I hated the idea that she would ruin this month, full of dates that were important to me, with a new baby.

I slept in the living room for the next few nights. But somehow, Sam and I made it through this. I could finally see that it was difficult for him, too. We managed to create our own odd kind of happiness again, even though I couldn't bear to think about October.

Soon enough I was reminded that you're allowed only very brief periods of happiness in Afghanistan. This seems to be one of the conditions of life there, like the dust and the wind. Some new horror is always waiting to turn the corner just when you've slowed your pace to enjoy the view. I simply hadn't a clue that the horror would be waiting for me in my own house.

One day I returned from the beauty school and found Sam sitting on our bed, his head resting in his hands. As for many of us, his command of a foreign language faltered when he had something really important to say. He blurted something about Ali and little Hama, but I had to keep asking him over and over what he was talking about.

"He kisses him," Sam said. "*Her.* Ali kisses her."

I couldn't figure out why he was so upset about a kiss. "My uncle used to kiss me when I was a little girl. It was harmless."

"Not uncle kiss!" He pushed me against the wall hard and put his mouth over mine, then pulled away. "This is like Ali kissing."

He had walked into Ali's room without knocking— he never knocks—and found them like this. If Sam had had any doubts about the nature of the kiss, they were swept aside by the way Ali had his hand up Hama's shirt and by the look of terror on her face. Sam didn't know how to say "breasts" in English— our little sexual code for mine was "apples and oranges." He said something about Hama's apples and oranges, but this time there was no playfulness about it.

I sat on the bed next to him, stunned. I had always been uncomfortable about the way Hama trailed Ali around the house, but that was because I didn't want her alone in a room with his male visitors. So I'd try to keep her with me as much as possible. Ali didn't stand in the way. He'd encourage Hama to stay with me and tell her that I was like her aunt. I actually felt more like her mother, because she'd cling to me as if she were a tiny child. Only at the beauty school did she relax.

"Did you tell him you'd kill him if he touches her again?"

He shook his head. "Ali is not family. Neither is Hama. I can make these orders only to family."

I stormed out to look for Ali, but he wasn't in his room. So I fixed myself up with a tumbler of whiskey, a pack of cigarettes, and plenty of magazines so that I could wait for him. He finally came in at around eleven o'clock, with Hama in tow. Her face brightened when she saw me on the couch, and she ran over to sit next to me. I ran my hand over her cheek. She was wearing bright red lipstick, heavy kohl, and eye shadow, all of it so harsh and unnecessary on her pretty little face that she almost looked like a child actor on vaudeville. I asked her to go into the kitchen and make some tea for us. She promptly skipped away.

"What are you doing with this little girl, Ali?" I demanded. "Are you really her uncle? Her uncle by blood?"

"Not by blood, no." He began patting his pockets for a cigarette. I didn't offer him one of mine. "I am a friend of the family."

"You're not her friend if you kiss her and touch her. You'll only ruin her reputation, and she'll never be able to get married."

"But Debbie, listen." He smiled and held his hands out. "I am going to marry Hama."

I felt sick and, if possible, angrier than ever. I was sure that he was lying. "You're at least thirty years older than she is, Ali. You're too old. And even if you were going to marry her, you have no business touching her like Sam saw you doing, not until after you're married. I might be a dumb American, but I know that much."

His face reddened. "What I do with Hama, I do with her parents' blessing."

"I don't want you to bring her in this house again. I don't want her in your room or with your friends. After she finishes her day at the beauty school, I want her to go right back to her parents' house."

I could tell Ali was angry, but he didn't argue with me. One of the other men who was renting a room came in right about then, and Ali whirled around and started shouting at him in Dari.

"Take her home." I walked into the kitchen and saw that Hama was standing by the sink, frightened by the loud voices from the next room. I told her to go home and stay away from Ali. She probably couldn't understand much of this, but she could see that I was upset. Then he shouted for her from the living room, and she ran out.

Sam and I decided that we had to find out more about Ali. Once we started asking around, the bad stories about this guy just kept coming. I felt sick that we had been too busy—and too trusting—to find out more about him before now. There were all kinds of rumors about his nasty activities. This explained the mysterious side of Ali. Why he didn't seem to have a job but always had money. Why he seemed to know well-connected Afghans all over Europe and the East.

But there wasn't a lot we could do about Ali. He was our partner in the Peacock Manor guesthouse, and we were stuck with him until the lease ran out. I really couldn't even insist that he stop bringing Hama into the house, but he did stop. I saw her at the school every day—I made sure she had a ride back and forth from her parents' house—and she was always so affectionate, so happy to be around me. I once took her away from the others and asked Roshanna to translate for me. "Does Ali still touch you in bad places?" I asked.

She hid her face.

"Tell me, Hama. Tell me what he does."

She started to cry. She pointed to her breasts and her pubic area.

"Don't let him do this, even if he is a friend of your family!"

She nodded and threw her arms around my neck. When she went back to class, I told Roshanna not to tell the teachers or the other students about Hama.

"They know this already, Debbie," she said. "They know she does bad things with this man."

"How?"

"So many ways!" Roshanna began ticking them off on her fingers. "She stays out late at night with him. You even come to school telling us how Hama is at parties. Good girls don't go to parties with men at night."

"I guess I should have figured that out," I muttered.

"She plucks her eyebrows," Roshanna continued. "Only women do this. And he gives her a cell phone just so he can summon her. You see how she never buys minutes so that she can call anyone else. It is just for him, to find her."

Ali still tried to charm me, but I avoided him. This made him furious. He never showed his anger to me, but I could hear him yelling at Sam—really, at anyone who crossed his path. He always seemed to be surrounded by a group of men who hung out in his room and in the living room. Then one day I noticed that they had brought a woman in with them. Ali introduced her as his fiancée, but I figured out after a while that she had to be a prostitute. Her cell phone rang about sixty times an hour, and it was always men calling. I knew this because she tossed her phone to me once and asked me to answer it for her while she was in the bathroom. I was glad he had this woman to keep him occupied—and away from Hama.

Our satellite phone rang in the middle of the night. I heard Sam knock the phone to the floor and rustle around to try to find it. He finally answered in Uzbek, and then he switched to English. I sat up, my heart pounding. If my family had something so important to say that they ignored the nine-and-a-half-hour time difference, then it had to be bad.

"Hi, Mom," my son Zachary said. "I've been having a hard time lately. I wondered if I could come and live with you."

"Sure." I yawned, falling back on my pillow. "Come to Afghanistan!"

I called him back in the morning to work out the details. I hoped that Afghanistan might affect him the way it had me: that he might forget about his own problems and start caring more about other people. So I booked him a flight and he was on his way. By this time, my family had found out about my marriage to Sam. As I'd feared, they had picked up a newspaper and read about it. I think my mother was actually relieved that I wasn't there by myself. So Zach soon joined us in the Peacock Manor and started volunteering teaching art and English at an orphanage for boys. I forgot all about Hama for a while, basking in the sight of my sweet son with his big crown of soft brown curls. Zach wasn't in Kabul for more than a day when boys his age started to show up and ask him to go out to games or movies or tea. I guess there weren't many American boys his age there, and everyone was curious. Then, several nights after he arrived, he came to a party at the beauty school. It was unusual to have him there, since males generally weren't allowed into the school or salon. After the party, Zach was talking with great animation about a pretty girl with red hair. I pulled out photos of the class, and he put his finger on Hama's face.

I teased Hama about this at school the next day. I

told her Zach thought she was beautiful. A few of the other girls teased her, too, but I saw Topekai whispering to Roshanna. "What is she saying?" I asked her in a low voice.

"She worries you don't understand that Hama is not a girl." Roshanna put her hand on my arm because she could already feel me bristling. "Not a girl, meaning not pure. She thinks you shouldn't let your son take an interest in her."

I looked across the room and saw Topekai watching us somberly. She frowned and shook her head. "Not good," she called across the room. "Only trouble."

Still, I could see that Hama was pleased by Zach's interest. I thought it was important for her to know that other men found her pretty. I didn't want her to think she was stuck with Ali or forever tainted by his actions.

But a few weeks later, Hama slunk into school with a black eye and a cut lip. She put her hands over her face and whispered through her fingers that Ali had heard about Zach and beaten her. A tiny woman wrapped in a big blue scarf followed her into the school. It was Hama's mother. As she pushed her scarf back, I could see that she'd probably had a pretty face once, but she had aged poorly. Like so many Afghan women, she looked twice her age. She had come to beg me to save her daughter from Ali, who had been giving her greedy husband money for the girl over the last year. The mother said she didn't know how the family would survive if Ali stopped giving them the money, but she knew that he was an evil man and she wanted to break her daughter away from him. Weeping, she took me by the hands and asked if I would have my son marry Hama and take her out of the country.

How do you tell a brokenhearted mother that you just don't do things that way where you come from? That you don't arrange marriages for your sons; you don't even do it to save a girl you love from being molested by a monster? I couldn't promise my son to her, but I did promise that I would always look out for Hama.

When Sam heard about this, however, he decided that marriage to Hama would be just the ticket for Zach. He already thought my son needed toughening—he thought all American boys did—and he figured that taking on a wife would be good for him. After all, he had been steered into an arranged marriage when he was about Zach's age. He felt it had made a man of him.

"You marry Hama," he told Zach. "She make good Afghan wife for you. Already, she has progressive Western ideas."

I could see my son weighing it in his mind for a day or so, then he sat down next to me and Sam when we were eating dinner. "I'll marry her," he said.

I wasn't terribly surprised that bighearted Zach went for this idea. He hadn't decided to marry Hama because he felt he needed to become a man in Sam's eyes. Rather, he was haunted by the thought of sweet little Hama being sold to Ali by her father. He hadn't been in Afghanistan long enough to know how often this happened. He didn't know that there were thousands—hundreds of thousands—of sweet little girls who had been sold to brutal men. He couldn't marry them all.

Ali didn't stop beating Hama when Zach said he would marry her. If anything, the beatings got worse. Every day Hama would come into the school with a new bruise or cut, all tokens of Ali's jealous affection. Zach was getting frantic. Here he had made the noble gesture of saying he would marry Hama, but it had wound up making her suffering worse. We were all still living in the guesthouse together, and Ali strolled in every night looking as smooth and urbane as ever, sometimes with a group of men, sometimes with the men and a few hard-looking women. I couldn't remember why I had ever found him charming or even handsome.

Then I had an idea that I thought might save Hama, one not quite as drastic as marriage. My friend Karen had been following Hama's story from Michigan through my e-mail updates. She had a lot of sympathy for Hama, since she herself had been in an abusive relationship with an older man when she was a young girl. So we worked out a plan for Hama to fly back to the States and live with Karen. We'd pool our money to cover her expenses and even start a college fund for her.

I sat Hama down after school one day and told her

the news, and she jumped up and danced around the room. "I am American girl!" she sang. She picked up one of the fashion magazines lying on a table, held a picture of a girl in skimpy clothes to her chest, and struck a pouty pose like one of the models. She looked like a little girl playing paper dolls, only she herself was the doll. I told her not to tell anyone, especially not Ali. And I told her to stay away from him, to drop the cell phone he had given her down a well and never let him summon her again.

It was as pretty a day as I'd ever seen in Kabul. Above my head, a green-and-blue canopy fluttered. My students' children wandered around the yard nibbling cookies and staring up at a forest of sunflowers. It seemed as if there were a million sunflowers, as if we were surrounded by a golden glow. The setting matched the glow in my heart. It was graduation day.

When it was time for the second class to graduate, in July, I was exhausted but happy. Against all odds, the Kabul Beauty School had survived to prepare yet another group of women for solid careers as beauticians. If anything, I believed the changes I had made to the curriculum were going to help this group be even more successful—and all this had been done at a fraction of the cost of the first class. In the final weeks of school, the girls had been working hard on their mannequin heads, hoping to win the "Most Creative" award. They went off in groups to the big outdoor market and came back with sequins, feathers, beads, ribbons, and all sorts of other materials to decorate their mannequins. After the girls went home for the day, I'd walk around and admire what they'd done. It was like being in the middle of a Mardi Gras parade—one where all the marchers had been cut off at the neck, but still.

This graduation was held in the backyard of the PARSA house. It wasn't as fancy as the first graduation. Not as many dignitaries showed up, although I was thrilled to welcome a contingent from Care for All Foundation, the relief organization that had brought me to Afghanistan that first spring. My students and their families were dressed in their finest. Baseera and some of the others came in beautiful silk Afghan gowns heavy with beads and embroidery. Some of the girls came in sexy sequined saris, and some—like little Hama—in their very best Western blue jeans with tailored white blouses. Sam had given me a pair of weighty gold earrings for the occasion. Between those, my long false eyelashes, and three pounds of hair extensions, I could hardly keep my head up. When the girls walked to the stage to get their diplomas, they carried their mannequin heads like babies and placed them gently on a table so that they all faced the crowd. The winning mannequin had a glittering map of Afghanistan spread across her eyes like a party mask, along with a luminous peacock on one cheek, its feathers curling gracefully along the neck.

• • •

After the second class graduated, I really tried to ramp up the salon business. I now wanted to make money not only to fund the third class and maybe a fourth but also to move away from Ali. We were still stuck with him on the Peacock Manor lease, but there was no reason that we couldn't move the school and salon and our own quarters sooner and rent the Peacock Manor rooms to someone else. I also wanted to put aside money for Hama's plane ticket to America while Karen and I figured out how to get her a visa.

Topekai, Baseera, and Bahar started to work more hours in the salon. I asked Hama to work in the salon, too, even though she hadn't turned out to be a very good beautician. I let her practice occasionally on Shaz, who often stood in the doorway watching my girls work. Shaz was looking better all the time. I had given her some clothes so that she didn't have to wear her old rags anymore. She had started smiling and talking more, probably because we finally figured out that she couldn't hear us if we talked on her left side. It turned out that she had lost the hearing on that side when a bomb went off. She still wasn't the greatest of cleaners, but I had hopes for her. She worked hard whenever I pointed her at something. She also came running after me with keys, important papers, even money that I left in the wrong place. I felt that she was always looking after my back, and it was a nice feeling. I was happy to let Hama help her feel a little bit girlie.

Then one day Hama was trying some powder on Shaz's rough cheeks when a cell phone with a tone I hadn't heard before rang. Hama dropped the powder on the floor. She ran to her purse, pulled out a phone, and huddled at the back of the room to talk.

"Is that a different cell phone?" I asked her when she was finished. She just ducked her head and went back to work on Shaz, but I was suspicious. Clearly, Topekai and Baseera were suspicious, too: they whispered together and spoke sharply to Hama. She finally admitted that Ali had given her another phone.

"Why are you talking to him?" I felt like slapping her. "Why are you taking his gifts?"

After that I started to catch sight of Hama in the Peacock Manor, usually at times when she thought I was either outside or still in bed. Once she was in Ali's room early in the morning, putting on her makeup. Another time I saw her come in with him late at night, wearing a sparkly dress with high heels. I also saw her in his room with a bunch of men, smoking a cigarette and laughing in an odd way that didn't sound like her. She'd try to hide when she saw me. When she'd come into work at the salon the next day, I'd tell her over and over to stay away from Ali. She'd nod, but she wouldn't look me in the eye.

It got so much worse. One day I heard her voice inside Ali's room and opened the door. There were Hama and her twelve-year-old brother with some of their clothes off, cowering against the wall. Hama's hand was under her brother's tunic, and she quickly snatched it away and hid it behind her back, shaking so violently that I could see it across the room. Ali was stretched out across his toushak watching them. "Leave them alone," I screamed at him; then I pulled Hama and her brother out of the room and called a taxi for them.

Hama started coming into the salon every day bent over in pain. I'd make her lie down and fix her some tea and try to talk her into seeing a doctor—I figured either Ali was beating her or she was pregnant. Finally, I got Roshanna in to translate so that I could figure what was going on. "Is he making you have sex with him?" I asked, but Hama just covered her face. "Hama, is he putting his *kar* [penis] in your *kos* [vagina]?"

"Nai, Debbie, nai," she said sadly. She reached her hand around and touched her bottom. I started to cry. She was so tiny—there was hardly anything to her— that this had to be terribly painful.

Her bottom wasn't much bigger than one of the cantaloupes they sold in the market, and Ali was a big man.

"This is very bad," Roshanna whispered. "Ali is not taking her virginity for himself. He must be planning to sell it to someone else."

"You can still get away from him, Hama," I said. "Karen is getting ready to make a good home for you in America."

But Hama didn't brighten this time when I went over our plan. She was falling away from me even then. I still don't know why. I don't know if she was afraid of Ali or if she already believed that being with him had taken away the possibility of any other kind of life. Maybe she loved him in some way that I couldn't understand, the way children who are beaten and ridiculed by parents can still suffer some sort of love for them. Ali's hunger for Hama had already crippled her. She called him all day from the salon when she thought I couldn't hear. I kept catching glimpses of her with Ali and sometimes with his friends near the Peacock Manor. She stopped hiding from me, and I stopped torturing her with my anger.

Hama still dragged herself to the salon every day. I was glad to see her—to me, her presence there was a sign of hope—but Topekai and Baseera were becoming increasingly hostile. One day Baseera just stopped coming in to work. I finally went to her home with Roshanna to try to find out what the problem is. Baseera invited us in, seated us in the women's part of the house, and brought in tea and biscuits, as if there was nothing wrong. But when I asked her why she wasn't working, she started to cry and spoke in a torrent to Roshanna.

"She wants to work, but she is afraid the salon is not a safe place for her," Roshanna explained. "Her husband also doesn't want her to come to work anymore. It is because of Hama."

I realized then that Hama's presence put everyone in the salon—and the beauty school itself—at risk. Moral extremists could decide to storm the salon and throw acid in everyone's face; the government could decide to shut us down forever if we had a known prostitute working there. If we were lucky, neither of these things would happen. Still, many people believed that beauty salons were fronts for prostitutes. To be honest, a few of them were. I couldn't allow Hama's presence to taint Topekai, Baseera, Nahida, and all the other women in Afghanistan who were trying to make a living as beauticians. I fretted about this for weeks. Then one day I read a story online about villagers not far from Kabul who had recently stoned and killed a prostitute.

I pulled Hama aside when she came into the salon. I told her that she had to make a choice between Ali and me. I told her that I had found a new house and was getting ready to move there. I was going to fix up a room just for her. I would tell my chowkidor to shoot Ali if he tried to come inside.

When I moved into the new house, I bought pretty curtains and painted the walls a nice shade of peach in the room meant for her. I put in a television and stuffed animals on the bed. I waited for her to come, because she'd said she would and her eyes had shone briefly when we talked about it. But she continued to be Ali's little girl at the Peacock Manor. I've seen her just once since then, at a party, dressed in flashy clothes that left her arms and neck bare. She was pouring drinks and smoking and letting the men touch her in a familiar way. I couldn't bear to stay.

Chapter 8

Everyone else was out of our new house, and I was looking forward to a long, hot bath with lots of candles. The door to the bathroom was closed, but that didn't necessarily mean anyone was inside. We always kept the door closed to seal in the heat. I knocked anyway, just in case Sam had come back without my noticing. No one answered, but when I opened the door I saw a strange man stripped to the waist and bent over the sink. He turned around to peer at me, dirty bubbles streaming from a beard that reached his belly.

"Get out!" I said. "This is not your house."

"Salaam aleichem." He quickly pulled his tunic back on and said something placating in Dari, but I wasn't having any of it.

"Take your bar of soap with you!" I noticed that he had used some of my toothpaste. I was glad to see he had his own toothbrush clutched in his hand. He reached for his unfurled turban, which was hanging on the shower rod, and wrapped it around his head. Then he rolled his toothbrush and soap into a dirty towel and slunk downstairs. I watched him from the upstairs window. He looked back at the house to see if I was following him, then opened the door to one of the outbuildings and darted inside. I figured Sam would have to flush him out later.

As I bolted the bathroom door, I decided I shouldn't

be too mad at the guy. After all, he was the reason that our rent was so low.

Sam and I had both been eager to get away from the Peacock Manor. I wanted to find another big house in a compound, but this time I didn't want to turn it into a guesthouse. I wanted to put the school and salon on the first and second floors, saving two rooms upstairs for our private use. I figured that I could have a bigger salon this way, one that would generate enough income to sustain the school. But Sam kept telling me that I didn't have enough money to rent a new building, and he was right. Rents in Kabul were sky-rocketing as local landowners figured out that foreign NGOs were desperate for space. I hadn't been able to save nearly enough for the move. What was worse, I had convinced my friend Chris to come to Afghanistan for ten days to help me paint the new salon and school that I didn't yet have. She was eager to do something to help Afghan women, so she had already bought a ticket for early December.

Three days before she was supposed to arrive, I was weeping all night at this new mess I had created. Chris would come to Kabul, and there would be nothing for her to do but hang out in the Peacock Manor and watch me work and fret about Hama. I had done everything I could think of to get enough money. I'd been praying for much of the last few weeks, but by now I figured that God thought I was an idiot. I needed exactly nine thousand dollars for rent and ren-ovation but had just over one thousand saved. But when I checked my e-mail later that day, a nice big miracle awaited me. There was a message from Mary MacMakin saying that Clairol and *Vogue* had just sent donations for the beauty school. The total came to nine thousand dollars.

So I had the money when Chris arrived but no house. Sam still hadn't found anything suitable in my price range. On the second day of Chris's visit, I was in meltdown. Sam and I were in our room at the Peacock Manor, and the power was ebbing so low that the lamps were all like flickering candles. It made a very dramatic setting for a hysterical beautician. "Find something in the next thirty minutes!" I yelled. "She came halfway around the world to paint this school."

He returned quickly with a new possibility. It was a big, white house with sturdy compound walls and a nice front yard that was cheap by Kabul standards. The owner lived in Herat and was desperate to find paying tenants. An old Talib squatter—the guy who startled me in the bathroom—had moved in, hooked up the electricity, and was running up huge bills that the owner had to pay. I told Sam to get the contract, and we started moving in the next day.

In addition to the squatter, who still made an occasional appearance, the new house seemed to come with a smiling plumber named Zilgai. I left him and Chris there to find workers and start painting while I dealt with an onslaught of Westerners needing highlights, cuts, facials, manicures, pedicures, and bikini waxes before they left for Christmas break. I was so busy it was as if someone had written my name and phone number in smoke in the sky, like in *The Wizard of Oz*. I could stop by the new house only a few times a day. Every time I did, it seemed that Chris was surrounded by a crew of eight men who couldn't believe that a woman could paint the ceiling without standing on a chair. I don't think they'd ever seen a woman this tall. They called her the "two-meter woman." In fact, it was Chris who finally scared the squatter away. She found a pile of his things tucked into a corner of the house, put them in a bucket, and handed them to him. He gaped up at her, bolted, and we never saw him again.

One day when I stopped at the house, Chris said she wanted a feather duster to do some special-effects painting. I couldn't recall ever seeing a feather duster in Kabul, but I described one to Zilgai and the painters using my Dari-English dictionary. Chris stood there flapping her arms like a chicken to try to help them understand. One of the painters finally nodded his head and said that he'd get it for me. He told me it would cost two hundred afghani, which I thought was sort of expensive, but I handed him the money. He came back an hour and a half later with a live chicken. Chris sighed and then pretended to stab herself in the heart to show them that she hadn't meant for him to bring a live chicken. No problem: the painter butchered it in the front yard and brought it back to her. She plucked out a few of its feathers and held them up to a stick. Then he got the idea; he finished plucking the chicken, bound the feathers to the stick with twine, then presented his improvised feather duster as proudly as if he were handing her a bouquet of long-stemmed roses. When I saw her using this thing later, I looked at the handle and asked her what wall she had painted red. "That's blood," she said. She and the painters had eaten the chicken for lunch.

Poor Chris! She was there at the absolute worst time of the year. The only good thing was that it wasn't what we call "terrorist season"—the terrorists tend to head back to Pakistan when the temperature drops—but it's a tough time in all other ways. It's cold and no one has central heating. It takes a long time to get the hang of the bokaris, too. Before you go to bed, you have to get them burning vigorously—not so hot that you can't sleep, but the fire has to be big enough to burn through the night. You don't want a dead bokari and a room so cold that you can see your breath when the mullah wakes you at four-thirty. Chris wasn't there long enough to master her bokari, so she was freezing the whole time.

Despite her miserable stay, Chris's handiwork resulted in a school-salon complex that was as soothing to the eye as anything in the States. She painted the main room in an Egyptian theme, with figures framing each big mirror that look like Cleopatra and her handmaidens—all equipped with mirrors, hairbrushes, cups of tea, and so on. The pedicure-manicure room was nothing short of splendid. She built a platform with sunken sinks for pedicures and covered the rest of the platform with Afghan carpets, then draped the ceiling with fabric so that, if you glance up, you feel as if you're in a beautiful tent. Then she painted the rest of the room so that it looks like an airy pavilion with light reflected from the sea—turquoise walls with faux pillars and trellises between them and intricate purple-and-white medallions on the trellises. Several months after Chris left, I had a group of NGO people whose street had been bombed come into the salon. They had woken up in the middle of the night to find themselves covered with shattered glass from their windows and came in for a day of much-needed pampering. I thanked Chris all over again when I saw these women stop trembling little by little in her beautiful turquoise room.

We moved everything over to the new compound by Christmas and gave the salon a new name—the Oasis. Since I knew we'd be able to do more business in this bigger, nicer space, I offered Topekai, Baseera, and Bahar full-time jobs in the salon if they'd help me train a new group of teachers for the next class. So I ran the salon four days a week and conducted school on the other three days.

We also hired more staff for the new compound: a sweet young cook named Maryam, a fierce little gingersnap of an Afghan girl named Laila as a translator, and a cheerful guy named Achmed Zia as our chowkidor. Soon Achmed Zia and the guys had wired the chowkidor hut with electricity, installed a television and a tinkling glass chandelier, and hung pictures of Bollywood stars all over the walls. The guys would hang around there together until well after sunset. In fact, I'd sometimes call Sam at dinnertime and ask why he wasn't home yet. He'd tell me he'd already been home for an hour and was in the chowkidor hut watching soccer. Sometimes they'd have eight men crammed into this space barely big enough for two.

"Don't talk to him until he talks to you," Laila said. "You must show him that you are the strong one!"

Topekai watched me with dark, serious eyes and put her arms around my neck. "You are my sister," she said. "What can I do?"

Baseera folded her arms and pursed her lips dismissively. "No man worth the crying, Debbie. No more crying today."

I only howled louder. It was a good thing that school hadn't started up again and that all my customers had left the country. My face was red and blotchy and swollen. At that moment, I was not a living testimonial to the beauty industry.

Sam and I had been having a tough time off and on ever since the beginning of October as my sense of dread about his other wife's pregnancy grew. I couldn't enjoy our anniversary because I was thinking about her staggering through her ninth month. I couldn't enjoy my birthday because I was afraid the baby would be born on that day and I'd be reminded of this painful barrier between me and Sam every time I got another year older. I relaxed a little after these two dates passed and waited for Sam to let me know what had happened. He said nothing. I finally asked him about the baby around Thanksgiving. He told me his other wife had delivered a few weeks before. It was a boy.

I knew how important boy children are to Afghans, and I was devastated. My Kabul friends kept telling me that this was the best thing that could have happened: Sam's parents would now be kinder to the first wife and stop pressuring Sam to have sex with her. My friends reminded me that I was still the favored wife, the one he wanted to live with. But in my darkest moments, I wondered how long this would last. Although Sam had not told his parents about our marriage, his mother had found out about it from a Kabul relative. She called Sam in a rage and told him that she heard he had married an old American woman. He lied and told her I was only thirty-two. She asked if we had had any children yet. He told her no—he said that, like all Americans, I had an operation when I was thirty so that I couldn't have any more children. I knew his mother would have been even more angered by the truth, especially the part about my being ten years older than he. Still, I wished Sam had been able to acknowledge me just as I was.

Now I was sobbing because he had been gone for hours—he always seemed to be gone for hours—and I was pining for closeness more than ever. It was my first Christmas season in Afghanistan, and I'd never been so homesick and depressed. Zach had gone back to Michigan, and I missed him more than ever. Sam knew how much this day meant to me, but he seemed to have forgotten all about it. So far, Christmas Eve day was cold, dusty, and noisy with the sound of generators banging up and down the street. Just like any other winter day in Kabul.

Someone must have called Sam to tell him how miserable I was. I looked up to see him hurrying in the door. He patted me on the head, a rare sign of affection from him in front of other people. "Of course, we will have Christmas here in this Muslim country," he said. "We will have best Muslim Christmas ever."

He rounded up the staff and told them we would have a party. He explained that Americans always eat turkey for Christmas dinner, so Achmed Zia obligingly called around for a turkey. Soon an old man arrived at the compound gate with six live turkeys tied at the feet and draped around his neck. I was supposed to pick two of them. The old man untied their feet and let them run around the compound, but I felt so terrible about their upcoming sacrifice that I put out piles of food for them. When it was time to slaughter the turkeys the next morning, Maryam the cook realized we didn't have a knife that was sharp enough. All the butcher shops were closed that day, so she tucked the turkeys under her arm, took them to the police station, and asked the police to cut their heads off. When she got ready to cook the turkeys, the power went off, and we weren't able to find a generator to keep the stove going. So Maryam prepared them in a big pressure cooker that rattled and shook on top of a fire Shaz built out in the yard. It looked more like Maryam was making a bomb than Christmas dinner.

On Christmas Day, Zilgai and his brother the florist came to decorate the house for me. They put plastic olive branches around all the doors. They made small forests in the living room out of plastic orange trees. I guess they thought the little oranges looked like Christmas ornaments. Then the party got started. All the women—the beauticians, the female staff, the wives, mothers, and sisters of the male staff—filed up the stairs into our living room, and all the men stayed down in the salon. In each room, someone popped in a CD of Afghan music. The dancing began.

I was watching Maryam and her sister twirl around each other when they suddenly stopped and shrank into the crowd. Sam was at my elbow with a bouquet of flowers and a huge box. "This for you!" he said. All the women clapped as I opened the present, then crowded around to look. They gasped as I pulled tissue paper away from a blinding red object. It was a traditional Afghan dress decorated with thousands of tiny mirrors and beads and sequins. "Wow," I said as I tried to lift it from the box and was almost pulled forward by the sheer weight of all those embellishments. "This is some dress!"

"Go put on." Sam waved me toward our bedroom.

It took me a while to get the dress on. I felt like one of those medieval queens who needed two or three attendants to get dressed, except that no one was around to help me. I finally got everything zipped and buttoned, arranged the matching scarf over my head, and staggered back into the living room. Sam was waiting for me wearing a Santa hat. Even though the CD player was still belting out Afghan music, he tried to get me to waltz. I could hardly move. My big-time-bling dress made me feel as if I were on Jupiter or some other planet where the force of gravity is stronger than ours. My muscles were starting to ache. But still, I cried happy tears because Sam had given me a Christmas present. "He loves you so much!" one of the women said as I lurched past in my husband's arms.

The door to the school slammed, but Mina didn't sing out her usual morning greeting. She slunk to the back of the house with her head ducked low. Soon I heard muffled sobbing. I was with a group of students, watching our three new teachers explain color concepts. Laila the translator and I exchanged puzzled looks, and then I tugged her into the hallway so we could find out what was wrong with Mina. She was hiding in the beautiful turquoise manicure-pedicure room. When she raised her head, we could see that she had been crying for hours. She hadn't even bothered to put on makeup that morning. This made her almost unrecognizable, because Mina always accented her beautiful almond-shaped eyes with about a quarter inch of liner. She and Laila spoke for a few minutes, then Laila turned to me. "She needs a place for her little boy."

"I thought she was taking him to her mother's house every day."

"She can't take him there now."

"Because . . . ?"

"Because they have disowned her. She must either find another place to take him or stay at home."

"Why did they disown her?"

"There is a fight with the husband about the dowry."

Sam had first brought Mina to the Oasis after we got busy when the foreigners returned from their Christmas vacations. She was a beautiful young girl with black hair and black eyes and the biggest smile in Afghanistan.

"My cousin Mina," he said. "You find a job here for her."

"I can't afford to hire anyone else." I tried to convey my condolences to the girl with a rueful smile, but she looked as thrilled as if I had just promised her a job as assistant to the president.

"You need extra cleaner. Shaz too old and expired."

Shaz was younger than I and was turning out to be a powerhouse of a worker besides. "She doesn't need any help, Sam."

"You don't have to pay Mina. She just do this and that."

"I can't not pay her."

"You take her, Debbie! She sit at home all day with baby and no electricity or heat."

So I took Mina. She left her child with her mother every morning, and gradually, she made herself indispensable.

Now that we had the bigger salon and school, a lot more work needed to be done to support them. I finally bought a washing machine and dryer because we were always running out of towels. But as it turned out, the new appliances didn't lessen the workload as much as I'd hoped. The washer didn't fill with water by itself. We had to get buckets of hot and cold water and pour them in to get the desired temperature. Then we'd turn it on and the washer would move the clothes around a little bit. To drain it, we'd take the hose from the back of the washer and let the water run out. We'd have to change into rubber shower shoes and roll up our pants legs to do this, since it always soaked the entire floor. It took two or three of us—Shaz, Mina, and I— to wash the towels. On most days, there wasn't enough power to run the dryer, either—if we turned it on, the blow dryers, the facial machine, and every other electrical appliance in the salon would just stop. So we usually dried the towels by hanging them over every available surface. The last thing we'd do every night was drape towels over the salon chairs and furniture, leaving the place looking sort of spooky and deserted.

Sam was happy at first that I'd given Mina a job, since his mother had given him strict orders to look out for her. But he wasn't happy when he noticed what she was doing. One day I was trying to explain to her that the bathrooms needed to be more thoroughly cleaned before the salon opened in the morning. I wanted my customers to feel as if they had escaped the Kabul dust completely for a few hours. Sam frowned as he listened to this, then said, "Mina must not clean bathrooms."

"Why not?"

"Not proper. No one from my family does jobs like this. Never hard cleaning, only light."

I sighed. It seemed I had run afoul of his family's honor again. "So what is she allowed to do? Can she sweep the floors?"

"No sweep floors."

"Dust?"

"Dusting okay. Serving tea okay. No toilets."

Mina didn't seem to care what kind of work she did, but—to settle Sam's caste feathers—I gave full responsibility for the toilets back to Shaz. Mina dusted all the shelves of beauty products and cleaned the mirrors every morning. This was actually a big help, as I had never been able to convince the beauticians that it wasn't beneath their dignity to keep our workplace clean. Mina would also help Maryam prepare meals for the staff, beauticians, teachers, and students. I'd often hear the two of them singing sweetly in the kitchen as they peeled eggplants or kneaded the dough for *aushak,* a kind of Afghan ravioli stuffed with leeks and scallions. Every time a customer would come into the salon, Mina would glide in right away with a big smile, two carafes of tea, and a handful of English words. "You wanna tea? You wanna black tea? You wanna green? You wanna sugar?"

Mina added a sort of madcap dash of fun to the place

that was as indispensable as her light housecleaning. Because she was Sam's cousin—not much more than a twelfth or fourteenth cousin, but still—she took more liberties around the compound than the other girls. One day she and Shaz were in front of the house shaking out the rugs and washing the patio down with a hose. Next thing I knew, the two of them were having a water fight. Water was splattering against the salon window, arching over to the side of the yard where some old styling stations were stored. Mina finally splattered Zilgai as he came trotting in the gate on his way to the kitchen. I had customers, but I couldn't help myself—I ran outside, grabbed the hose, and sprayed down Mina. As she stood there screaming and sputtering, I noticed how tiny she was now that her big, gauzy clothes were wet down. She dove for the hose and wrangled it back as the other beauticians and our customers stuck their heads outside and shouted encouragement. She sprayed me; then she turned and saw Sam coming in the gate in his suit and tie with his briefcase under his arm. He looked at us sternly, his dark glasses firmly in place—and then Mina aimed the hose at him. She soaked him top to bottom as he tried to divert the flow with his briefcase. He was one angry mujahideen after she finally stopped. He picked up his briefcase and stomped past us with little beads of water quivering in his mustache. Even I would never have had the nerve to do that.

But today, all the sparkle had gone out of Mina's face. Trouble had been brewing for months—no, for years—and she couldn't hide it anymore with her dazzling smiles.

Mina's family came from the northeast, up near Tajikistan. Her family had six girls and two boys, one of whom was older than Mina. Their father was a teacher, but his real distinction in their village was as a drunk. When he'd get paid, he'd immediately drink up the money and then sing in happy-drunk fashion until he got mad about something. Then he'd spend the balance of his inebriation fighting. Her mother somehow figured out how to get ahold of his money, and she'd hide it. He thought this was acceptable when he was sober, but when he started drinking, he'd fight with her to give him the rest of the money. He'd fight with his older son when he drank, too. Mina said he drank so much because he was sad that they were poor and that he owed so many people money.

During the war against the Russians, Mina's father had moved the family to Kabul. But when the mujahideen war had started, it wasn't safe for children to go to school and he couldn't keep his job. So he moved the family back near the Tajikistan border, into a room in his brother's house. Mina's uncle was wealthy, but he was grudging about taking in his brother's family and he treated them poorly. Her father couldn't find a job. Her family would have lean periods—sometimes days—when they had no food to eat. The uncle and his family would gather in the next room and eat by themselves. Mina told me once that she and her older brother used to stand outside the uncle's windows and watch them eat, clutching at the hunger in their own stomachs. Their aunt would come outside and chase them away, calling them beggars.

Finally, her brother got a job as a teacher in Kabul, and the family had enough money to move into their own rented house there. The brother got married, and he and his wife lived in an upstairs room. Mina would have been in eighth grade then, but her family was afraid to let her go outside for fear that the Taliban would snatch her up. Then one day a man came to the house and said he wanted to marry Mina. He wasn't Taliban, but her parents refused him anyway. She was only fourteen, and he was in his forties. Besides, the whole family thought he was too ugly for the beautiful Mina.

For three years this man kept asking for Mina's hand. She had stopped worrying about him, because she was sure her father would always say no. She had several boy cousins who were young and dashing. She hoped that when their families decided it was time for them to marry, one of the boys would convince his parents to consider Mina. Afghan girls and boys can't date, socialize, or even flirt openly. Still, a pretty Afghan girl can mesmerize a man from across the room by the way she tosses her scarf. Mina was hoping some of these cousins had been watching. She didn't want a forty-seven-year-old husband. Given the short span of life in Afghanistan, that would be almost like marrying someone who was ninety.

Then her brother borrowed money from the old,

ugly suitor for an investment that went sour. When the brother couldn't pay back the loan, the suitor demanded Mina as payment. Her father reluctantly agreed and handed over his beautiful daughter in order to protect the family's honor. Mina begged her parents not to make her marry him. By this time many young men had asked for her hand. Her father said no; she must marry the first suitor.

But after her wedding, resentment simmered among the men of the family and then boiled over. Mina's father and her brother began to fight because the brother had taken the very un-Afghanlike step of moving out of the family home. The brother was shockingly smitten with his wife, who convinced him to get their own house. Mina's father was offended. He got angry all over again at the son for defaulting on his loan; he had counted on getting a nice fat dowry for Mina but instead had gotten nothing. The father was angry at Mina's husband, too, because he had managed to obtain her for a relatively paltry sum. The husband was angry because he had lost his job after the wedding and now wished he'd never given Mina's brother a loan in the first place; he wished he still had that money to invest in a new business himself. All this anger was directed at the one person who was the least to blame and had no power to do anything about it: Mina.

As Mina continued to sob, Laila told me that Mina's father and brother were fighting again. The father had torn into the brother at dinner, telling him it was his fault that the father had gotten no dowry for Mina. The brother replied that he didn't care about the family's financial problems anymore. Besides, the dowry had nothing to do with him; he had defaulted on a business-related loan with Mina's husband. If the father wanted a dowry, he should take it up with the husband. So the father went to see the husband and demanded a dowry, which the husband couldn't pay. The upshot of all this was that the father said he would disown Mina until he got the dowry. He told Mina's mother that she was to have nothing to do with Mina or her son until he got his money. Mina and her mother were both in anguish over this.

"Where is the child?" I half expected him to be hidden under Mina's big black scarf.

"At a neighbor's house, but just for today," Laila said.

Later I explained the whole mess to Sam. He groaned at the burden of inserting himself into this situation, but since Mina was a relative—though a distant one—he told me he'd try. The next day Mina arrived at work with her little boy in tow. He was an adorably somber little boy with unruly red hair and kohl-rimmed eyes. "To fight off the evil eye," Laila explained to me.

How could I not let her bring the child to work? I didn't want him hanging around the building, though—there were too many sharp scissors and harsh chemicals. My chowkidor, plumber, and driver lined up to take care of him. I hardly ever saw the little guy during work hours throughout the dowry crisis. But one day a customer came in who worked for an NGO that was mighty insistent its employees stay away from locations that weren't heavily secured. "Pretty young chowkidor out there," she said drily.

I frowned. "He's at least thirty."

"More like eighteen months!"

I went outside to see what was going on and saw that Achmed Zia had locked Mina's son in the chowkidor hut while he went off to run an errand. The little boy was sitting on the floor watching television. I called Zilgai on my cell phone and made him stay with the child until Achmed Zia got back. After we finished work that day, the boy came into the salon with a little broom Zilgai had made for him and helped sweep up the hair.

Sam managed to settle the crisis for a while. I think he may have told all three of Mina's men—father, brother, and husband—that he was going to call in his ex-mujahideen friends and kick some ass if they didn't stop tormenting her. At least that's what he told me. I actually think he just paid the dowry himself.

But a few weeks later, Mina came into work sobbing again. This time she had a bruise that covered almost half her face and finger marks all up and down her arms. Once again she was caught in the crossfire between the men in her family.

An uncle who lived near Tajikistan—not the mean one from her childhood—had come to Kabul to visit the family. He especially wanted to see Mina. So she and her husband and child were invited to dinner at her parents' house. Shortly after they arrived, her husband started to fume because her father and uncle were drinking, and he told Mina that he wanted to leave. The uncle asked him to reconsider; he wanted to spend some time with his favorite niece. Mina put her hand on her husband's arm and begged to stay. This made her husband furious. He grabbed her by the hair, pulled her out of her father's house, then started to beat her right in her father's front yard. Her father stormed out of the house and ordered the husband away. He wasn't incensed because his daughter was being beaten; he knew that Mina's husband often beat her. No, he was mad because he wasn't the one doing the beating. A girl may be beaten by her father in his house but never by someone else in her father's house. So the husband stalked away in a sullen rage, taking their little boy with him. The hysterical Mina had spent the night with her parents.

I put my arms around her. "You can live with me. Or you can leave your husband and live with your parents again!"

She only sobbed harder. "If she does this, she will lose her son," Laila explained. "She can only have her son if she goes back to her husband. But now her father is threatening to dissolve the marriage. It is his right to do this, since the dowry was never paid." Even though Mina didn't want to go back to her old, ugly husband, she knew she'd lose her son if the marriage was dissolved. But once again she had no choice in the matter. Her father was the only one who could decide, just as he was the one who had decided that she had to marry this man.

So Sam talked to the father and the husband a second time. He somehow convinced the father not to force a dissolution. He wasn't related to the husband, so he told him that he would kill him if he ever beat Mina again. She and her son wound up staying with her parents for a week. At the end of that week, the husband came and begged mercy from the father, who gave Mina back to him.

She was still so very unhappy and frightened, even after things went back to normal. I knew Mina wanted to go to beauty school, and I saw that she was naturally gifted at hairdressing, but she had never asked me to let her into the school. So one day I invited her to have tea with me and Sam. "I have a surprise for you," I told her, anticipating the light that would come back into her eyes. "I'm putting you on the roster for my next class."

Sam translated, but Mina only shook her head sadly. "He says cannot do," Sam said. "Husband is not working. They need her housekeeper money."

"I have that all figured out," I exclaimed. "She can still work a few hours a day as a housekeeper, and I'll pay her a full salary. She can pay me back by working in the salon for a few hours every day after she graduates."

"You make her work for free later?" Sam asked incredulously.

"No, I'm only saying that because I don't want her to feel like a charity case! Tell her that if she works hard and is one of the top students in her class, I'll hire her as a full-time hairdresser."

When Sam translated this, Mina smiled again. She cried a little, too, but then was quickly skipping through the compound as if she were a carefree little girl again.

She joined my fifth class, and I immediately became anxious about my promise. I wasn't sure Mina could settle down long enough to learn the craft of hairdressing. She had some natural talent, but she was in a class with a lot of very competitive women who had both talent and drive. I knew that if Mina didn't emerge on the top and join my staff, I'd have not only her disappointment but also Sam's angry family, all the way from Saudi Arabia, to contend with. My teachers were the ones who were going to select the top students, and I couldn't interfere with their decision. It wouldn't be fair to the rest of the girls. But as the class started to wind down their work and move into the testing phase, I became more and more anxious about it. Mina herself was a streak of exuberant energy. A few days before the graduation, she was arranging with my girls in the salon to take still pictures and videos of her during the ceremony. She wanted to send copies to relatives all over Afghanistan.

"I'm so happy!" she exclaimed. "I've never achieved anything before."

Graduation was held on a sunny winter day in the Cleopatra room of the school-salon building. My students started arriving hours early, and how splendid they looked! There were enough rhinestones, sequins, seed pearls, lengths of gold braid, flecks of glitter, and chunks of flashy jewelry in that room to light up the dark side of the moon. My students wore fabulous outfits that they had most likely made themselves, along with some of the pointiest shoes I had ever seen. Mina wasn't wearing bling, but she was wearing breasts—or rather, a pileup of four padded bras underneath her sweater to give the impression of big breasts. My teachers, my Oasis hairdressers, and some of my former students were there, too, sitting in folding chairs along the side of the room like sensible matrons. This was the day for the new graduates to shine, and it seemed that no one else wanted to detract from their luster.

There was going to be dancing, so all the men were banned from the compound and the gate to the street was bolted. The girls brought their favorite CDs and danced for an hour or more, slinking and swaying and shaking around the floor in pairs as the rest clapped and sang along. They wouldn't let anyone sit—I was pulled to the middle of the floor, the teachers were pulled to the middle of the floor, some Western guests were pulled to the middle of the floor. All of this dancing was deeply sensual. As always, I loved watching how the music brought out another side of these girls. It was often the really quiet girls dressed in

282

somber clothes who turned out to be the most provocative dancers. On that day the formula held true: it was the tall, slender girl in a plain white tunic and white pants with her head tightly covered in a white scarf—even indoors—who had the most intense hip movements and suggestively fluttering hands.

We had to let a few men into the salon, but only for a moment. It was just Sam and Achmed Zia, rolling in a huge cake on one of the curler carts. The dancing stopped, and all the girls crowded forward to admire the cake's creamy white icing and real yellow roses. Then I stood in the middle of the room to make my speech.

"I'm so proud of you all." I tried to blink back the tears that would surely ruin my makeup and maybe even my silk dress. "Nothing in the world gives me as much joy as helping you become beauticians. I have never been around a group of women who work so hard to learn and become successful. You have changed my life by allowing me to be your teacher, and I know you will change Afghanistan for the better."

I say this to every class, and it is always true. Their determination always takes my breath away.

Then the girls crowded together and held hands as I got ready to announce the four best students. This is the hardest moment of the day, because they all want this distinction so much. If it were up to me, there wouldn't be any "best" students, but the girls insist on making the class competitive. I looked around at all the faces that had become so dear to me—and read the names from the list that the teachers had given me.

"Shukria!" I said, and the girl with long black hair threaded with sequins shrieked and took her place next to me.

"Mazari!" The slender girl in white stepped forward.

"Tordai!" A quiet girl with short, curly hair joined us in the center of the room.

The other students pressed against one another with agonized faces. I drew a deep breath, then shouted, "Mina!" She jumped up and down, making it hard for the girls who were videotaping her to do their job. I kissed each of the winning students and handed them their prizes: top-quality scissors and thinning shears. Then I handed out gift bags to all the students, my "salons in a box" that would enable them to work as beauticians anywhere: two towels, a blow dryer, large and small curling irons, a mannequin head, five cutting combs, two pick combs, two foiling combs, one styling comb, two hairbrushes, large and small round metal brushes, one washing cape, one cutting cape, one styling cape, one children's cape, one box of foils, one box of gloves, one set of rollers, one set of perm rods, one mirror, and a huge pile of other great stuff for doing hair, nails, and feet. These girls had probably never received such huge gifts in their lives. They shrieked so loudly as they went through their bags that my ears tingled.

Mina did her first pedicure on a paying customer just a few days later. She dipped the woman's feet in and out of the warm water as if they were rare arti-facts, with Bahar crouched next to her whispering encouragement. She did a nice job, too, and danced around later with her very first tip money in her pocket. She was radiantly happy. I had to assume her crummy husband was pleased with the money that she was bringing home.

But one day I found her sobbing in the back of the salon again. Her mother-in-law had moved into the house and was angry at Mina for working. She had riled up her son on the subject, and he was beating her again. Mina was bent over with pain from the beatings and what was probably an ulcer from all the stress. She was desperate to go back and live with her mother, but once again, she knew she would lose her son if her father dissolved her marriage. I decided that, since she was a full-time employee, she was entitled to sick leave, so I sent her to her parents' house. I con-vinced her husband to let her take her son with her for a two-week break. And I prayed that somehow things would work out for her, because I didn't know what else I could do.

Chapter 9

One night in late spring 2005, I was looking out our bedroom window. It had been an unusually dusty day in Kabul, and the sky was a solid gray. There wasn't a sign of stars or even the moon. It made me feel claus-trophobic, as if the air was so crowded with dust that

I couldn't catch a breath. Then I saw something sparkle across the sky.

"Look, Sam," I called across the room to him. "Shooting stars!"

Sam came and stood beside me at the window, then patted me on the shoulder. "No shooting star, Debbie," he said. "Is missiles. Someone is fighting again."

The warm weather was bringing the bad guys out of their winter hibernation. Not long after graduation, Afghanistan and even our own little neighborhood in Kabul were rocked by savagery. There was an attempted kidnapping on my street. Our local Internet café was blown up. A young woman who was working for a new Afghan television station was murdered in her front yard. Everyone suspected her brother of doing it because she was on TV without any head covering. An Italian aid worker named Clementina Cantoni was kidnapped in Kabul as she left her yoga class. There was rioting after news reports that American interrogators at the Guantánamo detention center had flushed a copy of the Koran down the toilet. In the most hideous incident of all, three Afghan women who worked for foreign NGOs were raped, strangled, and then dumped by the side of the road. A note attached to them said that this was what would happen to traitors and whores.

Everyone tried to keep their spirits up and carry on, even though the news was about as depressing as it had ever been. I put an advertisement about the salon in a little Kabul magazine geared to foreigners, and still more customers came, both Westerners and westernized Afghans. I like to say that Afghanistan is a place for mercenaries, missionaries, misfits, and the brokenhearted, and all of these came to my salon for pampering and gossip. I'd have five or six women at a time inside, and it almost seemed as if there was a contest to see who had the most amazing story. I don't think any beautician in the world has a more interesting clientele. These women were doing remarkable things under the most difficult circumstances. One was monitoring the health of pregnant women in villages so remote that she could reach them only by horseback. Another was helping traffic cops figure out how to enable children to navigate Kabul's streets safely. Another was working with Afghan journalists to build a news bureau. I thought what I was doing was important—I was preparing women to prosper in one of the best careers they could have in Afghanistan—and I still do. But sometimes when I listened to my customers talk about their work, I was truly humbled. And I was always happy to see all the business cards that changed hands. I felt that I was giving these women not only a place to relax but also a place to get to know others and maybe even to find partners for some of their projects.

And in the afternoons, after my girls went home, I continued to offer services for Western men. Some of them were the unlikeliest salon customers one could imagine—big, beefy hulks who had been hired to protect the important people in town. People commonly called them "shooters" or "Rambo wannabes," and some of my customers weren't allowed to go anywhere without one or two of these guys at their sides. That was how the shooters wound up as customers. One day I saw a shooter standing by my chowkidor hut, staring down the street, his muscles so huge that he couldn't even fold his arms. He wore something like a thick leather utility belt, except that this one was studded with weapons and ammo. "You want to come and wait in the lobby?" I called out the window.

He turned and shook his head. "Got to keep an eye out for the troublemakers." He had a nice smile that was nearly overshadowed by scruffy, lopsided sideburns.

"Come back when you're off duty. I'll trim up those sideburns for free!"

So he came back after all the beauticians left, and he brought a friend. Soon lots of shooters were showing up after business hours. Some evenings the scene inside the salon was just too funny. Two or three of these guys would come in, lay their guns down near the trays of curlers, and sink into my salon chairs so I could feather their hair, trim their cuticles, or maybe even slather facial masks on them. The fact that my salon capes were pink and featured pictures of Marilyn Monroe completed the picture. Sam loved these evenings. I'd call to tell him when his favorite shooters were in the salon. He'd rush right home so they could swap stories and compare guns.

As the weather got warmer, many of the Westerners

started to hang around the salon after hours, and we roared right into outdoor party season. It turned out that Zilgai the plumber was the best party boy in town. When the music got going, he and his friends would leap to the middle of the yard and treat everyone to some wild Afghan dancing. The Westerners loved these parties because many of them were stuck so much of the time in their own compounds that they never got out into the real Kabul. This wasn't exactly the real Kabul, either, but it was closer than anything they had experienced. I'd hire Afghan bands and have Maryam make Afghan food; Sam would invite his Afghan friends over, and we'd dance into the night. If the Westerners had visitors who'd come to town for a few days to work or consult or whatever, they'd call to ask if the party was on that night.

At one of these parties, I introduced Sam to a guy who was working in the opium poppy eradication program. "He's one of the poppy killers," I said.

"Poppy killers?" Sam's eyes widened. He almost shuddered as he looked at the guy. "Debbie, I thought you loved dogs!"

There was a writhing knot of men just outside my gate. They had come running from all over the street to watch the man with the long black beard berate Achmed Zia, my chowkidor. Even the goats who were pawing through the pile of garbage down the street wandered over to see what was going on. Achmed Zia shot me a worried look. I could see that the bearded guy had been drinking, but I didn't think he was particularly dangerous, just stupid. "What's he making such a fuss about?" I asked Laila.

She cocked her head at the man, then shrugged distastefully. "He is saying that he will kill Achmed Zia."

"Why does he want to kill Achmed Zia?"

"Because you have moved the chowkidor hut from one side of our gate to the other. He says that it is his wall on the other side of the gate."

I pushed through the men and stood next to Achmed Zia. "Tell him it is not his wall!"

Laila barely came up to his shoulder, but she lit right into the man. It was like seeing a Kewpie doll—not only a Kewpie doll but one wearing five-inch-high, toeless heels in order to show off her pink, opalescent toes—launch an assault. The black-bearded man frowned at her, then started yelling again. Laila turned back to me. "He says that he will kill you, Debbie, and the rest of the foreigners who came to your house."

"Well, you tell him I'm going to report him to the police!"

We had been going back and forth like this for a while—he was going to kill us, we were going to bring the law down on him—when one of his brothers arrived. He was a scrawny, sallow guy with a misshapen ear. He just looked at me grimly and pulled his drunken brother back into their compound.

We already knew that these neighbors were trouble. All the rest of our neighbors were friendly and decent, but these two were from a family that was notorious up and down the block. The vegetable dealer around the corner had told me that they would snatch up a handful of beans or a head of cauliflower and just walk off, snickering when he'd protest. The guy who had a little dry goods store at the end of the street— we called him Karzai, because he always wore the same kind of fetal lambskin hat that the president of Afghanistan wore—had complained about them stealing from him, too. Karzai smoked hash all day in his store and was always wreathed in smoke, but these guys were capable of spoiling even his cheerful buzz. My girls had also complained that these neighbors made offensive comments if they passed them on the street.

Sam and I had had our first run-in with these guys a few weeks before. We weren't getting enough electricity, and our lights were so dim at night that it was hard to see anything. We called the city about it, but the guy on the phone kept saying "tomorrow" every time we called. We finally had one of Sam's uncles put in a bigger cable from the main power box to our house. I don't know how he wasn't electrocuted, but lots of things in Kabul are fixed this way. If you can call it fixed: we had brighter lights at night, but there were also flames shooting out of my outlets. Anyway, the bad neighbors were outraged. They stood on the ground shouting at Sam's uncle as he stood there on top of the building wrestling with live wires. We figured they just didn't want him to be able to look down into their compound and see their women.

Not long after that, Sam and I were watching television in our room over the school after work. Suddenly, we heard the sound of about thirty guns being cocked at once. I grabbed my shoes and scarf and was getting ready to run outside to see what was going on, but Sam pulled me back. "You want to get yourself killed?" he hissed. So we went across the hall to a small room where I'd set up the ob-gyn table for massages and peeked out the window. On all the rooftops around our house, men in dark clothes with their guns drawn were creeping toward the bad neighbors' compound. Then they jumped down from the roofs and rushed inside. We watched for about an hour and a half while the guys in dark clothes came in and out. The women of the house were swarming around one of the outbuildings, and we could hear them crying. Then we saw the guys in dark clothes drag a bunch of handcuffed men outside, put them into cars, and drive them away.

The next day I was going nuts. The hairdresser in me just *had* to find out what had happened. I put on my scarf and went to the tailor, but he didn't know what had happened. I went to the flower shop and the little beauty salon up the street, but they didn't know. I went to Karzai. He jumped up and saluted me as always, but he didn't know. He probably didn't even know what day it was.

Finally, Achmed Zia found out what had happened. The police had suspected that our bad neighbors were connected to the Clementina Cantoni kidnapping, so what we saw the night before was a raid. The police didn't find Clementina, but they found a cache of weapons and drugs. They also found two Afghans who had been kidnapped. That was their lucky day— the police would probably never have bothered looking for them. But it made those of us who lived on the street realize just how bad these guys really were.

About a week later, and after the bearded thug came and yelled at us about the chowkidor hut, I overslept and stumbled downstairs in my pajamas, even more groggy than usual. The first thing I saw was Achmed Zia with blood running down his chin. He had punch marks all over his face, his shirt was torn, and his lip was split open. "What the hell happened?" I asked. "Who beat you up?" He didn't need a translator. He just pointed morosely down the street, toward the bad neighbors' house.

I've never been a morning person. I need my coffee, my cigarettes, and a little bit of downtime before I start my day. I get really pissy without those things. If people want to agitate me, they have an easier time doing it in the morning, especially if I'm at that certain dangerous point in my cycle. I went into a mindless rage. I grabbed my head scarf and Sam's machine gun, and with all my staff trailing along behind me, I stomped down to the bad neighbors' gate in my pajamas and started kicking it. No one came, but I could see the gate gaping open, as if it were barely latched. And finally, I just pushed it and went inside.

The bad neighbors' women streamed out, and I

demanded to know where their men were. Not here, they said. I kept shouting that I wanted their men. I could see all the neighbors crowding around the gate. I was still shouting, using up every word I knew in Dari—probably even the words for "carpet" and "hairbrush." Then three men pushed through the crowd at the gate and came inside. Two of them were the ones who had hassled us about the chowkidor hut, and the other was a tall, handsome guy I had seen on the street before. I knew they were brothers, even though they didn't look at all alike. The three of them just stood there, smirking. That made me even madder.

"Which one of them hurt Achmed Zia?" I asked my staff. No one seemed to know or want to say, so I grabbed the good-looking one by the shirt. I turned my head slightly, so I could see my staff. "You guys go call the police. I'm going to make sure they stay here."

Then things got a little humorous. My staff stood there with their faces crinkled up as Laila translated. They talked among themselves. It seemed that no one knew how to call the police. No one ever called the police in Kabul because doing so was pointless—they never came. And there's no all-purpose emergency number like 911 to call in Afghanistan. So all of my staff except Achmed Zia wandered off to try to figure out how to call the police station, leaving me with the criminal brothers at gunpoint. At least they were no longer smirking. Finally, the police actually arrived. I don't know if it was because I was an American or because they already had an interest in the bad-neighbor family. The other neighbors were more surprised by the appearance of the police than they had been by my assault on the criminals' house in my pajamas.

The police took the three men away, and I went home to get my coffee, dress, and start working on customers. I was right in the middle of putting highlights in a missionary's hair when Laila came running into the salon. "The criminals' mother is here!" she announced.

Clustered outside our gate were the bad guys' mother, grandmother, several aunts and wives, and all sorts of children. Their whole extended crime family had arrived to plead for me to drop the charges. Their mother was a tall woman with a sad, ravaged face, dressed as if she were going to a funeral. "I'd dress like I was going to a funeral, too, if I had sons like hers," I told Laila. "Tell her that I will not drop the charges."

The mother kept trying to take my hands, but I put them behind my back. She spoke to Laila in low, placating tones, but Laila snapped right back at her. "She says that she will have her sons write you a letter of apology!" Laila was clearly enjoying her role as the intermediary.

"What good will that do me?"

"She says her sons will not bother you again."

"Since when did a woman in this country have any

control over her men? They probably treat her as bad as they treat everyone else."

I'm not sure if Laila translated this, but she said something and all the thugs' women started to talk at once. "They ask if you will drop the charges as a favor to them."

"Nai!" I shook my head at the crowd of women. "Nai, nai! Your sons are nothing but thugs, and they've been bullying everyone on the street for too long. If I can get them into prison, that's where they're going."

I went back inside and continued working, but I could tell by the noise coming in the door that the women hadn't gone home. If anything, it sounded as if more people had joined them. I walked to the front door and looked outside. Sure enough, there were now about twenty people milling around outside the gate. Achmed Zia and Zilgai stood facing them with their arms crossed, and I could see Laila scolding an old guy with a fat gray turban. I was starting to feel as if my house was under siege and, for the first time that day, wondered if we were safe. Plus, all these damn people were interfering with business! One of my customers called to say that she and her driver had cruised past the gate but were afraid to stop when they saw the huge crowd. "It looks like you have some kind of riot outside your house," she said. "Unless you're giving away some really great shampoo samples."

I got on my phone and called Sam. I called the American Embassy. I called the Afghan women I knew whose husbands worked in the government. I called the minister of the interior. I tried to find someone who could help me with this. While all these people were scrambling around trying to come up with the name of someone who might be able to keep these guys in jail and prevent their family from killing me, I got a call from the police asking me to come and tell them more about what had happened.

Down at the station, a big policeman in an olive drab uniform greeted me as if we were already friends. "Sit, Miss Debbie, sit!" he said, gesturing to a chair. Another policeman came into the room with tea. Through Laila, we exchanged the usual pleasantries about the weather and the traffic. Then he got down to business.

"We know these men well," he said. "We think they're part of the same crime family who kidnapped Clementina Cantoni. We didn't find evidence of her in their house, but we still think they're connected."

"Are they terrorists?"

"Yes, but not Taliban. These ones just do it for the money and the power."

I grimaced. "So you're going to send them to prison?"

"We will try. But they have told me they wish to press charges against you, too."

"Against me?" I was wondering if maybe I had yanked off too many chest hairs from the one I'd grabbed. I couldn't figure out any other way I might have hurt them.

The policeman reddened a little and looked at the papers on his desk. "They wish to file immorality charges. They say that you stand naked on your balcony."

Laila burst out laughing. "Very funny," I told her. "Tell him to ask those guys what the tattoo on my ass says."

I don't think she chose to translate that for the embarrassed policeman. I told him this charge couldn't be true. I didn't stand naked on my balcony, not ever. And even if I had, those creeps wouldn't have been able to see me from their compound. He nodded his head, as if he were ashamed that he'd even brought this unpleasant matter up.

On the way back to our van, I saw some of the international peacekeeping troops hanging around, leaning against their tank. I had met one of them somewhere, and I stopped to explain what was going on. I told him I was afraid that the thugs' family might try to get back at me for having them arrested. "Next time you're out patrolling, can you come down my street and stop in front of their house? Maybe point that big gun at them?"

He gave me a funny look.

"Hey, it's not like I'm fighting with my neighbors because they let their grass get too high. They're criminals! Ask the cops."

He shrugged. "I'll check with my boss."

Laila and I were about to climb back in the van when one of the policemen came running out after us. "Ah, I see you have a van here," he said.

When we nodded, he explained that the police station did not have a vehicle large enough to transport my three thug neighbors to the prison facility across town, which was where they belonged. Since I was the one pressing the charges, would it be possible for me to help the police by driving the thugs over to the prison in my van—with a security presence from the police, of course? He was a very small policeman with an anxious smile. I unaccountably found myself saying yes. He dashed back into the station, then returned with the three suspected kidnappers at the end of his gun. After they climbed into the middle seat of my van, he jumped in and closed the door behind him. So he was my security presence!

This may have been my most insane experience in Afghanistan. The little policeman was giving directions to my driver. The thugs were talking on their cell phones to their family, pausing every once in a while to turn around and smile in a comradely way at me and Laila, who were sitting way in the back. Finally, one of them turned around and handed me his cell phone. "Hello, Debbie!" a voice on the phone said. "I understand you have some trouble with my brothers. How about you let them go this time and it never happens again?"

From the neighborhood gossip, I knew that they had another brother—and he was reputed to be even bigger and badder than they were. He was supposedly hiding because the police wanted him for some other crime. I clicked the phone shut and tossed it back into the middle seat. The little policeman was carrying on a conversation with my driver about the best way to reach the prison—which roads had too much traffic at this time of day, which ones had terrible potholes, that kind of thing. He was paying no attention to the thugs, who were getting bolder and bolder in their entreaties to me. The handsome one turned around and patted me on the knee. "We're not so bad. Why, we gave one of your friends a ride to Wardak and we didn't kill her!"

The bearded one turned around. "If you don't let us go, this will be a big problem for us. You'll see—we will be good neighbors from now on."

Finally, I called Sam on my cell phone and told him what was happening. He said, "You are a crazy woman! Get out of the car before they kidnap *all* of you."

As it turned out, we were only a few blocks from our street. So I told the driver to go home and let all of us out, Laila and I as well as the little policeman and the thugs. Sam called the police and told them to come back and get their prisoners, but they never did. The thugs went home and were welcomed noisily by their family. I think Achmed Zia finally had to give the little policeman a ride home.

A few days later, five tanks from the international peacekeeping force rumbled down our street and groaned to a halt in front of my compound. I ran to the bad neighbors' house and banged on the gate until one of the brothers stuck his head out. I pointed to the tanks and told him that if his family bullied anyone on the street again, I'd have their house blown up. Of course, I didn't really have that power, but they didn't know it. To my knowledge, no one in the neighborhood has had any trouble with them since. They became as cordial and well mannered as my old neighbors back in Michigan. And as far as I knew, the police never had enough evidence to connect them with any terrorist activities.

It was a Thursday afternoon, the time of the week when my beauticians did nothing but joke and twit one another about sex. Friday is the beginning of the weekend in Afghanistan, so practically the whole country has sex on Thursday night. Friday is called *joma,* Thursday night is called *rozi joma.* On that evening, the women cleanse themselves thoroughly, remove their pubic hair, and prepare to give it up to their husbands. In keeping with national custom, my girls would start to giggle and wink every Thursday afternoon and ask one another if they were ready for rozi joma. Bahar usually grimaced and turned her head when the teasing started. She'd tell everyone she hated sex, and she hated her husband.

But this afternoon Bahar sat in front of one of the mirrors and started freshening up her makeup. Baseera leaned over her shoulder and made kissy noises and said something so lewd that it made Topekai blush. But instead of grimacing, Bahar got a huge smile on her face. She sashayed around the room while all the rest of them clapped their hands and called out, "Rozi joma!"

I pulled Laila aside. "I thought she hated her husband."

"She has fallen in love with him again," Laila assured me.

"How can that be, when he's so mean to her?"

Laila flashed her Kewpie doll eyes at me. "Oh, Debbie, he's changed! She took him to a doctor and he takes some medication for his problems. Now he's a good man again."

I first met Bahar when I was interviewing prospective students for the beauty school. It was one of those days near the end of winter when the sky all of a sudden dumped a foot of snow on the city. There was no snowplowing equipment in Kabul—still isn't, to my knowledge—so life pretty much came to a halt. When people attempted the roads in their cars, they just slid into the sewers and made an even bigger mess of the streets.

We had over one hundred applicants for the class, but because of the snow, only about twenty showed up that day for the interviews. I knew those twenty had to be really serious, and that gave them an extra edge. The funny thing is that I probably wouldn't have admitted Bahar based on her history. She was already making about forty dollars a month—not a bad salary for Kabul—as a kindergarten teacher and had no background in hairdressing. I tried to admit only the women who both really needed this opportunity and could profit the most from it. Women with jobs usually went to the bottom of my list, so that was a lucky snowfall for Bahar.

She was about twenty-eight then, with a sweet face and gentle manner. She soon became one of the very best students. Bahar had such a nice way with people that I knew she'd do well as both a teacher and a beautician in my salon. This was a bright and ambitious class, though, and there were four women who would also do well as either teachers or beauticians. So I started getting more in-depth histories from them. When I heard Bahar's story, I realized I had to help free her from her crazy husband. Like so many women, she was still threatened by terrorism, even though the Taliban were gone. She faced it daily from the man she had married.

I think that he had once been a good husband and that she had loved him. They lived with his parents, who were quite old, and Bahar happily cared for his parents as well as their two children. Her husband had been a police officer in Kabul before the Taliban came to power, and they let him stay on in the job. But this quickly turned out to be very tough for him. He was often required to enforce their ridiculous edicts about white shoes and music and such. Worse, he had to stand by and watch as the Taliban brutalized men and women for the tiniest infractions and help maintain order during public executions. At some point, he ran afoul of a group of Taliban and they turned on him. They beat him so badly that he suffered a brain injury that caused all sorts of complications—depression, memory loss, and uncontrolled rage. He couldn't work anymore.

He became a monster. He'd lock Bahar and their children in one of the rooms in the family house and leave, sometimes for days. His parents were in the rest of the house, but they were so senile that they didn't notice anything was wrong. There was still food in the house, so the parents foraged and fed themselves. But Bahar and the children had nothing to eat. Worse still, Bahar was pregnant with their third child. Her husband locked her up without food so often that the baby was starving in her womb. He beat her often, too. There was no one she could turn to for help—certainly not their Taliban overlords, since they never thought wives had valid grievances against husbands. Bahar's third child was born with disabilities, doubtless because of this abuse. She is six years old now and still can't walk.

When the Taliban were driven out, Bahar was finally able to get out of the house. She fought with her husband and told him she was going to work because he couldn't work. Her family finally had enough to eat again when she got the job as a kindergarten teacher.

She started working at the salon after graduation. Her specialty was manicures and pedicures, and her light, gentle touch pleased the customers. They tipped her well, and her monthly income shot up from forty to nearly four hundred dollars. The only problem was still her husband. He used to call her cell phone all day long to demand that she explain what she was doing. Sometimes she had to rush out in the middle of the day because he was in the grip of one of his rages and was beating their children. She'd startle and flinch when her phone rang because she was still so afraid of him.

But as she made more money, Bahar became stronger and more independent. There were several times when I heard her speak sharply to her husband when he called and tell him not to bother her. Finally, she stopped answering the phone if he called too many times. Even when he wasn't calling, she expressed nothing but disdain for him.

Then one day Bahar asked me if she could take a week off from work. She said she'd been saving her money to take someone in her family to an important doctor in Pakistan. I figured she was taking her child, so I didn't ask further. But at the end of the day when Bahar was primping for rozi joma, I followed her outside to take a look at her husband. He stood waiting in his clean, dark shalwar kameez, his beard neatly trimmed, his face kind and proud. I didn't even recognize him. Somehow the doctor in Pakistan had managed to return him to some version of the man he had been before the Taliban beat the decency out of him. I had never met this version, but clearly, Bahar was overjoyed to have him back.

The satellite phone rang in the middle of the night. On the third ring, I crawled across Sam's body to answer it. It was some man speaking Dari, so I knew the call didn't have anything to do with trouble in Michigan. But I had other worries when the phone rang at night, so I jostled Sam and laid the phone on top of his ear. "It's not about Robina, is it?"

He raised his head and listened. "Not about Robina. Nothing wrong."

Still, I had a hard time going back to sleep. I always worried about Robina and her sisters at night.

I had met Robina a few months after we moved to the Oasis. She walked into the compound one morning as I was sitting outside drinking my coffee. None of my beauticians had arrived yet, and I thought she was a customer. She wore a stylish blue jacket and shoes that looked as if they had come from Italy. I thought she might have been one of the UN workers— maybe from France or Spain—who had dodged security precautions and braved the dust to get a manicure. But when I looked her over at a closer distance, I could see that she didn't need a manicure. Everything about her was already impeccably groomed.

"Good morning," she said. "This is Oasis?" She held out a copy of the *Afghan Scene*, the local magazine that ran my ad for the salon.

I nodded.

"I am here for job?"

Lots of Afghan women had asked for jobs in the salon, but I didn't want to hire anyone who hadn't been through some sort of beauty school. I made an exception, though, for Robina. I could tell just by looking at her that she would know how to cater to my Western clientele.

Robina was thirty-three and had recently returned to Afghanistan from many years of refugee life in Iran. She came to me as an experienced hairdresser. She added a whole new look to the Oasis, with her heart-shaped face, high cheekbones, artfully highlighted red hair, and fashionable clothes. Although Topekai had a strong following by then, many of my customers weren't always sure if my other two beauticians could fix their hair the way they wanted. In part, this was because Baseera and Bahar didn't have a high-fashion look. My customers didn't hesitate a second when I told them that Robina would handle their cuts or color. Customers like to see a beautician who has the sort of look about her that they want themselves.

But it wasn't just Robina's look that made her different from my other beauticians. Everything about her was different—everything, that is, except the difficulty of being a woman in Afghanistan.

Robina's family had left Kabul when she was five years old, just before the war against the Russians started and long before anyone had even heard of the Taliban. They'd settled in Iran because her father was a great fan of Shah Mohammed Reza Pahlavi, a pro-Western ruler whose modernization efforts included suffrage for women. But the shah also generated huge resentment among both Islamic clerics and democrats. His overthrow in 1979 paved the way for Ayatollah Khomeini and the revolution that would wind up creating an Islamic republic in Iran. Robina's father, however, saw the shah as a force of enlightenment in the Middle East. He even named one of his daughters after the shah's third wife.

Growing up in Iran, Robina had advantages that most of my girls couldn't have imagined. She had loving parents who weren't at all displeased to have three daughters; they doted on their daughters as much as they did their three sons. Her family was also fairly prosperous, so she and her sisters never went without food or other necessities. Her father was a wholesaler of clothes and perfume, and he'd bring home samples to his wife and daughters. The women of the family covered themselves with big scarves when they went out, especially as Iran became a harsher climate for women. But at home they wore slacks and short-sleeved shirts, just as if they were girls in Michigan.

And unlike most parents of Afghan girls, Robina's mother and father weren't about to force her to marry anyone she didn't like. Iranian boys asked for her hand; when she didn't want them, her father sent them away. Afghans who lived in Iran asked for her hand; when she didn't want them, her father sent them away, too. Afghans who lived back in Kabul asked for her hand. Her father begged her to say no, because he couldn't stand the idea of her moving so far away. She did say no and continued to live at home. There, she and her sisters had a kind of social life that simply didn't exist in their homeland. They were allowed to go out with groups of young men and women—

together!—for picnics, hikes, and tame little parties.

Iran had welcomed Afghan immigrants at first, but the welcome ran out as more and more Afghans poured across the border during the wars. Soon the Iranian government began slapping restrictions on the Afghans living within its borders. It became difficult for them to find jobs, own homes or cars, or even have telephones. Robina told me that many Iranians became hostile to the Afghans in their midst, complaining that Afghans were taking all the good jobs and making the schools too crowded.

Robina's younger sisters wound up getting pieces of a university education, but Robina went instead to special courses run by the United Nations to teach dressmaking to Afghan women. While she was there, Robina got a reputation as someone who was outspoken about the ill treatment of Afghans in Iran. She was warned that she could be killed for talking like that. She continued to have strong opinions and express them but finally gave up dressmaking. Her father was afraid she would ruin her eyes, and besides, she found a beauty salon near her home that was willing to train her as a hairdresser.

This caused problems within the Afghan immigrant community, because many there thought beauty salons—especially Iranian beauty salons—were fronts for brothels. So Robina became less connected to the Afghan community and more connected to her new profession. Even though the government was cracking down on Iranians who gave jobs to Afghans, the woman who ran the salon looked out for Robina. If a government official sniffed around the neighborhood to see if there were any Afghans employed there, the salon owner would swear that Robina was either a friend or a customer.

But things continued to become harder for Robina and other Afghans in Iran. Her father lost his job as a wholesaler. He went into an industrial business with an Iranian but was robbed by his partner and had no legal redress. Two of her brothers became tailors, but they had a hard time getting enough work to support the whole family. Robina was just starting in the salon business but hadn't built up enough of a clientele to help the family much. Then both of her younger sisters found jobs in one of the only areas open to Afghan girls: they worked as babysitters to a British family doing business in Iran.

After two years the British family told Robina's sisters that they were being transferred to the United States. The sisters were distraught about losing both their jobs and their kind foreign friends, but the Brits said that they'd love to have the girls follow them to America and continue working as their nannies. They told them that Robina could even come along as a chaperone. The Brits would try to find sponsors for the girls, and then they would all have to get visas. The big drawback to this plan was that there wasn't an American embassy in Iran. It had been closed since the hostage crisis following the shah's overthrow. If they wanted to get visas, the girls would have to go back to Afghanistan and work through the American Embassy there.

Since it was only getting harder to be an Afghan in Iran anyway, the three sisters decided to seize this opportunity for a better life in America, even if it meant a brief stopover in Kabul. They had heard only bad things about Kabul—about how dirty and crowded it was, about all the destruction from the wars, about the poverty. They had heard it was the worst place in the world for women, but they decided to take a chance. Their mother wept and begged them to stay in Iran, but their father trusted that they were strong and smart enough to make their way. He figured it was just for a few months, until they got their visas for America.

So Robina and her sisters did what just about no Afghan women ever do: they traveled on their own, without a male escort. They were met at the airport by relatives and stayed with them for a few weeks. Then they found their own apartment and moved into it, only the three of them.

It's hard for Westerners to understand just how revolutionary this was. It's almost a rite of passage in America for girls to move to another city and get an apartment with friends as young adults. But in Afghanistan, this sort of independence was unheard of—it was an abrupt departure from the way things have been done for thousands of years. It was the kind of thing that sent out shock waves around the sisters wherever they went. Just about everyone assumed that they had to be prostitutes if they were living on their own. When they interviewed for jobs and people found out that they lived on their own, they got phone calls from the men at the companies wanting to take them out to dinner, out to parties. This is the kind of behavior Afghans associate with prostitutes.

I'll bet ten thousand dollars there was not another group of girls living on their own like this anywhere in Afghanistan. I'll bet there still is not. Western girls, maybe. Afghans who had been living in the West for most of their lives, possibly. But not Afghan girls who had never left the East. In a way, Robina and her sisters had been made more vulnerable because they had been raised by parents with progressive ideas about women. The problem was that these ideas didn't match the culture to which they were returning.

Ultimately, their plan didn't work. The Brits lost their jobs in America and moved back home, so Robina and her sisters had nowhere to go. They couldn't go back to live in Iran because they had given up their identification cards when they moved to Kabul, and it was so expensive for Afghans to get visas for Iran that the sisters even had a hard time visiting their parents. Basically, Iran just didn't want them anymore. The sisters were forced to stay in Kabul and continue to live on their own. They knew it was dangerous, so with the help of foreign friends they raised enough money to send the youngest sister to college in India. Robina didn't want to leave until there was enough money to send her other sister away, too.

You would think that other Afghan women would be full of sympathy for Robina and her sisters, but you'd be wrong. Even *my* girls, who were themselves breaking so many barriers by going to school and becoming breadwinners, even they looked coldly at Robina when they heard that she and her sisters lived alone. Then Robina made it worse by breaking another taboo: she went out on a couple of dates with a Western man. That was enough to make all the rest of my girls shun her as if she had the avian flu.

This wasn't the only time there had been divisions among the girls, although I was often clueless about these tensions as they were going on. In a way, I had deliberately worsened these divisions by making sure each class was diverse. Back when I was struggling just to keep the beauty school running, I hadn't even known that it *wasn't* diverse. Then Sam walked in one day when the third class was in session, looked around, and scowled. "Why is everyone in the school Hazara?" he asked. I didn't realize that they were, but it turned out that two of my teachers were Hazara, and they had helped me select a class that was all Hazara. From that point on, Sam sat in on all the interviews and helped me make sure that I wasn't inadvertently favoring one ethnic group over another. We balanced each class not only by ethnicity but also by religion and region. But the ancient conflicts among these groups sometimes spilled over into the school and salon. Then I'd have to stand in front of the students and give them a Rodney King lecture.

"Can't we all just get along?" I would plead with them. "How is Afghanistan going to prosper if those of us in this one little place can't put our differences aside?"

I didn't notice how the others slighted Robina until Laila pointed it out to me. How they would suddenly dart into the lunchroom and leave her behind. How they would be whispering in another room while Robina was reading a book, trying to ignore them. Sometimes I didn't even need Laila to tell me when things were amiss. I'd find Robina sobbing in the back room. Things had to be pretty bad for her to drop her highly polished, professional demeanor.

The tension inside the salon finally eased for Robina, at least a little. Maybe it was because Laila decided to throw her bantamweight ferocity in Robina's corner. Laila was the only other unmarried woman working for me. She also had progressive parents, who wanted her to continue her studies and weren't going to force her to marry anyone she didn't want. But unlike Robina, Laila hadn't grown up in comfort. During the wars, her family had fled to Pakistan, where life was tooth-and-nail tough. There Laila was a wage earner even as a tiny child. She spent five hours a day weaving carpets that paid the family's monthly rent. Now Laila was living with her parents in Kabul, but she knew how tough it was to be a single woman out on the streets every day. To keep the men from bothering her, she fixed a glare on her face as she headed out her parents' door every morning and maintained it until she got to my compound. Sometimes it took a while for her face to relax into a smile. She was a formidable ally for Robina.

Still, Robina needed bigger guns to protect her and her sister outside the salon. They had chosen what seemed to be a perfect apartment. It was in a secure location—right next to the Ministry of Agriculture— with a locked entrance and a nice landlord. But the landlord became less and less nice as he realized that no father or brother or husband was coming to take his rightful place in their household.

Robina had been telling me every day of the landlord's escalating unfriendliness. Then the phone rang one morning when the salon was closed and school was getting ready to start. I was clamping mannequin heads to the countertops, and I didn't even recognize the voice at the other end of the phone. "They push me," the voice gasped. "They push me down the stairs!"

"Robina?"

She had woken up that morning to find that there was no water coming into the house. Robina was famously clean—she came to the salon every day with her own mug wrapped in foil—so the thought of not being able to wash was intolerable to her. She knocked on one of her neighbors' doors to ask if they had water, which they did. She went to see the landlord to ask why the neighbors had water and she did not. He shrugged in a sullen way. She asked if the water valve to their apartment had somehow been shut off, because this is often what landlords do when they want to harass a tenant. Then he exploded with rage, calling her and her sisters whores and donkeys—the latter because he was Pashtun and they were Hazaras. His whole family poured out of their apartment and pushed her until she fell down the stairs.

Sam and I went right over. I took some bandages and ointment and a package of Wet Ones that I saved for emergencies. Sam went to yell at the landlord. We had brought Zilgai along with us, and he turned the water back on. Sam later went back to see the landlord with a friend who is a general, who told the landlord that Robina was a distant cousin and that he wanted the landlord to look out for her. Generals carry a lot of weight around here. Better to come with a general than to come with a policeman.

Things were better for a while, but the fact was that Robina and her sister were in mortal danger. They didn't belong in Afghanistan, even though it should have been their country as much as anyone else's. There are many kinds of terrorism, and Robina and her sister had to brave the persistent daily kind aimed at women who break away from the social order. Maybe all the different kinds of terrorism are, in their essence, the same. I don't know. All I know is that every time the phone rang when Robina wasn't in the salon, I was afraid someone had come after her and her sister again. I was afraid they'd been raped or murdered or both.

Chapter 10

Maryam the cook hadn't come to work for the second day in a row. As lunchtime drew near, I could see some of the students looking longingly at the door of the manicure-pedicure room, where Maryam usually set out their food. They'd been doing spiral perms on our long-haired mannequin heads for a good two hours now, winding twenty-inch strands of hair in hundreds of small lavender perm rods, taking care not to twist or crimp the ends of the hair, making sure that each curled strand had the exact same tension and angle. Some of the students were so tired that they looked as if they needed to put their arms in slings. I knew they had to take a lunch break, so I gave up on Maryam once again. I called Achmed Zia and told him to go out and buy Kabul burgers—nan wrapped around salad, fried potatoes, hard-boiled eggs, and some kind of meat—for all of us.

Topekai and Baseera were sitting next to each other on green plastic lawn chairs, momentarily oblivious to the hour as well as to the crush of students around them. Topekai held both hands in front of her and turned them as if she were steering a large, unwieldy rocket ship through space. Her eyes widened with horror and then clamped shut as she described the scene to Baseera in rapid Dari. She squealed and shuddered with pretend impact, and the two of them laughed. The students stared, and I wondered for a

second if they thought this demonstration had anything to do with spiral perms. Then I remembered
that—unlike me—the students could actually understand everything being said, even if they weren't yet
familiar with the situation. Topekai and her husband
had purchased a car. She was learning to drive and had
smashed into something.

I had asked Topekai and Baseera to come and teach
class since one of my regular teachers was sick. I also
thought it would be great for the students to get to
know two successful Afghan hairdressers. "Tell them
about giving your husband money," I instructed
Baseera, wanting to distract the students until Achmed
Zia returned with the food. So she told them how she
used to have to beg her husband for as little as twenty
afghanis. Sometimes he wouldn't give it to her, and
sometimes he couldn't. After she graduated from
beauty school and started to work for me, she stopped
asking him for money. Not only that, she realized that
he sometimes had no money. So she had started to
leave the equivalent of twenty dollars in his pocket
every now and then. She never outright gave him the
money, because that would shame him. Still, he knew
she made more money than he did and he seemed to
appreciate it. In fact, they were also pooling their
money to buy a car. Both Baseera and Topekai had
more freedom than most Afghan women. They
worked as late as they had to every day and shared the
chores of child rearing and housekeeping with their
husbands. Topekai had always been a strong woman,

but in the three years that I'd known Baseera, she'd also become strong.

I wasn't sure how much Baseera told the students about her new life, but they looked impressed. Some looked disbelieving as well. Three of them had just moved back to Afghanistan after spending most of their lives as refugees in Pakistan. They had grown up hearing stories about the wonders of Afghanistan from their parents, but they were finding their homeland harsh and unyielding. Back in Pakistan, there was electricity all day and all night long, as well as reliably running water, decent roads, and good schools. They didn't have to cover their heads and account for their every move outside the home. But Pakistan had started to crack down on Afghan refugees and make it harder for them to find jobs, so their fathers and hus-bands had insisted that the girls accompany them back to Kabul. There was 40 percent unemployment in Kabul, but at least no one was telling the men that they couldn't apply for jobs just because they were Afghan. For these girls, though, the move was a cruel step backward. They had told me that the beauty school was the one thing that gave them hope.

Achmed Zia finally returned with the Kabul burgers. The girls rushed into the manicure-pedicure room, once again cheerful and chatty. As I trailed along after them, I saw that the floor in the lobby hadn't been swept yet. Shaz hadn't swept it yesterday, either, and there was already so much dust on the floor that I could see where the girls had disturbed it in their dash to lunch. "Where is Shaz?" I asked Topekai and Baseera. "I know she came in today, but why hasn't she done anything with this floor?"

I saw a look pass between them, and I groaned. "Not out meeting Farooq, is she?"

"Nai, Debbie," Baseera said quickly. "I think she works in your private rooms now." She pointed to the house in the compound next to the beauty school, where Sam and I had moved our quarters. The beauty school and the salon took up all the space in the original house now.

"Folding scarves again?" It seemed as though every time I went looking for Shaz these days, she was sitting on the floor of my closet folding my scarves or my underwear. "Why does she fuss so much with my damn scarves?"

Again I saw a look pass between them. I set off to find Shaz, resolving to talk to her about Farooq one more time.

About four months earlier, I had noticed what seemed like a positive change in Shaz. She came into work one morning wearing lipstick, a touch of kohl, and a pretty new green paisley scarf. When she removed it, I saw that her short, dark hair had been brushed carefully and arranged with two sparkly combs. I called all the beauticians over to exclaim about how nice she looked. She didn't exactly look pretty—her skin was pitted from hardships I couldn't even imagine, her eyes and mouth were too small for the fullness of her face, and she had the body of a rugby player. Still, there is something alluring about the care that a woman takes to make herself look nicer. Maybe it's the attention to detail, or maybe it's the hopefulness implied by the act of enhancing what you already have. In any case, I was touched and charmed by Shaz's new look. I thought it showed that she cared a little bit more about herself. Foolishly, I congratulated myself for having had something to do with it.

Usually all the staff left together at the end of the day, and Achmed Zia would drive them home in our van. A few months later, I went into the salon one day after I thought everyone had gone home and found Shaz still working on her hair. "Did Achmed Zia leave without you?"

I was ready to fly into battle on her account. I thought I'd seen the other girls act a little snippy toward her in the last few weeks. Sometimes hostilities among the girls were expressed beneath the threshold of my limited Dari; sometimes all I caught was a haughty look or a mean tone of voice that somehow made it through the clamor. Sometimes I'd talk one of the girls into telling me what was going on. More often, they kept these rivalries and tensions to themselves. They never complained to me about one another, even if the grievance was legitimate. Even if it somehow affected me or the beauty school.

"Why didn't they wait for you?" I demanded.

"No problem, Debbie," she said, blushing. She put on her coat and scarf, patted me on the arm, and walked out to the gate. Something about the way she patted my arm—as if she were telling me to stay behind—made me suspicious, so I followed her. She heard me kick a pebble across the driveway and rushed back to pat me on the arm again. "No problem," she repeated anxiously. She backed toward the gate smiling and waving at me, but I kept following her. "What's going on?" I asked. "What don't you want me to see?"

Finally, she turned and dashed through the gate. Outside the compound walls, a battered black sedan was shuddering into gear. She climbed into the backseat and pulled her scarf over her face. Before the car drove off, the driver turned to look at me in a familiar way and gave me a little wave. He was as battered as his car, with a broken nose and a heavy mustache made crooked by a scar on his lip. He nodded his head and then sped away.

The next morning, I grabbed Laila as soon as she walked in the gate. "Who was that man picking up Shaz last night?"

Laila was still scowling from her walk past the bad neighbors' house. She pulled off her head scarf and regarded me coolly. "He is her boyfriend, Debbie. His name is Farooq."

I remembered having heard the name. "I thought he was her cousin!"

"Cousin can be boyfriend, too," she reminded me. "But he is not even cousin."

"How long has this been going on?"

"I don't know. Long time, maybe."

"Why didn't you guys tell me?"

She just shrugged as she folded her scarf into a neat, tightly pinched little rectangle.

Since Shaz was married, this was a serious breach of decorum—the kind that could get her killed. If her husband found out, he could bring charges against her and have her stoned to death. I was furious at Shaz for being so stupid. I planted myself near the gate so I could talk with her as soon as she arrived. I was planning to tell her that she had to choose between Farooq and her job. But when she slipped in the gate, I felt so bad for her that I burst out crying. She was still wearing her jaunty little bit of makeup, but it couldn't disguise her sadness. I knew how it felt to be trapped in a bad marriage; I knew how one can yearn so terribly for love.

I could see a few of the other girls watching us from the window, so I pulled Shaz to the back of the compound. I didn't want to shame her any more by having them watch or Laila translate for me. Laila and the others were sometimes very uncompromising in their judgment of women who stepped outside the sexual boundaries, no matter how much they liked to joke about sex. If this weren't Afghanistan, I would probably have been happy that poor, homely Shaz—stuck with a grasping, old husband in another city—had found a boyfriend. But it was Afghanistan, and I didn't want to risk losing her to a mob. "No Farooq!" I whispered to her. I picked up a stone from the ground and pantomimed it bashing my head in. "No car with

Farooq, no phone with Farooq. Too dangerous!"

She nodded and walked to my house wearily. She removed her pretty green paisley scarf and wrapped a gray rag over her hair to protect it from the dust that she would raise shaking out carpets. The other girls looked at me as I entered the salon but knew enough not to say anything critical of her.

Of course, my pantomime with the stone didn't change things. Although I made sure that Shaz joined the others in the van for a few days, I didn't have time to do this every day. Besides, she managed to see Farooq even when she did ride in the van. Achmed Zia came to tell me one day that she had asked him to let her off at a new location. When he looked in his rearview mirror, he saw her getting into Farooq's car. And she talked to Farooq on her cell phone whenever she could. I'd often catch her hiding in an empty corner of the house talking to him, her face lit with guilty pleasure. I even caught her once using my cell phone to talk to him because the battery on hers was dead. "No Farooq!" I shouted, but I saved the number so that I would know if she ever tried to call him again on my phone.

As I walked upstairs to my closet, I expected to find Shaz talking to Farooq. But she was sitting on the floor with a dreamy look on her face. She had emptied out the contents of my scarf box and my underwear drawer and was folding everything up into neat little piles. "Didn't you just do that yesterday?" I asked.

She stared at me as if she was trying to remember who I was. "Nai."

"Are you feeling okay?"

She still looked confused.

"Do you need some tea?"

"Nai."

"Come downstairs and sweep the floor when you're finished here." I pantomimed this, and she nodded. She started to get up, then sank back down again. Then she picked up a red sheer scarf and stretched it out languidly. She held it up in the sunlight, then fluttered it down to the floor and stroked it with her fingers. "Shaz, hurry up. I'd rather have you sweep the floor."

I walked downstairs feeling as though I were missing something and nearly collided with Maryam as I walked into the lobby of the beauty school and salon. She looked as if she were in mourning. Her eyes were puffy and raw, and she was tightly wrapped in a big, black shawl. Maryam was always the most lighthearted, sweet-tempered person in either compound. She sang when she peeled vegetables. She sang when she plucked chickens. She sang when she washed dishes. She had a good marriage, a good family, a good job. The only time I'd ever seen her unhappy was once when everyone left the houses for one reason or another, leaving her alone in the kitchen. She panicked when she discovered that she was alone and cried when we returned. Now she looked as though she had been crying for the last two days. "Where's Laila?" I shouted at the closed door to the salon. I knew that I needed help to understand this, whatever it was.

Maryam sat down on the stairs to sob, and Baseera and Mina came running out of the salon. Laila walked in from the porch. "Something is terribly wrong," I told her. "Find out what it is."

Laila bent down over Maryam, who spoke rapidly from behind clenched fists. Then Laila straightened up again. She and the beauticians talked back and forth for a few seconds. "We know part of the story already," she said.

It seemed that, two days before, Achmed Zia had been driving Shaz and Maryam home when one of the van's tires blew out. The spare was also flat, so he was going to leave the girls in the car while he went to get the spare repaired. Then Shaz offered to call Farooq and see if he could give the two of them a ride. She asked to use Maryam's phone to make the call, claiming that she was out of minutes. So Farooq came, and soon they were hurtling along one of the dirt roads that led to the neighborhood where both Shaz and Maryam lived. All of a sudden, Farooq slowed down at a corner, and Shaz opened her door and jumped out. Farooq sped up again, driving down the streets so fast that Maryam couldn't get out of the car. As he drove, he looked up at the frantic Maryam in the rearview mirror and told her that he was in love with her. He told her he had seen her when he was picking up Shaz outside the compound, and he knew he had to have her for himself. He wanted her to leave her husband and go off with him.

I interrupted. "Why would Shaz jump out of the car to let him be with another woman?"

"Farooq told her she must do this to prove that she loves him," Laila asserted. "He tells her he is attracted to Maryam and asks Shaz to let them be together just this once."

"Why would she go along with that?"

Laila grimaced. "Because she is crazy, Debbie. Crazy with love and crazy with the drugs."

I grabbed the railing of the stairs and sat down next to Maryam. "What are you talking about? She smokes hash out there with the men?"

"She is an opium addict. She takes a little pill under her tongue every day, then she goes off by herself to fold your scarves. Farooq is the one who gets her the drugs."

"But she's such a hard worker! How could she be a drug addict and still work so hard?" I couldn't make sense out of this.

Maryam lifted her head and spoke again to Laila. I would have never recognized her voice if I had heard her speaking on the phone. All the lightness and warmth was gone. Laila and the girls listened with looks of horror, then fixed their eyes on me expectantly. "There's more? What else?" I asked.

Farooq had finally let the hysterical Maryam out of his car, and she'd walked home. She was late but told her husband that the van had broken down and that she hadn't wanted to wait there alone while Achmed Zia got the spare fixed. She said she hadn't been able to get a cab because she didn't have enough money, and she hadn't been able to call her husband because her cell phone couldn't get a signal. The cell phone systems in the city were down so often that he didn't bother to question this. He also didn't wonder about his wife's agitation, because he knew how easily she became frightened and that she didn't like walking through the streets alone. But later that night he checked her cell phone to see if it was working again. There he found a long, lurid text message from Farooq saying how he wanted Maryam more than ever after their brief time together. Farooq said that he knew now she wanted him in the same way. Then Maryam's husband threw her phone across the room and left the house, shouting that he would divorce her if she was spending time with another man.

Right about then, Shaz opened the lobby door. She was still looking a little bit dreamy, but she shrank back against the outside wall when she saw Maryam. Laila and Baseera shouted at her a few times, but she refused to come inside. Then Mina shrieked. She had been looking at Maryam's cell phone and recognized Farooq's number. She had been getting a lot of harassing calls on her own phone, and they were all from this same number. The last thing Mina's husband needed was another reason to beat up on her, and she started to cry at the thought that Farooq could leave an incriminating text message on her phone. Laila and Baseera also pulled out their cell phones. They found the same number in their own phones, in the logs for both incoming and outgoing calls. Each remembered that Shaz had asked to use her phone in the last few days. It seemed that Shaz was delivering all the girls over to Farooq, so desperate to please him that she'd play the pimp. The lobby echoed with screaming and crying, and the few customers who were in the salon that day tiptoed past us warily. Achmed Zia finally came to the door and poked a worried head in.

Two days later I fired Shaz. I had tried to get her to take us to Farooq. Sam was ready to pay him a visit and threaten to kill him if he harassed any of my girls again. But Shaz wouldn't do it. Her face closed up and she shook her head; she wouldn't meet my eye. She sent piles of dust flying as she swept and beat carpets, trying so hard to show me that she was indispensable. She *was* nearly indispensable, and I loved her, but I couldn't let her hungers endanger the rest of my girls. When she left, I felt as if a part of me went walking out the door.

I wanted to talk to someone about this, someone who could help me make sense of it. The first person who came to mind was Roshanna, of course—she had been my friend ever since I came to Afghanistan. She had helped me decipher each mystery that arose from my conflict with the culture and from my ignorance of what the Afghan women had been through. But I couldn't ask Roshanna, because she was gone.

After the traumatic night of her engagement party and consummation, I had gone home and spent the day crying. Sam was out of town and hadn't been able to come to the party with me, but I called him and told him what had happened. "She will be fine," he assured me. "She marry nice Afghan man this time, go to country where there never was Taliban."

So I told myself to stop worrying. The consummation had been a nightmare, but she would walk off into a new day with her husband. I cried a little more, though, knowing how much I would miss Roshanna.

Her husband left for Amsterdam three days after the engagement party, as planned. Within two months, Roshanna had a visa and was preparing to follow him there. Her family and I took her to the airport and sobbed amid the potholes as she disappeared inside.

She called her brother two weeks later in a panic. It turned out that when she arrived in Amsterdam, it was her mother-in-law who was waiting to greet her. The older woman explained that things were not quite as she had presented them back in Kabul. Roshanna's new husband was not actually a successful engineer; he was just a clerk at a large Dutch company. Moreover, he didn't live at his parents' house full-time but would be around only twice a year. He was not at home then and would not be for another four months. Roshanna told her brother that she had been a virtual slave to the family those two weeks, scrubbing floors, cooking and serving meals, doing whatever her mother-in-law ordered. She had been banned from all forms of communication, as many Afghan brides are. They're supposed to cut off contact with their families for several months so that they can adjust to their husbands' families.

The brother was outraged and wanted to jump on a

plane right away. But Roshanna's family couldn't track the new husband's family and didn't know how to find her. They didn't have enough money to hire a detective, so they just waited. I waited along with them and worried every day about her.

Finally, after months had gone by, she called. She told her family that things had changed yet again. Her husband had come back. He took her by the hands and asked her if she loved him as her husband, even if he was just a lowly clerk and not an engineer, even if his family was not wealthy. And of course, being Roshanna, she said yes. Then he began to laugh. He told her that he really was an engineer and that his family really was wealthy. They had been testing her. Now that he saw how devoted she was to him, regardless of his position, he knew they would be a happy couple. She told her family that they could stop worrying about her. Her life was good.

I haven't spoken to Roshanna since she left Kabul. I still wonder if she was telling her family the truth or just trying to save face. They tell me they don't hear from her anymore, either. When I see them, we try to be cheerful for one another and pretend that she must be doing very well indeed away from the dust of Kabul.

In my darkest moments I wonder if I did Roshanna any good by spilling my blood on her consummation night. Sometimes I wonder if I'm doing much good at all here. There are many of us Westerners who want to help Afghan women, but our efforts don't always help them in the ways that we hope they will. There are so many ties that bind these women and hold them back, and many of the ties aren't even visible to the Western eye. It takes a long time to understand how the complexities of these women's lives differ from the complexities of ours. Sometimes we can't help, even when we understand these complexities. The culture is changing so much more slowly than their dreams are.

I saw a reflection of the moon in my glass of wine and took a quick sip before it moved on to someone else's glass. We were having a starlight picnic in our front yard with a small group of friends, both Afghan and foreign. It was a lovely night. We had dragged the living room rug outside, ringed it with toushaks and candles, and piled the middle of the rug with platters of fruit and cakes. I hadn't bothered to hire a band, but music drifted out from a CD player propped in the window. Sometimes we sang along.

I was in the middle of a funny story. Sam had brought kebabs home for dinner the night before, and there had been a lot left over. In the middle of the day, he'd sent Achmed Zia to the door of the school to tell me that Sam was having a business meeting at his office and that he wanted to serve the leftover kebabs. But the girls and I had already eaten them, so I called Sam on my cell. I was watching one of the students attempt a fancy updo on her mannequin, so I didn't want to talk too loudly. When he answered, I whispered, "We ate the meat."

"Debbie? Debbie, is that you?" said the voice on the other end.

"Yeah, I wanted you to know the meat is gone."

"What?"

"We ate the meat!"

There was silence on the other end of the line, then the voice said, "Debbie, you're kind of scaring me. Is this some kind of code? Am I supposed to evacuate the city or something?"

"Sam?" Then I looked at the phone and saw that I had called one of my male customers by mistake. "Oh, my God, is this Viani?"

He and I laughed for about ten minutes. I called him later in the day and whispered, "We ate the meat," again. He whispered back, "The eagle has landed! Abort mission! Abort!"

As I told our friends the story, they got it right away. Where else in the world would you hear someone whisper "We ate the meat" and assume right away that it's a coded warning to get out of the city? Did this mean that we were all crazy to live here? We laughed and laughed. Then Sam's cell phone rang, and he motioned for us to quiet down. My heart sank as he switched from Dari to Uzbek, because this probably meant his family was calling. Sam walked away to continue his conversation. When he came back, I could tell that he was upset.

"Is everything okay with your family?"

"Okay." He picked up an apple and began cutting it into small pieces.

"Why did they call?"

"My father, he is right now at Saudi airport. He will be here in morning."

"Is he going to be bothered that you live next door to a beauty salon?" asked one of our friends incredulously.

Sam groaned.

"Have you met him before?" another friend asked me.

"He not know about wedding," Sam said. "Only mother know."

"She didn't tell him?" I asked. "He still doesn't know about me?"

When Sam shook his head, all my happiness drained away. I had never been able to forgive him completely for not telling his parents about me on his own. Now I knew he had still been hiding me after nearly three years of marriage.

But I tried to make the best of it. The salon was open the next day, and there was no way that Sam could avoid it: you can get to our private compound only by walking through the beauty school compound. As the beauticians and customers arrived, I told them what was going on. When Sam called to tell me that he and his father were driving down the street, all of us dashed into the room where I stored the hair color products. We held our breath and clamped our hands over our mouths. I heard Sam and some men pass through the yard, then I heard him slam the gate between our home compound and the beauty compound. "It's safe now," I told everyone, acting as if I found all this drama great fun. "Papa Sam has landed."

"Is his name Sam, too?" a customer asked.

"I don't even know his real name."

"This is so exciting," said another customer. One half of her head was done up in neat foil packets; the other half bristled with an inch of gray roots. "I'm going to have to come back next week to see how it all turns out!"

I decided to let Sam have a quiet twenty-four hours with his father. I made my own dinner plans that night with friends, and he took his father out to a restaurant. Later on, he called me at my friends' house and told me he had taken Papa Sam back to our house. He wanted to pick me up so that we would arrive at the house together. But as we pulled up to the gate, Achmed Zia walked over to the car. Some of Sam's mujahideen friends had come over and were sitting in the yard with Papa Sam. "Stay here," Sam told me. "Let me move Father into house."

"Are you going to introduce me to him then?"

"Yes, but inside house. Not in front of crowd."

As soon as he left, the car started to fog up with my anger. If Papa Sam was like all other Afghans, I knew I'd be stuck waiting in the car for hours. There is no such thing in Afghanistan as simply saying good night to guests and going inside. Papa Sam would have to serve them tea or soft drinks, make sure they had biscuits and fruit, ask about their families and the villages where their grandfathers lived and their male children and so on. I figured that if Sam came back out at all, it would be to try to sneak me inside the house using an entrance from the alley where everyone kept their generators and garbage. After about ten minutes, I climbed into the driver's seat and sped away by myself. My phone started to ring, but I ignored it. I roared around the city for twenty minutes. When I returned, Sam was pacing outside the compound. Now he was in a rage.

"You couldn't wait?" he shouted.

"Are you going to tell him about me? Make your choice: either I am or I am not your wife tonight!" I shouted right back.

He pointed inside the car at my head scarf, which had slid down to the floor. "Put on scarf and come inside!"

We walked into the yard. Papa Sam sat among a group of men, a round, toothless little man with a turban that was almost as big as he was. He didn't rise to greet me; men in this culture don't usually stand when women make an entrance. But several of the other men stood, greeted me warmly in English, and clasped my hands. They were all General Dostum's men, whom Sam knew from his fighting days. They visited our house often. I had considered it a major turning point in our marriage when Sam had introduced me to them a year before, then invited me to sit and have tea with them in our living room. When an Afghan man entertains his friends, his wife usually

336

stays closeted in another room until the men leave. I knew it was an honor when Sam introduced me to Dostum and his men, because Dostum was Sam's hero. These men were like family to Sam. I figured that this was nearly as important as an introduction to his real family, that it was as good as declaring his love for me to the world.

As the men settled down again and I took my place on a toushak, they switched back into speaking Uzbek. I couldn't follow any of the conversation, and I couldn't smoke with Papa Sam there, so I picked forlornly at a biscuit. I could tell that Sam was furious because his friends had probably overheard our quarrel and were assuming that he didn't know how to control his wife. Well, fine, I thought: they should know that by now. I saw Papa Sam steal an occasional look at me, and I wondered if he recognized me. I had actually met him when Sam and I still lived in the Peacock Manor guesthouse. He had shown up for a surprise visit that time, too. Neither Sam nor I was ready to tell our families about our marriage, so we played an exhaustingly silly game of hide-and-seek for the few weeks that Papa Sam was there. We were constantly ducking in and out of rooms so that his father wouldn't see us together. We told him that I was a visiting teacher working with the school, and he shook his head with alarm that I was living by myself. I almost blew my cover by making him breakfast one morning when the cook didn't show up. If he remembered me, he was probably puzzled that I was still hanging around his son. I hoped he didn't think I was a prostitute.

It seemed that one of Dostum's men had been talking for an hour straight. Old war stories, I thought to myself miserably. It was clear that Sam wasn't going to suddenly stand up and introduce me as his wife tonight. Equally clear that all these men were probably going to ignore me for another three hours. All I wanted to do was crawl into my bed, but I didn't know what kind of story Sam had concocted about me this time; I didn't even know where I was supposed to sleep. I sighed, and Papa Sam looked at me quizzically. He said something to one of the other men, and the tenor of the conversation suddenly changed. All the men were looking at me and chiming in with comments. One of them pointed to Sam and then to me. Sam looked down at the grass, but Papa Sam smiled.

"So now he knows," one of Dostum's men said with a big grin. "He says welcome to the family. He says he has always known, even two years ago, but he was waiting for Sam to tell him."

Sam turned bright red, and I started to cry. Then I walked over to Papa Sam's toushak and dropped at his feet. I took his hand and kissed it, then placed it on my head. Sam had once told me that his children did this to greet him. "My own father died four years ago," I told Papa Sam in my bad Dari. "I am hoping that you will be my father now. I have been wanting this ever since I married your son."

He put his hand on my hair and stroked it. I continued to cry, and when I looked up, I saw that he had tears running down his grizzled cheeks. I saw that Sam and even some of the scarred old mujahideen were wiping away tears. I was finally Sam's wife. I was finally out of the closet.

The next morning, Papa Sam was waiting for me in the living room. He had taken down all the pictures from the walls so that he could pray without having to look at *haraam* images of animate things. He must have shuddered when he took down my painting of naked cherubs. He was ready now for his son's wife to make his morning tea. He told me that he had gold jewelry for me back in Saudi Arabia. He hoped I would come soon to meet the whole family, including the first wife and her eight children. Or maybe he could bring them all to Kabul to meet me and see the compound! He said he thought it was a good thing that Sam had taken a second wife, and he hoped I would bear him many sons.

I drove Papa Sam to a local coffeehouse. The two of us sat down with our caramel-flavored lattes. He looked with interest at the people around us, but I didn't notice them. I was contemplating all the joys and demands of being a true Afghan daughter-in-law with no small measure of terror.

The end almost came a few weeks later. Not the end of my marriage; that drama continues on and on. But it was nearly the end of the Kabul Beauty School.

We had a good-size crowd in the salon that day. All

the girls had customers. Robina was blow-drying an American woman who had about ninety pounds of long blond hair. Mina was giving a pedicure to a French baker who had just moved to Kabul, and Bahar was giving a manicure to an Afghan-American woman who was working for the United Nations. Topekai was cutting the hair of a lawyer who was getting paid big bucks to suffer another summer in Kabul. Baseera was upstairs giving someone else a massage. I was trying to talk a missionary into highlights.

Suddenly I heard footsteps pounding along the driveway and looked outside to see Sam flying by the windows. Then he was inside the beauty building and flung open the door. "They're going to put us in jail!" he panted.

All my beauticians and my customers stopped what they were doing to turn around. Sam was leaning against the doorframe, his cell phone crushed to his heart. His shirt was hanging out, and even his sunglasses were askew. I had been trimming the nape of the missionary's neck. She pulled away from me slightly, as if she no longer trusted me with the razor.

"What are you talking about?" I don't think I'd ever seen Sam so upset.

"They want you to pay twenty thousand dollars in back taxes."

"I don't have to pay taxes," I told him. "I'm an NGO."

"No taxes on beauty school." He waved his arm at the room. "Taxes on salon!"

"It's all the same thing," I explained. "I fund the school with money from the salon, which is a teaching salon anyway. There are no profits."

"They say you are enterprise."

"I'm a *social* enterprise. It's in my NGO contract."

Topekai's lawyer jumped into the conversation. "I'll e-mail you a document about social-enterprise tax law. Sounds like you're operating in accordance with it, though."

Sam ignored her. "Debbie, they say they stand outside watching everyone who goes in and out. They're not playing."

It took a few days to figure out what was going on. I still don't completely understand it. It seemed that some governmental entity had decided to assess me for what they claimed were thousands of dollars in yearly profits. This kind of shakedown happens every now and then in Afghanistan because laws and taxes and all the staples of government are pretty new. There is also widespread and growing distrust of foreign NGOs because the Afghans don't understand why everything is still such a wreck when so much money is supposedly pouring into the country for reconstruction. Money wasn't pouring into the beauty school, and I could show anyone who was interested a survey demonstrating that our students' family incomes rose 400 percent after graduation. But even though the claim against us was bogus, it would still hurt. Sam and I would have to make an appearance at the same court that tried people who made false passports and counterfeit money. The beauty school would suddenly become the talk of the town, but in a bad way. The damage to our reputation would reverberate even if we won our case. Fathers and husbands wouldn't allow their daughters and wives to attend the beauty school anymore. And if we lost the case—because that was also a possibility, even though we were in full accordance with current tax law—I would go to jail for two years. Sam would go to jail for five years.

I consulted with friends who were lawyers in Kabul. The consensus was that if we waited until we were formally charged, we would lose everything. So we took the time-honored legal recourse of a modest payment to someone who promised that the charges against us would make their way into an incinerator.

I was able to breathe again, but only briefly.

As I write this, in May 2006, both the Kabul Beauty School and the Oasis Salon are closed up tight. There have been widespread rioting, burning, and looting in the city following a tragic accident in which U.S. military vehicles crashed into civilian cars and killed several people. As an angry crowd gathered, U.S. troops and Afghan police fired—over the heads of the crowd, they said—but some civilians were killed and many more were injured. Some foreign NGOs were burned down. The Karzai government imposed a nightly curfew similar to the one in effect shortly after the Taliban were driven out. I haven't seen the city this tense—or the residents this angry and frightened—in all my years here. Our compound is safe because General Dostum's men arrived shortly after the rioting began. Their presence ensured that we wouldn't be burned down or overrun, but it was hard to get used to the idea of bearded men and machine guns taking up the space that my beauty students usually occupy.

I can only hope that calm will return and that all the people who want to help rebuild this country can continue doing just that. The Kabul Beauty School's part in all this seems small in comparison with many of the other efforts, but it is nevertheless huge. I know how the lives of the women who have come to the school have changed. Whereas they were once dependent on men for money, they are now earning and sharing their wages. Whereas they were once household slaves, they are now respected decision makers. Not all of them, not all of the time. But enough to give them and so many other women here hope.

Here's a funny story. People often send product donations to the Kabul Beauty School, and I dutifully open every box and distribute the contents. Sometimes the donations are salon products. Those are always welcome, because we run through that stuff quickly—it's not even easy to replenish our stock of good shampoo here. Sometimes the donations are intended for the girls themselves. We've gotten handbags, bolts of fabric, and knitted scarves, and the girls have appreciated all these gifts. But one day I let Laila open one of the boxes, and she carried it over to me with a perplexed look on her face.

"What are these things?" she asked as my other girls gathered around.

So I looked inside the box and saw—thongs! Lacy thongs, leather thongs, satin thongs, thongs with embroidered flowers. I bent over the box and laughed for a few minutes before trying to answer. "Knickers," I finally said. "What ladies wear under their clothes."

Laila translated for the others, and they all frowned. "No, Debbie," Baseera said. "These can't be knickers."

"Yes, some women like to wear these. They think they look sexy."

Topekai picked up a pair of the thongs and dangled them in the air. "They don't cover anything."

"That's kind of the point. There's a little coverage in front, but the back is thin like this so you don't have panty lines under your clothes."

"This part goes between—?" Mina patted her bottom, and I nodded.

They hooted about those thongs for weeks. They threw them at one another and occasionally pulled them over their heads when they were feeling really silly. I think the housekeeper finally threw them in the fire. Now, that's an example of a wrongheaded attempt to help Afghan women.

But not too long ago I went with a group of friends to Istalif, the village in the mountains where they make the beautiful turquoise-glazed porcelain. We wandered around looking at mugs and platters and pitchers, and each of us bought a few things from the merchants who sit in the sun and wait for visitors. We stopped at one of the old warlord palaces nearby and visited a greenhouse full of geraniums where the gardener posed for a photograph between a huge poster of Ahmed Shah Massoud and a red heart that had been painted on the wall. We wandered near a spring that Sam claimed had healing properties, and he scooped up a jug of its water to take home.

As we were driving back down the mountain, we passed a long line of children who were marching down the muddy road toward a soccer game in one of the cleared fields. All the children were wearing brand-new rubber boots in different bright colors. One child had purple boots, another had red ones, another green, another yellow, another orange, and so on, turning the mountain road into a rainbow of children's feet. I knew that somewhere in the world well-meaning people had collected those boots and sent them off to Afghanistan. Those people knew that there had to be children here who could put those boots to good use. Maybe they even knew that the children would stomp with joy because of this kick of color beneath them.

On my good days, I know the Kabul Beauty School will take my girls much farther than rubber boots.

If someone had told me only a few years ago that I'd be living in Afghanistan and running a beauty school, I would have laughed. But as soon as I set my foot on this soil, I knew I'd somehow managed to come home. I've been renewed by the spirit of this place and roused by its challenges. I've been blessed with family, and I'm rich—especially rich—in sisters. I sometimes wonder if I've done as much for them as they've done for me. They helped me heal my broken heart and believe in myself again, and I keep trying to repay them for the love they've been so eager to share. Afghan women have so much healing to do themselves. They have been held in the dark for so long, and during the darkest years they suffered more than even I can imagine. But the darkness has been pulled back a bit. The light is starting to fall on them now. They need the rest of the world to look, watch, and make sure nothing puts out that light again.

Acknowledgments

I feel like I am at the Oscars, with a long list of people I need to thank and not enough time to thank them. There have been so many people who have come into my life and supported me on this project. This book could not have been written without the help of my good friend Kristin Ohlson, a wonderful writer with a generous spirit who came to Kabul and experienced for herself the daily challenges of the beauty school, and who was with me every step of the way as I struggled to put this story together in the midst of my chaotic life. Thank you for your hard work and for your dedication to the writing of this book and for the long hours spent helping me organize my journals, thoughts, and experiences. We went through some fun times and some hard times together, and in this process you have become a dear friend. You are a wonderful and talented woman.

A special dedication to my sweet husband; without him at my side at each step, I am sure that I would have fallen on my face even more times than I did. You can always make me laugh when I am down. You are as rugged, harsh, and loving as this country. You embody Afghanistan, and through you I have learned how to love again.

I would like to thank my mother, Loie Turner, and my two sons, Noah Lentz and Zachary Lentz, for allowing me to come to Afghanistan and fulfill my lifelong dream. You have supported me in everything that I've been through. Mom, you have always been my rock and foundation. You taught me that I could do anything I put my mind to and encouraged me even when you didn't agree with my decisions. When I was crying half a world away, you always made me feel like you were right here supporting me.

Zach, you are as crazy as your mother. You jumped at the chance to come to Afghanistan when everyone told you it was an insane idea. I hope and pray that you have learned as much as I have from living here. I know that being in Afghanistan was hard on you at times and that there have been many occasions when you were frustrated with Kabul, but thanks for sharing them with me.

Noah, I have missed you very much. I know that it was difficult not having me at home. There have been times I felt like I was letting too much time go by away from you for a country that isn't even my own. I know how much you hate dirt, and this place would have made you crazy. But the e-mails you wrote and the phone calls you made just to tell me you love me helped me through the day.

A huge thank-you to my wonderful best friend, Karen Kinne, and her children, Josh, Gabe, and Claire. Karen, you stayed online with me while the bombs were dropping like flies; you made me laugh and didn't leave me while I was scared to death. Thank you for taking care of my life in the States while I am in Afghanistan. Knowing that you are there has made it easier for me to do my work here. Thank you, Karen, for being the best friend I ever had.

To Christine Gara, my lawyer and decorator, thank you for traveling to Kabul to help me paint the school with a dead chicken. Thank you for forgiving me for no hot water and not being able to shower for a week. Not only have you made a difference in my life, but you have shown the women in the Kabul Beauty School what it means to be a strong, independent woman. You have changed many lives.

Thank you to Gay-LeClerc Qaderi, who taught me how to be a wife to an Afghan husband without losing myself. You are still teaching me, and you have become indispensable in my life.

To Betsy Beamon, what can I say? You are as crazy as I am. We have gone down some rocky roads, and having you in Kabul let me know I always had someone whom I could trust and who understood me. Thanks for calling just to ask, "Deb, you all right?" Sometimes the answer was yes, sometimes no. But knowing you were a phone call or a taxi ride away never failed to make me feel less lonely.

Nick and Halima are the reason I am happily married to my wonderful Afghan husband. There are days when I thank you for that and—I'll admit it—others when I don't. You have been instrumental in our marriage and have helped us get through some pretty hard times. You showed us how to cross those cultural roads without hitting too many land mines. You will always be the mom and dad to us.

I would like to thank Mary MacMakin for her vision and her dedication to the people of Afghanistan.

I would like to thank Sima Calkin and Lindy Walser, two wonderful hairdressers who used their own money to come teach and support the school. You gave me time to take well-needed breaks. I can't tell you what it meant to me that you would leave your lives in the States to come here and help.

The constant presence of John Paul DeJoria and Luke Jacobellis at the John Paul Mitchell System gave me the confidence that I could overcome any hurdle. J.P. and Luke, you can never know how important you have become in my life and how safe you have always made me feel.

Vogue and Clairol never left my side. These companies were always there like the Rock of Gibraltar. Without their generous funding, the school would have been lost. I would also like to thank all the companies and all the people who have contributed to the school with supplies or money.

To all my customers in Holland, Michigan, whose hair got too long and whose roots grew gray because I was always gone: thank you for your loyalty when I came back, and thank you for your continuing support and prayers.

To my agent, Marly Rusoff: you believed in me when no one else did. I don't even know how to begin to thank you. Without your guidance and support, I would never have been able to do this.

To Jane von Mehren, my editor at Random House: somehow you knew that my story was worth telling and you gave me a chance to tell it. You took a risk with me and there are no words strong enough to express my gratitude.

Wow, what a team at Random House. I don't think I even knew what a team was until I had the chance to meet all of you. You are so kind and supportive and made me feel like a queen. I feel like one of the luckiest people in the world to have a publishing company and team like you to work with.

Finally, I would like to thank all the foreigners and the Afghans who came to our salon when we didn't have hot water to wash their hair or electricity to blow it dry and never complained.

But most important, I want to thank all the women who have come through the Kabul Beauty School. If we had a dime for every tear shed at the school, we would all be millionaires. One of the wonderful things about Afghan women is that they never let someone cry alone. Without your honesty, friendship, love, and willingness to share your stories, there would have been no book. Thank you for letting me into your lives and allowing me the chance to share them with the rest of the world so the real stories of Afghan women can be heard. You have always treated me more like a sister than a boss or teacher. Always know that I count you among my family, and that I will never be the same because of you.

Center Point Publishing

600 Brooks Road ● PO Box 1
Thorndike ME 04986-0001 USA

(207) 568-3717

US & Canada:
1 800 929-9108
www.centerpointlargeprint.com